HILLBILLY HEART

JOHNNY CASH Hendersonville, Tn.
June 12 '92

Billy Ray,

I was very impressed recently to hear you give God the credit for your success. It's good to be re-minded where _all_ goodness comes from.

Thirty-six years ago I was working with Elvis and saw him take the same kind of flak you're taking now.

Congratulations on the way you're handling it all. In your case, as in Elvis' the good outweighs the bad.

Let 'em have it. I'm in your corner.

Johny Cash

Johnny Cash sent this letter to me in June 1992.

Letter courtesy of The John R Cash Revocable Trust

Billy Ray Cyrus

HILLBILLY HEART

New Harvest
Houghton Mifflin Harcourt
BOSTON   NEW YORK
2013

His truth shall be your shield
and your buckler.

— PSALM 91:4

Opportunity often comes disguised
in the form of misfortune,
or temporary defeat.

— NAPOLEON HILL

Expect a miracle.

— PAPAW CYRUS

This book is dedicated to the dreamers.

PROLOGUE

WHO KNOWS HOW THIS stuff works?

Not me.

I'll tell you a story. In 1993, I was shooting a video for "In the Heart of a Woman," the first single off my second album, *It Won't Be the Last*. We made the video in the center of the Navajo Nation in the Grand Canyon. I had never seen a natural landscape any more dramatic, beautiful, or spiritual than Canyon de Chelly National Monument. Its towering sandstone walls and ancient dwellings are magical.

After the shoot, one of the tribe's elders introduced me to a little boy who had Down syndrome. When I asked if he had an Indian name, he quietly answered no.

I noticed a picture of an eagle on his T-shirt and said, "Well, you're Soaring Eagle."

Suddenly, the elder bent down, scooped up a handful of dirt, threw it in the air, and said, "Huh, Soaring Eagle!"

The tribe repeated it. "Soaring Eagle."

The boy's face unfolded into a grin of pure joy. It was a beautiful sight, every bit as magical as the land where we stood.

• • •

Several hours later, I was back on a plane to Nashville and eager to see my soon-to-be wife, Tish, and our six-month-old daughter, Miley. Even though I was working on my second album, I was still riding the rocket of the "Achy Breaky Heart" phenomenon, and it was a crazy time for me. I don't think I slept for a year, maybe longer. Indeed, by the time I got home from the video shoot, I had been up for a couple of days, and I guess I looked like it, too. Tish sent me straight to the bathtub and told me to use the soap.

Afterward, as I sat in the bedroom, re-acclimating to being home, I flashed back to that little boy I'd met in the canyon. I wanted to tell Tish about him, the way his smile had come from inside and taken over his entire being, and how fortunate he had made me feel about being a new daddy to a healthy baby girl.

Suddenly, those emotions turned into words. They filled my head, and I found a pen and piece of paper and wrote them down as fast as they came to me.

When they stopped, I had a poem. I titled it "Trail of Tears" and showed it to Tish.

"What do you think?" I asked.

"I think I'm going to buy a frame and hang it on the wall," she said, and that's exactly what she did. We later moved and the poem came down.

Almost three years went by before I thought about that poem again. It was late 1995, and I was enjoying the early morning on top of the hill by the fire I had built that sits in the shadows of my teepee. It's like a church to me — where I escape and think and get in touch with timeless stories that emanate from the land. It's a surefire place to get perspective on things.

I don't remember why I went out there that particular morning, whether anything was bothering me, but I do recall myself thinking about the Indian families and children who had been marched across nearby land in the 1830s, along what became known as the Trail of Tears. The trail ran close to my land. I pictured those uprooted families — daddies and mamas like myself and Tish, and their children, tears in their eyes, fear in their hearts, many of them barefoot, marching through mud and snow — and that's when I remembered my poem about that little boy, Soaring Eagle.

The words came right back to me, only this time I heard them with a bluegrass melody reminiscent of the old Earl Scruggs and Bill Monroe records that had provided the soundtrack to my early childhood. Up there, all by myself, I put words to music and sang that song for the first time ever.

I had a show that night in Canada. On the plane, I noticed guitarist Don Von Tresse, who had written "Achy Breaky Heart," had brought a mandolin. I had never played mandolin before, let alone a right-handed one. But I picked up Don's beautiful little instrument, turned it around for my left-handedness, strummed once or twice, and said to the guys in my band, "Listen to what I wrote today."

> *Too many broken promises*
> *Too many Trail of Tears*
> *Too many times you were left cold*
> *For oh so many years*
>
> *Too many times you walked away*
> *And was made to feel ashamed*
> *And though you only tried to give*
> *You were often blamed*
>
> *How can this world be so dark,*
> *so unfair, so untrue?*
> *How did the cards of life*
> *fold right on top of you?*
>
> *God in Heaven, hear my prayer*
> *If you are still above*
> *Send the children hopes and dreams*
> *And lots and lots of love*
>
> *For this I only ask of you*
> *To conquer all their fears*
> *And let them soar like eagles*
> *Across the Trail of Tears.*

I played the poem exactly as I had heard it. And now it was a song, and the guys in my band were into it.

Ordinarily, we rehearse a new song for a few weeks, if not longer, before adding it to the set list. But I was eager to share "Trail of Tears," and so we worked it up during sound check and performed it that night. As I told the audience, I needed to share it with them. Why else would that song have come to me?

For me, sharing music is what I'm all about. As I write this, it's been twenty years since "Achy Breaky Heart" became a multi-million-selling smash hit around the world, transforming me in blinding speed from a hard-working barroom country rocker into a household name. Since then, I have released thirteen albums, more than a dozen hit records, starred in two hit TV series, made two handfuls of movies, and recently starred on Broadway in the hit musical *Chicago*. Best of all, I have been married to the love of my life for nearly two decades and raised five children in a business where few people do either one.

I'm not saying it's been a smooth ride. From the beginning, I battled for respect from Nashville, and like a lot of people, I've also battled myself.

I have asked why a kid from Kentucky who wanted to be a pro baseball player started to hear voices telling him to buy a guitar, and then started to hear songs, and then ended up with the life I have today. On the one hand, I followed my dream and worked hard and never gave up. On the other hand, I don't claim to understand a thing.

I'm not the best songwriter. I'm certainly not the best singer, either. What I do is bring honesty to my music. I also bring a conviction that sharing my music is my purpose. I honestly can't think of any other way to explain what's happened to me thus far in my fifty-one years. In this book, you will see what I mean. I will share stories from the whole extraordinary ride — the good, the bad, the off-key, and the stuff that still doesn't make sense. You'll learn about my family and our crazy life. You'll see that I'm a guy who occasionally needs to disappear into the woods till my head clears. And you'll read a few stories that might make you believe, as I do, in a power greater than any of us.

I'm constantly asked how I write songs, and I never have a satisfying answer. I don't know that any songwriters do. Telling you about "Trail of Tears" is about as close as I can get. As I said earlier, I don't know how this stuff works. All I know is, I have lived the majority of the songs I've written. They are my truth. This book is a lot like those songs. The stories ain't always pretty, but they're real.

PART I

Country as Country Can Be

CHAPTER 1

·•◦•·

"Life Ain't Fair"

L IKE ANYONE ELSE, I can think of a hundred different things in my childhood that shaped me in one way or another. But one moment stands out as decisive and defining not just for who I became but also for the ways it caused me to look at the world, the way people behaved, and what I was going to understand about myself.

It was a Sunday afternoon, and I was sitting in the passenger seat of my dad's car. I was about ten years old, a stocky boy with long, dark, floppy hair and a smile I was reluctant to break out. I was still a kid, but growing up fast.

I was clearly all boy, a good athlete and given to finding trouble if it didn't find me first. Still, my dad, Ronald Ray Cyrus, recognized I was a little sensitive on the inside — more thoughtful than soft — and I had been going through a bunch of stuff that had me thinking. It was beyond my control, and what I would call a worst-case scenario for me and my brother, Kevin Lynn.

(By the way, everyone called him Kebo, and I was known as Bo. For some reason, my dad always called us by those nicknames, and they just kind of stuck.)

Anyway, my feelings were no secret to my dad. A few years earlier, he and my mom had split, and even more recently my dad, who had remarried, had filed to get custody of me and my brother.

It had been a mess, and now my dad was taking me for a drive so we could talk. I have a hard enough time expressing myself at age fifty-one, and back then it was even harder. My dad noticed I was on the verge of tears, and struggling emotionally.

"What is it, son?" he asked.

I took a deep breath to summon my courage.

"Why can't we just be a normal family?" I asked. "Why's everything always messed up?"

My dad pulled over to the side of the road and put his truck into neutral. He looked into my eyes. To his credit, he told me the truth.

"Son, life ain't fair," he said. "It ain't fair. Once you understand that and accept it, the better off you're going to be, and the sooner you can move forward."

Acceptance of life's hard knocks was a way of life for my kinfolk. They came out of the mountains of eastern Kentucky and southern West Virginia and settled along the banks of the Big Sandy, the Little Sandy, and the Ohio Rivers. I would get to know the region well when I played the bars and honky-tonks there. It was known for railroads, steel mills, coal mines, and farms, cornerstones of the industries that built and fed America — and the Cyrus men labored in all these fields.

My dad was a rigger for Armco Steel in Russell and Ashland, Kentucky, when I was born on August 25, 1961, the second of Ronald and Ruthie Cyrus's boys. My mom was a big-hearted woman from the Appalachian hills, a little spitfire barely past five foot who played piano by ear and had been such a talented performer in high school that her senior class had named her "Most Likely to Succeed and Run a Hollywood Studio."

On the day I was born, my papaw Eldon Lindsey Cyrus, who stood several inches over six feet and weighed well over 200 pounds, perfect for a fiery Pentecostal preacher, looked through the glass partition of the hospital nursery and tried to read the name on my ID bracelet. It said BABY BOY CYRUS. But he thought it said BILLY RAY CYRUS.

"What a perfect name!" he declared.

Since my mom's father was William and my dad's middle name was Ray, it made sense to him.

"But it actually says 'Baby Boy Cyrus,'" my mom corrected.

He didn't listen. He had already made up his mind.

All of my earliest memories from our home at 2317 Long Street in Flatwoods, Kentucky, are related to sports, church, girls, being rebellious, and music — most of all music. On Saturday nights my papaw Casto, my mom's father, and my uncle Clayton came over and played bluegrass and folk classics such as "Won't You Come Home Bill Bailey," "Rolling in My Sweet Baby's Arms," and Bill Monroe's "Blue Moon of Kentucky." My mom was on piano, her father played fiddle, and her brother played guitar. Sometimes my dad hit on a little drum while my brother and I listened and sang and jumped around.

When they took a break, we switched on the radio and listened to the Grand Ole Opry, though I remember one night at my papaw Casto's home when everybody laid down their instruments, turned up the radio, and listened to a heavyweight boxing match between the champion, Sonny Liston, and a very confident Olympic gold medalist named Cassius Clay. One other thing I remember about that night — my papaw had a gas fireplace where the heat came out of the floor. I stood on it too long and burned a hole in my sock.

My papaw Casto was a character. He worked for the Chesapeake and Ohio Railroad, riding in the caboose. He enjoyed a beer or two, or three, and inevitably called me over to ask if I wanted to hear something funny, which usually meant an off-color joke.

"Did you hear the one about a little bee?" he once asked.

"No, sir," I said.

He pulled me close and dropped his voice to a whisper.

"A little bee flew across the sea and landed on a martin pole, stretched his neck, shit a peck, and closed up his farting hole."

Another time, he asked, "Did you hear about the guy who gave a speech to ten thousand people?"

I shook my head.

"Ten thousand people!" he continued. "Ten thousand people . . . *ten thousand people.* Can you imagine? Then some old wino in the back hollered, 'Hey, buddy, what about ten thousand people?' And that ol' boy looked up and said, 'Ten thousand people . . . and that damn bird had to shit all over me.'"

That one still makes me laugh.

On Sundays we went to the tiny white Pentecostal church where my papaw Cyrus preached. Eldon Lindsey Cyrus filled that church with the spirit of the Holy Ghost and gospel hymns. As I said earlier, he was an imposing man, with a commanding presence, and when he pointed to the little sign in front of his pulpit, EXPECT A MIRACLE, you believed him. I did.

He was a rebel in his youth. He probably would have ended up in the steel mills or coal mines if fate hadn't steered him in another direction. He drank coffee, smoked cigarettes, and chewed tobacco, all considered sins back in those days. Then one day when he was out riding his horse with a huge chaw tucked inside the cheek of his mouth, he felt the calling of the Lord. He heard a voice from beyond or high above tell him to become a preacher.

He immediately spit out his chaw, rode home, and took steps to become an ordained preacher. He spent the rest of his life spreading the good word. And the words he preached were taken straight out of the Bible. I looked up to him, as did many people. He found a lesson in everything, as did my dad, but as a kid, I especially liked listening to my papaw, thinking it was cool that he had talked to God, and I took every opportunity to ask, "Papaw, tell me about that time you heard the voice of God."

Sunday was also the day we listened to my dad's gospel group, the Crownsmen Quartet. My dad had many talents. He was strong, smart, wise, tenderhearted, and charismatic. He was also one heck of a gospel singer, a very passionate and respected entertainer. His quartet was renowned throughout the tristate area for their south-ern gospel harmonies. Whereas most gospel groups sang one emo-tional, inspirational ballad after another, the Crownsmen Quartet were known for their high-energy performances.

Starting when I was four years old, my dad would bring me on-stage and have me join them on "Swing Down, Sweet Chariot." I know you are probably thinking isn't that "Swing Low, Sweet Char-iot"? But my dad's group sang, "Why don't you swing down, sweet chariot / Stop and let me ride / Swing down, sweet chariot, stop and let me ride / Rock me Lord, rock me Lord / Come Ezekiel / I gotta home on the other side . . ."

It was my first taste of harmony, and I loved it. My dad got a kick out of having me sing with him, hearing my tiny but expressive oom-pah-pas. I would experience the same feeling of pride years later when I brought my daughters, Miley and Brandi, onstage to sing with me.

My favorite song in their set was "I Want My Loved Ones to Go with Me." It was the group's slowest and saddest song. Written by papaw Cyrus, the tune told the story of a man growing up and learning to appreciate what was really important in life. Toward the end, my dad would stop singing and speak the words as a slow recitation. In a plaintive tone that had people hanging on every syl-lable, he said, "And now I have my own sweet family, a wife and little children dear, and only God knows how I love them, and how I love to have them near."

That song moved me inside. It moved my spirit. And as I got older, I would ask, "You got Papaw's song on the list?" I wanted to make sure they were going to perform my favorite.

My dad would smile.

"Yeah, bud, it's in there. Are you going to sing 'Swing Down, Sweet Chariot' with us?"

It's my impression that the harmony extended to our home. My mom was the hands-on field general. Ruthie wasn't all that big, but she was tough. She was an expert skeet shooter as well as a seasoned musician. You know that old saying dynamite comes in small packages? That describes Ruthie, who was both feisty and loving. She never failed to take in a stray animal, feed one of my friends, or nurse a dead plant back to life just by loving it. That said, she never took any shit, either.

My dad was the more laid-back of my two parents and a very wise man. He saw a lesson in just about everything and concluded most of his thoughts by saying, "And the moral of the story is . . ." I know I inherited a sense of that. Dad was both a friend and a father, the same way I try to be with my kids. He worked hard, often pulling double shifts at the steel mill so that we could make ends meet. Sometimes I would wait up for him, and even though he must have been exhausted, he would get out the Oreos, pour us some cold milk, and watch some cartoons. As I got older, he never failed to ask how I was doing and if I needed something or if there was anything on my mind I wanted to talk about.

To this day, it's one of the things I miss most. I mean you can have all the conveniences and luxuries money can buy, but you can't bring back having your dad there when your back is against the wall and you want to talk with someone who knows you better than you know yourself, and knows about life, too. That was my dad.

My brother, Kebo, was side by side with me through the majority of my childhood. Although older than me, he was slight in stature and smaller than most kids his age. He used to get picked on now and then, and I instinctively stuck up for him, even if it was his fault. Conversely, he could talk me into anything. One night, he convinced me that it would be fun to hide in the ditch in the woods, holding a fishing line connected to a plastic baby doll. When a car came around the curve, he told me to pull it across the road.

With Kebo's encouragement, I did exactly that, scaring the crap out of one driver who jammed on his brakes, probably convinced he'd narrowly missed hitting a kid. I got scared and never did that again.

Kebo and I spent Sunday mornings driving to and from church in my mamaw and papaw Cyrus's four-door Buick. We passed the time in the backseat by trading miniature football helmets, toys, and plastic rings we purchased in the machines at the gas station and Hills department store. We also spent many hours in the nearby woods, fishing, tracking down animals, and exploring. We found arrowheads and climbed trees, sometimes pretending to be Daniel Boone, other times pretending we were Apaches or Cherokees. Our great-grandmother was part Cherokee.

I know I'm painting a kind of idyllic picture of my childhood, but that's the way I remember it, until the strains of my mom and dad's fighting became more common than not. Looking back, I know these were the moves people who had married young had to go through as they realized they were different as adults than they were fresh out of high school. I hated hearing the fighting. It tore me up. I didn't understand what was going on. Nor did I understand why my parents seemed to want to hurt each other.

It didn't help that my dad was thought of as the Elvis of Southern Gospel. His chiseled good looks and angelic voice were catnip for gospel groupies. After one performance, my mom found lipstick on my dad's collar. Soon after, she recruited her best friend to help spy on my dad. She put Kebo and me in the backseat of her car, and the four of us parked outside a bar in Ironton, Ohio, called the Auger Inn. It had a hand-painted sign in front that read AUGER IN . . . STAGGER OUT. I don't recall what she saw, but it was something incriminating. She also spied on him at the Crownsmen's performances.

I remember some major blowouts. Nothing made me more upset than seeing my mom cry. One day, my brother and I came home from school and immediately sensed a dark cloud hovering above our house. Instead of asking me about the activities in my first-grade class, my mom stood with her arms crossed and told Kebo to take me into our room and lock the door. She explained, "Your dad and I are going to have a fight."

Indeed, my dad came home and the fighting started. It was horrible. Kebo and I heard plates break, furniture overturned, and a fist go into the wall. Unable to take the screams and cries any longer, I bolted out of my bedroom and wedged myself between them. Everything stopped. In the stillness following the battle, my father glared at my mom and said he was going to leave. Hearing that, I jumped up and wrapped my arms around his chest and wrapped my legs around his waist, clinging like a little monkey.

Without saying anything, he walked past the living room, which was in total disarray, and outside, down the five green steps, and past the birdbath. Finally, he wiped his tears, kissed me on the forehead, and got in his car. Kebo stood nearby, and my mom watched from inside the door. My dad turned on the ignition, backed out of the driveway, and disappeared over the hill. He never returned again to live under that roof as a family.

From then on, there was no question that life ain't fair.

CHAPTER 2

Back When I Was Young

I DON'T KNOW WHY I liked to torture myself. But I did. Unless I had a ballgame, I still went to every Crownsmen Quartet performance, and each time, as I had always done, I asked my dad if the group had Papaw's song on the list. Except now, my dad's emotional reading of the lines about his "own sweet family, a wife and little children dear," destroyed me inside.

I suppose I intuitively understood the power music had to move people, even when it hurt, and man did hearing him say those words hurt. I couldn't reconcile those lines with our vastly different reality. After the split, Kebo and I spent weekdays with my mom and weekends with my dad, who eventually bought a home on fifteen acres in Argillite, Kentucky, about ten miles from Flatwoods. I prayed they would get back together and make our family whole again. But that day never came. Instead, I found myself torn between two worlds.

The divorce didn't stop my parents from fighting. Whenever my dad dropped us boys off at the end of the weekend, Ruthie would find all sorts of reasons to let him have it. Once, before he married Joan, he made the mistake of coming to the house with his new girlfriend. When he pulled up to the house in his girlfriend's shiny new convertible, with his girlfriend next to him, Ruthie went ballistic. She grabbed the lady's jet-black bouffant by the roots, yanked her out of the car, and literally kicked her ass. Kebo and I and all the neighbors watched. My dad managed to separate them and get his girlfriend back in the car.

After he peeled out of the driveway, Ruthie apologized to the neighbors for her unladylike behavior.

"Ruthie, if it makes you feel any better, you stomped her ass right there in the ditch," one of the neighbors said.

On July 17, 1970, my dad remarried: a very nice woman named Joan Ward. She was educated and wore nice clothes. She had been married before and had two daughters, Cheri and Lisa, both older than Kebo and I. On January 19, 1972, Joan gave birth to my little sister, Angela Leigh Cyrus. Not long afterward, my dad was driving me back to 2317 Long Street when he said he was "getting ready to make a move."

I didn't know what he meant.

"I'm getting ready to make a move so that you and your brother will live with me all the time," he explained.

I suppose he thought he could give us a more stable life at his place, but my heart sank. I wanted to say, "Daddy, please don't do anything. Everything is fine like it is." It wasn't fine, or maybe it was in its own way, but I couldn't imagine leaving 2317 Long Street or my mom. Nor could I begin to tell my dad about the pain, anger, fear, and other complicated emotions that were going through my head at that moment.

Like a lot of kids who feel overwhelmed and confused, I was sullen and moody, and with all those feelings inside me, I didn't know how to express myself. So I just sat quietly. That's what I did with my dad. I just shut down.

To his credit, he didn't press me. He kept driving, and after a while he turned the radio back on.

But his notion turned into a custody battle. Soon a hearing date was set and Kebo and I were told we would have to go into court and talk to a judge about where we wanted to live. It was scary. Each of my parents spoke to us privately about wanting what was best for us, while intimating that it would be best if we chose them. "You do see why living with me and Joan and Angie would be best for you, right?" my dad asked. My mom said, "Now you guys tell me. Y'all want to stay here, right?" As far as I was concerned, there was no right decision . . . only wrong. Someone's feelings were gonna get hurt. But I knew my mom needed me.

I was aware of when the court date arrived. From the bits I heard, relatives from my dad's side painted my mom as inferior to my dad, and some of our neighbors went in and did the same in regards to my dad. It was ugly. The last cards in the deck were me and Kebo. No one wanted us boys to be put in the position of talking to the judge, but finally that day came. Papaw Casto drove us to the courthouse in his red Ford Falcon. I don't think we spoke a word the whole time.

For some reason, though, Kebo and I never made it inside. To this day, I'm not sure what happened, but we pulled up in front of the courthouse, got out of the car, with our hair combed and dressed in our nicest clothes, and someone came out and spoke with my papaw. A moment later, he told us to get back in the car and drove us back to 2317 Long Street, where Kebo and I lived for the rest of our childhood and beyond.

Back then, especially in a God-fearing town, divorce was uncommon and brought a great sense of shame. It didn't help that my grandfather was the town's preacher and his church was a focal point of the community. At school, I was the only kid whose parents were divorced. I heard the kids whisper about me. *Cyrus's parents are divorced. Does that still make them Christians?*

It didn't help that I was insecure about my appearance. Nothing on my face seemed to fit right, not my ears (they stuck out), my eyes (too big for my head), or my teeth (they were crooked). Ruthie kept my hair short, in what was called a butch cut. One day in first grade, a bunch of big kids from the eighth grade formed a circle around me and laughed. The oldest of them was a very hairy, scary midget. He scared me the most. He pushed me and said, "Come on, fight me. I'm your size." He pushed me again. "Come on." I broke free and ran home. That night I started saying a new bedtime prayer: "Dear God, I know I'm ugly, but when I grow up . . . just make people think I'm funny. Amen." It became known as my "nightly prayer."

I found refuge in the nearby woods, where I learned the calming effect of Mother Nature. One of my favorite things was to pretend I was Geronimo. Papaw Casto had given me an old rifle that no longer worked, and it looked identical to the one Geronimo is holding across his knee in the famous photograph of him from the Smithsonian. Instead of walking directly to school, I detoured into the woods and climbed a tree that my brother and I called "the song tree." We used to sit in its branches and make up songs. If I could sit in that tree and imitate the calls of the birds or see a deer or a rabbit or a squirrel or even a red-tailed hawk, I was happy.

I would sit in the tree for five, ten, or even twenty minutes — however long I could until I heard the first warning bell from school. By the time I reached the baseball field at McDowell Elementary School, the second bell would be ringing. I would usually make it to class just after everyone else had sat down.

"Boy, why are you always late?" my teacher once asked.

"I ain't late," I replied, heading straight to my seat without stopping. "I'm right on time."

Money was tight in our household. My dad's small salary mostly went to his new family, and Ruthie cleaned houses for a living. Somehow she always managed to find an extra hamburger to fry up if Kebo or I had a friend drop by; or if I needed a new football helmet, she made sure I got one. But we were practically the only family in all of Flatwoods that didn't have a telephone. I dreaded the beginning of the school year when the teacher made each student stand up and say his or her name, address, and phone number. Again, I heard the whispers. *Whoa, Cyrus doesn't have a phone? Yeah, he's the one whose parents are divorced. Wow, no phone. They probably still use an outhouse at his place.*

One of the saddest days of my life was when my mom sold her beloved piano, which had belonged to her mother, so she could pay the power bill and buy us clothes for Christmas. I think it was the saddest I ever saw my mom. Later on, when I started Russell Middle School, I met kids from Bellefonte and Kenwood, the two rich areas, and I realized how much of a divide there was between us and them.

We couldn't even afford a membership at the community swimming pool. When the summer heat and humidity got unbearable, Kebo and I cooled ourselves off with a garden hose on the front lawn, trying our best to ignore the laughter and the sounds of classic rock blaring over the loudspeakers at the nearby pool.

My best friend was Robbie Tooley. He showed up in third or fourth grade, the new kid in a school where we all knew each other, each other's parents, and each other's grandparents. Something else made him stand out, an aura, the way he immediately claimed a space for himself. Whatever it was, Robbie had it. His clothes were nice, his hair was slicked back, and he seemed self-confident, especially for a new kid. He was so different that I had a feeling someone was going to try to take him down a few rungs. Sure enough, they did.

By the end of the first week, word circulated that a couple of the school's bullies planned to take him down a notch or two after the last bell. There was a pond along the path everyone walked home, and word was they were going to confront Robbie there. Robbie got the message, too. Rather than cower or take another route, though, he made it known he planned to fight back.

I thought he was crazy.

After school, I followed the crowd to the pond. But instead of watching the new kid get beat up, I watched Robbie kick the crap out of two tough guys who thought they were going to teach him a lesson. It was the coolest thing I'd ever seen, like a scene out of the movies. Afterward, as Robbie dusted himself off, I stepped forward, helped him pick up his books, and told him my name. We were best friends from that day forward and that helped me.

My poor mom was the definition of snakebit. Bad luck seemed to dog her. Even now she recalls, "If I had one good day, four bad ones followed." Kebo and I didn't help. She had a succession of boy-friends after she and my dad divorced, but we scared most of them off. As the unofficial Ruthie Protection Squad, we pulled out all the stops whenever we decided one of her dates wasn't good enough, including one guy who owned a car dealership and was crazy about Ruthie.

He even gave her a car — a used car we nicknamed Ragsy be-cause we stuffed the gas cap hole with a rag. I don't remember whether we ran him off or she wasn't interested in him. Another one, a perfectly nice gentleman, gave me a terrific birthday pres-ent, an official leather NFL football signed by the commissioner, Pete Rozelle. Under different circumstances, it would have been the greatest gift in the world. But I was in Ruthie Protection mode. I went into my bedroom, got out a hunting knife, and cut the ball into shreds. Then I returned with the mutilated ball in my hand, grinning like a crazy clown.

The poor guy grabbed his coat, kissed Ruthie good-bye, and bolted for the front door. We never saw him again.

I know my mom deserved a life, but it didn't feel right for an-other man to come into the house where my dad had lived. Now, I like to say that if I hadn't run all of them off, Ruthie never would have meet Cletis Lee Adkins, a former railroad man turned truck driver for Ashland's Wolohan Lumber. Cletis — or Red, as I and everyone else called him — spent his last nickel to make sure Kebo and I had milk to drink, clothes on our back, and other comforts most kids took for granted. He was one of the best men I have ever met. But before I let him know I felt that way, before I admitted it to myself, I put him through hell.

On the day he and Ruthie got married in the church, we observed the occasion by actually getting into a fistfight in our front yard. It rained hard that day, which seemed appropriate to Kebo and me. After the ceremony, we drove home. It was still pouring, and the yard was a wet, muddy mess. When Kebo announced that he was going out to play, Cletis went into full stepfather mode and ordered him to think again.

"You're not my father," Kebo protested. "You can't tell us what to do."

Us? I hadn't planned to go outside. But now that Kebo had drawn a line in the mud, I wanted no doubt about whose side I was on.

"Yeah, you can't tell my brother what to do," I chimed in.

Cletis begged to differ, and the argument quickly escalated from raised voices into a shoving match and then into a full-scale war. There I was, trading punches with a man more than three times my age and twice my size, as the rain drummed down on us in the yard. And Kebo? He cheered me on from the safety of the porch, while Ruthie stood with her hands covering her face, horrified, screaming for us to stop.

Gradually, all of us acclimated to our new extended families. Ruthie and Cletis also had a son, Michael Joseph Adkins, my little brother, who we called Mick. If Cletis and Ruthie's wedding day was a disaster, I look back on Mick's arrival as a blessed event. Today, he is one of the few people I trust whole-heartedly. Our house on Long Street continued to be where all of Kebo's and my friends came after school to hang out or play ball.

By contrast, my dad and Joan's home in Argillite was way out in the country. They had a full house, too, with Angie and also Joan's mother, who we called Mammie. Being situated in the middle of nowhere, on fifteen acres, gave their home its sense of place. Kebo and I would spend hours exploring the land, looking for arrowheads and artifacts. One day we came upon a family living in a shack way out on the back edge. We were shocked by the decrepitude of their place, which made our home at 2317 Long Street look like a palace.

These folks defined Appalachian poor. The dad was an alcoholic, and the mom was haggard-looking from taking care of at least eight kids. The oldest two, Calvin and Jimmy, were the same age as Kebo and me. They were friendly, but they were so dirty and smelled so bad that we would run away from them.

This turned into a game. Kebo and I and our dog, Hank, a collie that was a dead ringer for Lassie but smarter, would spend the whole weekend hiding from those boys. We were like Daniel Boone and the Indians.

One day Kebo and I hid in a cave. We could hear Calvin and Jimmy rustling through the trees nearby. Hank had stayed sitting outside the cave, so they knew we were inside. After they found us, we all went back to my dad's house and Kebo and I washed off with the hose. Then we told Calvin and Jimmy to do the same.

As we cleaned up, I realized that we were all just boys having fun. It was a revelation. I had grown up worrying about what people thought of me for not having a phone or spiffy clothes, and lo and behold if God didn't bring two boys into my life who were worse off than me.

Calvin and Jimmy became our close friends. Kebo and I brought them to our Long Street home a few times and they flipped out. They'd never been out of their neck of the woods. Flatwoods was like a big city to them.

They were impressed that Kebo and I had our own bedrooms. In reality, we had shared a room until I threw my bed in what had been an oversize storage closet and hung a couple of black-light posters: one of Jimi Hendrix and another of a Bengal tiger. A few years later, I added the famous poster of Farrah Fawcett in a red skintight swimsuit.

Before *Charlie's Angels,* my favorite TV shows were *Batman, The Green Hornet,* and *Daniel Boone.* Then, *Get Smart, Sanford and Son,* and *Chico and the Man.* On Saturday mornings, my brother and I never missed *The Pink Panther;* I also loved *The Bullwinkle Show, Bugs Bunny,* and *Tom and Jerry.* Thinking about it now, those cartoons were pretty violent. I bet it's against the law to make them like that today. But that's beside the point.

I loved movies, too. When I was five, my three girl cousins took me to see *Bambi* at the Paramount Arts Center, a place that would later change my life. Back then, I was a squirmy little thing who wouldn't stay in his seat. As my cousins tell it, one of them said,

"Billy Ray, if you don't stop jumping and sit still, we're taking you home," and I just looked at them and said, "Don't make no difference to me." And kept jumping.

My dad also took me to a couple of drive-ins, where we saw *Planet of the Apes* and *The Good, the Bad and the Ugly*, starring Clint Eastwood. Those movies made an impression on me. To this day, Clint is still my number one box office badass. I also was a fan of *Billy Jack*, and my favorite of all time is the made-for-TV classic *Brian's Song*.

In my house, though, neither TV nor the movies could compete with music. We were a music-loving, music-playing family. A radio or a record player was usually on in some room. My boyhood soundtrack was a mix of Waylon Jennings, Willie Nelson, Merle Haggard, Glen Campbell, and Johnny Cash. I also listened to my share of Grand Ole Opry and Roy Clark and Buck Owens on *Hee Haw*. You weren't truly country without your music.

When I was eight, I started a collection of 45s. I'll never forget that day, because it was a tragic one. My mom, my brother, and I had saved three flying squirrels that had been deserted in their nest. We fed them with a medicine dropper for about three days. Then, for some reason, they died. To cheer me up, my mom took me to Hills department store and I got to pick out a record. I bought "Hitchin' a Ride" by Vanity Fare.

The first album I bought was Ike and Tina Turner's *What You Hear Is What You Get: Live at Carnegie Hall,* featuring their version of "Proud Mary." But I mostly bought 45s and eight-track tapes, including classics by Lynyrd Skynyrd, Charlie Daniels, the Ozark Mountain Daredevils, Earl Scruggs and Bill Monroe (bluegrass made me feel good), and Pink Floyd (that was my late-night go-to, and *loud*).

Then there were sports. I was a fan of the Cincinnati Bengals football team and an even bigger fan of the Cincinnati Reds baseball team. In those days, their stadiums were about a three-hour drive from Flatwoods up US 52 in Ohio, and though we couldn't afford to go to many games, those were my home teams, especially the Reds.

In the early '70s, they were known as the Big Red Machine. Their team consisted of all-stars and future hall of famers Johnny Bench, Pete Rose, Joe Morgan, Dave Concepcion, George Foster, Ken Griffey, Cesar Geronimo, and Tony Perez, along with manager Sparky Anderson. Bench was my favorite, since I played catcher in Little League. One day, Pete Rose signed autographs at a car dealership in Ashland and that was the biggest event that had ever happened near us, other than the day Santa Claus jumped out of an airplane to promote Hills department store and got stuck in a tree.

My mom took me to the car lot where Rose was signing autographs. I waited in a line that snaked around the entire place. After getting my signed picture, I got in line again, figuring it couldn't hurt to collect a few autographs. On my third time through, Rose complained loudly about me to the car lot owner. Then, in language more suited to the locker room, he directed his irritation in my direction.

"What the —" he said, dropping the F-bomb once or twice. "How many damn times are you going to come through here, boy?"

My mom wasn't about to let some hot-tempered, hotshot ballplayer talk that way to her kid. With hundreds of people watching in stunned silence, she lit into Charlie Hustle the way he was known to speak to umpires. I almost felt sorry for Pete. But I was too busy trying to wiggle out of her clutches and block her punches, because for some reason, she found it necessary to punctuate every sentence by slapping me upside the head.

"Don't you ever talk to my boy that way!" she said.

Slap!

"If anyone's going to discipline my son, it'll be me. Not some asshole like you!"

Slap!

"Hell, I don't even know why the boy would want your autograph."

Slap!

I was doing my best to get to the car. I didn't know which was more embarrassing: getting cussed out by Pete Rose or beat up by my mom. She was a force to reckon with. Later, after we were home, we laughed about the episode. I realized my mom had had a pretty good afternoon, and a pretty serious right hook. In terms of hits, she was three for three — a perfect day at the plate.

CHAPTER 3

A Series of Adjustments

MY DAD STARTED THE Crownsmen Quartet with guys just like him: riggers at Armco Steel, men who were tougher than tough and as solid as the steel they made, with good singing voices and a passion for performing gospel. Like my dad, who'd served in the air force, most had been in the service as young men before taking jobs at the mill. They all worked the late shift, and during their breaks they would sing.

They performed on Sundays throughout the tristate area. Churches. Revivals. County Fairs. One time they appeared on *The Happy Goodman Family Hour,* a gospel music TV series that aired every Sunday morning. I think they were one break away from being like the Oak Ridge Boys. It just didn't happen for them.

But music was always a sideline for my dad, who would have been a lifer at the steel mill if not for his sense of fairness. He would get stuck on a problem until he figured it out, and one time he got stuck on a problem at work. It was the early 1970s, and he saw the steel mill cheat a guy who'd lost his legs in a work-related accident out of money they owed him. It affected him deeply and turned into a calling, similar to when my papaw Cyrus heard a voice tell him to become a preacher.

Helping that injured coworker ignited my dad's determination to stand up for working men and their families. He became their voice. In a short time, he put himself through school, quit the mill, started working for the AFL-CIO, and set a goal of getting elected to political office.

His patience was typified by the way he taught me to drive. As a little kid, I sat on his lap as he drove the last mile or so up the gravel road leading to his house in Argillite. He worked the gas and brake and let me steer, though I'm sure he kept a finger or two on the wheel. As I gained more control of the vehicle, as well as respect for what it meant to get behind the wheel, he gave me more independence.

In the morning, as he drank his coffee, I would ask if I could take the truck to get the newspaper. The first time he said yes was one of the greatest days of my life. I ran outside, started up his truck, and drove down that gravel road to where the paper sat. From then on, it became a routine.

The truck had an eight-track cassette player, and my dad had three eight-tracks — Merle Haggard, Johnny Cash, and Glen Campbell. Every time I drove, I played one of those cassettes. Around the time I was twelve, he had switched to a Buick and my morning excursion began to include a few daring zigzags across the dry creek, just enough to excite me and not damage the car. I'd be listening to Haggard's "Workin' Man Blues," and I couldn't help it. I had to do something a little crazy. It just made me feel good — the song, that is.

Once I got a hold of some Led Zeppelin, like the song "Black Dog," I got a little crazier, pressed harder on the gas pedal, and did what I call loop-de-loos — 360s — while laughing as the back tires spit out clods of dirt and grass. It was simple fun, but also, looking back, it was the beginning of my foolishness.

I was not much of a student. This became abundantly clear the year my aunt Sue — my father's sister — was my sixth-grade math teacher. (An interesting side note: She had married Clifford Hatfield — yes, those Hatfields of Hatfield and McCoy fame; and, somewhere down the family tree, I'm a blood relative of the Mc-Coys.) Anyway, one day in class, Aunt Sue politely said, "You may want to avoid being a mathematician when you grow up," and I didn't argue with her.

My academic career may have peaked the following year, when I gave a speech in history class on Chief Joseph of the Nez Perce. It included a recitation of his famous surrender speech, ending with "From where the sun now stands, I will fight no more forever." I got an A, and at the end of the year when the teacher assigned us to rewrite any speech as a satire, I picked that one and rewrote it as a declaration of what I wanted to do that summer.

"I will go fishing," I wrote. "I will go skinny-dipping. I will play baseball. I will ride my motorcycle." And here I took a long, dramatic pause. I sensed the entire class was hanging on my words. What ignorance was I going to impart? I didn't let them down as I said with breathless melodrama, "From where the sun now stands, I will learn . . . no more . . . forever."

All my classmates laughed, and so did my teacher, Mr. Holt. He gave me an A — and more important, he encouraged me to be creative.

But my most important lessons came when I was riding around with my dad while he was teaching me to drive. One time I was trying to back out of a tight spot. I kept going back and forth, back and forth, turning the wheel one direction, then the other. Laughing, he said, "Remember this day, Bo. Life is a series of adjustments." My dad's front seat was always filled with a mess of papers; if you were to get in my car today, you'd find the same thing — CDs, songs I'm working on, and reminders of meetings. But his were notes about people and the problems that really mattered to them.

One day, out of the blue, my dad announced, "We're going to pay a visit to John Samson and see how he's doing."

I'd never heard of John Samson. I asked, "Why?"

"He got cheated out of all them funds he's supposed to be due for that black lung he caught in the coal mine, and he's going to need some help fighting for that money."

Later, we visited Sister Sheila out on Route 1. Her culvert was stopped up from a flood and my dad was trying to get it cleared. He explained, "If we don't get that fixed, her creek is going to overflow again and all the gravel will wash out of her driveway."

My dad didn't just talk about helping people and getting things done. He lived it. Whether I realized at the time, I took that powerful lesson to heart, as I did so many other lessons from the school of real life.

Another branch of my education revolved around a baseball diamond or a basketball court. I celebrated when the Big Red Machine won their first pennant, listened to the Muhammad Ali–Joe Frazier fight on the radio, and mourned the 1970 plane crash that killed seventy-five people from the Marshall University football team. That crash happened less than twenty-five miles from my house, and it was the most tragic event that happened close to us.

When I was in seventh grade, I made what seemed to be a monumental decision in my burgeoning athletic career. I stopped playing basketball. The coach was stunned. "Cyrus, you could be the best player on the team," he said. "Are you sure?"

I was. I didn't tell the coach this, but I felt bad when my mom and dad were trapped on the same bleachers, under the same roof, during my basketball games. Other sports were played outside and in spaces that allowed more distance, especially for my mom.

"Sir, I think I should just focus on baseball and football," I said.

"Is that what you really want?" he asked.

"I think it's for the best," I said with the utmost sincerity, trying to show that I had given this a lot of thought.

Sports kept me confident and focused. Robbie Tooley and I tore up the football field. But baseball was my favorite because it brought out the warrior in me. Although I started out playing all positions, I had settled in at catcher by the time I was eleven.

As soon as I strapped on my gear, I turned into a field general, a quarterback . . . and a scrappy one at that. My teammates called me Blood. I'd fight at the drop of a hat. If a batter struck out on the third strike, I'd show him the ball, as if to say, "Here it is, here's what you missed," just to rile him up and get under his skin. Or if a runner slid into home plate with his cleats high, I made sure he got tagged first. As long as he was out, that's all that mattered.

I needed that toughness when Papaw Casto died suddenly after a massive heart attack. Not only did my heart overflow with sadness like I'd never known, but I was also passed over at about that same time for the baseball all-star team even though everyone knew I was the best catcher in the league. Crushed, I rode my bicycle to my papaw's grave at the Flatwoods cemetery.

I remembered my dad's words — "Life ain't fair." But my papaw would have had something else to add. He was a baseball fan and had come to nearly every one of my games.

"How could this have happened?" I said. "I miss you so much. I know if you were here you'd tell me something to make me smile."

I sat there for a long time, looking at the grass, slapping at insects buzzing past, and listening to the quiet. Before leaving the cemetery, I said a prayer.

When I arrived home on my bike, the coach of the all-stars was there, talking with my mom and Cletis in the front yard. When he saw me, he stuck out his hand and said, "There's my all-star catcher."

I stopped in my tracks. "What the — ?"

"We were looking at the team and realized you weren't on it," the coach said. "Everyone assumed you'd made it. We need you, son. You're our catcher."

I broke out my supersize grin, looked over at my mom, then at Cletis, then at the coach, and finally up at the ceiling. "Thanks, Papaw," I said silently.

It wasn't the last time I would think someone up high was keeping an eye on me.

CHAPTER 4

Silence Speaks Louder than Words

I WAS NEARLY A fourteen-year-old fugitive. A developer began building homes in the woods at the end of Long Street. I watched the bulldozers clear the trees and level the land. I was horrified and angered. That was sacred ground. I couldn't fathom the loss of my sanctuary, the wooded retreat where I went to hide out and think. It was also where Indians had lived and hunted for hundreds of years before anyone thought of putting in dozens of one-story tract homes.

Even if it was legal, it felt wrong, so I did my best to stop the pillaging. I snuck out at night and put dirt in the bulldozer's gas tank. I also tore up the insides of a few tractors. I prayed I wouldn't hear the sound of those diesel engines starting up in the morning.

Unfortunately, while I may have annoyed some folks when they showed up for work, they continued, unhindered. Soon the woods disappeared and houses were built. One day I saw a guy who'd moved into a new house take a bird's nest out of a tree and bust a bunch of baby bird eggs on the sidewalk. I thought he deserved payback.

Late one afternoon, I went out there with my friend Joe Preston. I knew the builders stored cans of sulfuric acid for dissolving extra concrete. We took a couple of cans and walked back to where the baby-bird killer lived. We threw the acid against the side of his house and wrote ugly things about killing baby birds on the walls and fence in red paint. It looked like blood.

As we turned to run away, I noticed the neighbor's bathroom window was open, with a large jar of Vaseline on the shelf in front. In a single motion, I grabbed it and chucked it on the sidewalk, where it shattered. Back then, the jars were made of blue glass and it made a horrendous mess.

That night, the police came to the house. My brother knew about it and said the state police were taking fingerprints. Joe and I snuck through a couple of backyards and saw the cops. By this time, I felt bad about having torn up that guy's property. It was a horrible thing. Maybe we had taken it too far. But I didn't want to go to jail and neither did Joe. So we decided to leave town . . . on our bicycles.

We headed out toward Greenbo Lake. We spent a good part of the night on our bikes, but at some point we turned back and went to Joe's house. After making sure the coast was clear, I went back to 2317 Long Street. Nothing happened, no one asked any questions, and I never brought it up.

For me, it was the rare escape.

I wasn't a bad kid, but I sure wasn't an innocent one. Getting in trouble was my way of dealing with the conflicts of being from a broken home. My parents' lives were so different, and it created a mess of confusion for me. I dreaded conversations with new people, knowing that they'd eventually ask me about my family and if I had any brothers or sisters.

Always trying to be honest, I'd say, "Yeah, I have one brother by my mom and my dad, one brother by my mom and my stepdad, one sister by my dad and my stepmom, two stepsisters from my stepmom, and one stepsister from my stepdad."

Every month, my mom and Cletis struggled to pay their bills. My dad and Joan did better. It was hard for me to reconcile having hardship and joy in the same family. I guess that's where the phrase *broken home* comes from.

· · ·

A year or so later, my dad made his first run at public office. He lost, but I never heard him say so. Instead, he made it seem like he'd learned what it was going to take to win the next time. "Everything was in God's timing," he said. Then he added, "There are only two things in the middle of the road — yellow lines and dead possums."

That's one of the truest sayings, ever. I still say it to this day.

In 1975, my dad ran again, for the Kentucky House of Representatives, from the ninety-eighth district, and this time he won. We worked hard on his campaign. Kebo and I put up posters all over town, so I attributed the win, at least in part, to my staple gun. I don't remember my dad celebrating his election. Not even a victory dinner. He went straight to work the next day.

Soon afterward, he quit the steel mill and went full-time with the AFL-CIO. As he canvassed the state, his passion for helping people took on an even more pronounced purpose.

Not long before, my papaw Cyrus got an infection in his lungs and passed away. He was eighty-five. His was the first funeral I attended where he wasn't preaching. It was strange to not have either of my grandfathers in my life anymore. After my parents divorced, I'd leaned on my grandfathers, and while it was sometimes a curse to be known far and wide as the preacher's grandson, there were definitely benefits, too.

Take for example the day Mrs. Fight, the meanest teacher at McDowell Elementary, caught me and my brother bombing her house with apples. She was an older, heavy woman, with gray hair. My dad remembered her as mean from when she had been *his* teacher. Kebo and I were getting even, I guess. As soon we heard her yell at us, we ran away.

We didn't expect her to chase us. She was a scrappy old lady. We ran to my papaw Cyrus's house and went inside just before Mrs. Fight arrived. She knocked on the door a few minutes later and let my grandfather know what had happened. "Preacher Cyrus, them boys right there just pelted my house with apples. I want you to bring them out on this porch and whip them!"

My papaw stood between us. I was imagining the paddle with

holes in it she kept in her classroom. She had beaten me, as well as my brother, my dad, and hundreds of others through the years. But she wasn't going to get us this time.

"Mrs. Fight, you know boys will be boys," he said, stretching out his frame to its fullest six feet three inches before closing the door on her.

What could she do? He was the preacher.

Payback came a few years later when I was playing with matches and accidentally set my papaw's bathroom on fire. To this day, I can still see the hurt in his eyes as he stood in the doorway, surveying the damage, after I had put out the flames.

"What did I do to make you hate me?" he said.

Without waiting for a response, he walked away. It was the most severe punishment I have ever been dealt. If I could take back one moment of my life and trade it in, that would be it.

After my papaw was gone and no longer preaching, I quit going to church and took my juvenile delinquency to a whole new level. I was fourteen, and many kids that age were starting to experiment with alcohol and marijuana. Only I didn't experiment: I just went straight for it.

There was a guy who lived with his folks a couple of houses down from mine. He was five or six years older than me and, as far as I was concerned, the coolest dude on the planet. To me, he was like the Fonz on *Happy Days*. I saw him one day with a sack of grass and yellow rolling papers. I didn't even know what it was, but I watched, completely enthralled, while he rolled what I thought was a cigarette. I forgot to mention he had a yellow Corvette to match his papers. He also had a motorcycle and pretty girlfriends . . . lots of them.

I wanted to be just like this guy. Every now and then he gave me a smoke. Or sold me one. He also introduced me to beer — little green bottles of Big-Mouth Mickeys. Sometimes we chased them with a shot of whiskey . . . or moonshine.

My mom usually kept a bottle of Jack Daniel's Black Label or

Wild Turkey in the kitchen cabinet, and Cletis had a fridge in his work garage filled with a beer called Bavarian. It was the cheapest beer he could buy. But it was cold — and free! — so I helped myself.

I'd always had a daring streak, but the whiskey was like putting a match next to a can of gasoline. Toss in a soundtrack of ass-kicking southern rock with a double shot of outlaw, turned up loud, and it was a recipe for a big batch of trouble. I thought it was fun to pelt people's homes or trailers with rotten apples or eggs at midnight. The evening wasn't a success until I got the police to chase me. The blue lights were icing on the cake to a job well done. Mission accomplished.

Without my papaw or church in my life, I didn't have any fear of consequences. One of my favorite activities was streaking. As soon as I heard about this fad of people running out in public without any clothes, I jumped on the bandwagon. I ran all over Flatwoods. I even went to Hills department store and bought Ray Stevens's record "The Streak," which became my national anthem.

My friend Robbie was usually running alongside me; other times it was Joe Preston or another buddy named Jeff Vest. I ran through the middle of town; people laughed and screamed. It was fun to see how far I could get running naked before the cops gave chase. That was the goal. To get chased.

We did get caught one time, me and Joe. We told the cops our clothes were in the woods. They knew who we were; we had a reputation. Laughing, they let us get our jeans and T-shirts before driving us back to my papaw's house, where my grandmother still lived.

"Cyrus, don't let us catch you hanging out in town again," one of the cops said.

"Literally," the other one cracked.

Despite the warning, my wild side and petty vandalism continued. I threw eggs, tomatoes, and persimmons (when in season) at homes and trailers. The sound of persimmons bursting as they smashed against the outside of a trailer sounded similar to a gunshot. If we threw them fast enough, we could approximate the sound of a machine gun — or so we imagined.

Then I started to shoplift. We had three department stores nearby, Hills, Hecks, and K-Mart. My frequent partner in this crime was a friend from the football team. He was the kicker and I was the holder. We were already a duo of sorts. When the weather turned cold, we wore large down coats that we called puff jackets.

"You got your puff jacket?" was code for "Let's go steal stuff." We slipped whatever we could inside those jackets and walked out of the store as if we weren't able to find what we'd wanted. This was my acting debut; I just didn't know it. We were loaded down with 45s, LPs, and damn near anything else we wanted. We got so skilled that we took orders from our buddies and sold the stuff back to them at a discounted rate. We considered ourselves redneck Robin Hoods.

Robbie only came with us one time, but it turned out the one thing he wasn't good at was shoplifting. We went to K-Mart, and he also wore his puff jacket and he put a bunch of stuff in it. I was on lookout at the front door when I heard our gambit announced over the loudspeaker: "Shoplifter. Aisle 12." Then an update. "He's at aisle 10 now. It's a man in a blue jacket." Then: "He's headed toward the side door and throwing stuff from the jacket."

That's when we took off. Robbie managed to escape through the parking lot, and we picked him up down the road where there were no lights. He was wet and sweaty from running his ass off and he looked scared to death. As he caught his breath, Robbie swore he'd never shoplift again.

One weekend I was having dinner with my dad at his house. It was just the two of us. Kebo had graduated high school and was off doing his own thing now, and I can't remember where Angie, Joan, and Mammie were that night. My dad and I were talking, when I heard Calvin and Jimmy yelling outside. They were too far away for me to understand what they were saying. I went to the window and saw them running across our horse pasture as hard and as fast as they could.

"Look there," I said. "Calvin and Jimmy are having a race."

My dad turned around and looked.

"No, it seems like something might be wrong, Bo," my dad said.

I stepped outside to holler at them, and that's when I understood their scream: "Our house is on fire! Our house is on fire!"

"Dad, their house is on fire!" I yelled. "Call the fire department!"

I shot into the backyard and joined them in the field. We turned around and ran back up the creek to their house. We raced through a hollow, through the creek bed, and along a path that wound back to where two Appalachian foothills came together. When we finally got there, we saw that their wooden house was ablaze. The sun was setting; we were literally in a valley of shadows. Their house, which dated back to the 1880s, was a fiery hell. I had never seen anything like it.

As we got closer, I heard something that sounded like a young girl's voice. The voice was faint, and creepy, like something out of a scary movie, but I could clearly hear the words: "Help me. Help me, Mommy." I looked around for Calvin and Jimmy and found them over to the side, counting all their brothers and sisters.

"Everyone there?" I yelled.

"Yep," Calvin said, adding to his parents, "Daddy? Mama? You OK?"

Then where the hell was that little girl's voice coming from? When we were younger, Kebo and I would camp out in our barn with Calvin and Jimmy, and they frequently told us about a ghost that lived in their house.

"Last night the ghost came downstairs and took all the clothes that Mama had for Sissy and Bubba out to the well," Calvin once said.

"And hung 'em on the clothesline," Jimmy had added.

"Y'all are just trying to scare us," I'd said.

Another time, Calvin and Jimmy said their father saw a Ford Model T from the late '20s driving up the creek one night. I investigated and I found a carving of a Model T etched deep in the bark of a huge old beech tree by the creek. When I showed my dad, he shrugged it off.

"Oh, you know Clyde," he said. "One night he might see a pink elephant and carve that into a tree. Given how he's been known to have a little drinkie-winkie, he's liable to see anything."

Maybe so, but that still didn't explain the voice I'd heard in the fire. Nor would I get an explanation that night. The fire trucks were unable to get up the hollow and Calvin and Jimmy's house burned till there was nothing left. I waited for my dad to say something about this tragedy, something that would make sense out of it. I wanted him to at least tell me that Calvin and Jimmy and their family would be OK.

Instead, we sat up late that night, just me and my dad, not saying much of anything. Johnny Carson came on TV, and we watched him together as we always did on the rare occasions when we were in the same house, in the same room, at the same time. But this time we never laughed, not once.

When the show ended, my dad turned off the TV and we sat in the dark, enveloped by stillness of the night, the absolute quiet. Finally, my dad got up to go to bed, without mentioning anything about what had happened earlier. I was surprised. It was the only time my dad didn't seem to know what to say, though now, as a father myself, I realize he'd said it all.

Sometimes silence speaks louder than words.

CHAPTER 5

A Higher Authority

KIMMY BLEDSOE WAS MY very first girlfriend. We started dating when I was three years old. I'm serious. Her family lived in the house next door to mine and that wasn't close enough for us. We weren't happy unless we were sitting on the sofa next to each other. We shared a little stuffed monkey that we referred to as our baby and took it into the woods, where we pretended we had a house of our own.

One day, a couple years into our friendship, I came out of the woods and my dad said, "Where have you been, son?"

"I was down in the woods, kissing Kimmy," I said.

"Where did you kiss her at?" he asked.

"Down the woad," I said, my speech impeded then by a few missing teeth.

"No, where did you kiss her at? On the lips?"

"No. Down in the woad, tupid."

My dad loved that story and told it for years, always laughing as he recalled asking me where I had kissed her and then embellishing with an exaggerated accent, "Down in the woad, *tupid*." But that romance ended when Kimmy and her family moved the summer before first grade. After that, I was unattached until I was eight or nine and noticed Regina Carroll had grown some boobies.

Starting in third grade, we were on-again-off-again boyfriend and girlfriend. Sometimes we were just friends. We played football or basketball together. By junior high, she had turned into an exceptional athlete (and would go on to star on every team in high school and stand out at the University of Kentucky). On Friday nights, we roller-skated at the local rink and held hands. Afterward, I walked her home, and somewhere between the rink and her house we'd end up in the woods, fooling around.

She taught me a lot. I'm not sure I taught her anything except that she could jump higher than me and shoot better.

My mantra was "play it by ear," and that's how it was with me and sex. It kind of happened, and I learned.

By fifteen, though, Regina and I stopped kissing each other (with a few exceptions, just because it was fun). I had a few different girlfriends in high school, but not anybody steady until the end of the summer between my sophomore and junior year. That's when Susie Secrest not only entered my life but also took it over.

She was younger than me, coming up from the eighth grade to be a high school freshman, and she put out the word that she had a crush on me and wanted to date me. Up till then, I had never been in love. I didn't have time for that foolishness. Oh, I might meet someone at the pizza shop or roller rink every now and then and have a game of hide-the-weenie. But that was it. Then it was back to work.

At first I felt that Susie was too young and flat-out wrong for me. She was from a religious family in a prosperous neighborhood called Kenwood, and I was from the other woods, Flatwoods. There was a difference. I knew her parents wouldn't dig me. But that didn't matter to Susie. She was smart and persistent.

It was August, and I was in the middle of two-a-day football practices before the school year started. I played defensive and offensive end. Robbie Tooley was the center. We worked out in the morning and then again late in the afternoon. It was hot and humid, temperatures routinely soaring into the nineties and hundreds. As far as I was concerned, the tougher the conditions, the better I liked it — except wearing a helmet and chin strap in that heat made my face break out something terrible.

One day after practice, I looked up and saw Susie staring at me. She was blonde, with brown eyes, and she'd made the cheerleading team as a freshman. She stepped forward without my noticing and was straddling the front tire of my bike, a leg on both sides.

At first, all I saw was a pair of hot-pink gym shorts right in front of me, at eye level. As far as I was concerned, I was looking at the most beautiful, sexiest thing I'd ever seen in my life.

"Please, Bo, won't you take me to my street," she said, motioning to my dirt bike. "I won't cause you any trouble. No one will ever know."

"I don't know," I said. "What if your mom and dad drive by? Or someone they know?"

"No one will find out. Just ride me to my street."

I had no willpower at this point. I surrendered. The word *no* disappeared from my vocabulary.

"Yeah, sure," I said, and it was game over.

We stopped along the way in the woods and kissed, and between then and dropping her off, I fell in love.

Even though I had strong feelings for Susie, I still played hard to get through most of my junior year. Susie was a good girl; I was from the wrong side of the tracks, and I wanted to spare her and her wonderful family the heartache and disappointment of a doomed relationship. I didn't see how we could possibly work as a couple.

I had other reasons, too, and I couldn't articulate them other than to know that Susie was such a good girl and I had some issues. Here's the proof: A few days before Christmas, I stole a 3-D picture of Jesus from Hills department store and gave it to my grandmother Mamaw Cyrus for Jesus's birthday. She loved it! Thank God she didn't ask where I bought it so I didn't have to lie to her.

I still don't know how I could've stolen it in the first place and then given it to her. Anything would've been better than a 3-D Jesus. What had happened to my conscience? Had my spirit left me?

My heart was in the right place. I wanted to give my mamaw that magnificent three-pronged spectacle of Jesus on the cross, the Lord's supper, and then I think if you moved in one more direction he was kneeling at the rock. You can understand why she loved it — and why I felt terrible.

But if I could do that, how could I be with someone as nice as Susie?

Obviously I needed to learn a lesson. I had a little car that I called the Gray Mouse. It was a Vega that I wished was a Pinto or vice versa. I got it used for around $700. It wasn't nice, although it did have wide tires and was jacked up a bit in the back, which gave it a unique look. After Cletis and I put in some shag carpet and a decent stereo, it was a pretty good little redneck potluck.

One afternoon between baseball practices, I was driving to the barbershop in Russell to get a haircut. I was in a hurry, driving way too fast, and I hit some water in the road, hydroplaned, and flew off a hilltop.

After my car rolled to the bottom of a ravine, I sat still for a minute, figuring out which way was up. I got out and ran back up the hill. At the top, I looked back down at my car and only then did I realize how lucky I was to be alive. The Mouse was mangled. It looked like King Kong had grabbed hold of it and crushed it like a soda can. The windows were broken, doors were gone, and the frame was bent.

All I could remember was that as I rolled over and over down the hill, everything around me was white. As I surveyed the damage, I heard a voice: "Now we're even."

I looked around. No one else was in the vicinity. It was just me out there on that country road. I put my head in my hands and thought that in my distraught state of mind, I must have been hearing noises. But, as soon as I tried to reason it away, I heard the voice again, this time more clearly and more unmistakable.

"If you ever steal again, I'll have to take your life. For now, we're even."

• • •

When I told Susie about the voice, she said what I was already thinking: "It was God."

"I don't know for sure," I said. "But if I ever did hear the voice of God, then that was it. And I'm freaked out."

"Don't be," she said in a tone of voice that held the comfort of a genuine believer. "He just needed to get your attention. God does that sometimes. You're out of control, and he was watching over you."

"I know, but — "

She put her finger over her lips. "No buts. Just listen and accept his word."

Easier said than done. But I accepted her appraisal of the situation, along with her advice, and as the baseball season got under way, Susie and her dad started coming to my games. I think she began to feel the stirrings of a mission. She didn't say it, not yet anyway. But that's what I thought. Her dad, whose name was Bill, had also been a catcher back in school. Like me, he'd harbored aspirations of turning pro. He seemed to enjoy the games and watching me play.

Afterward, we'd talk about the game. He asked great questions about situations that only another catcher would pick up on. Then Susie's family started inviting me over for dinner. A few times they let me sit at their house and watch TV when no one else was there. Basically, they welcomed me into their home.

By summer, Susie and I had grown even closer. My resistance had melted. I gave her my high school ring, and after that, as best as I could tell, we were going steady.

But then I let her down in August at Greenbo Lake. I was again in the midst of two-a-day football practices. As always, it was miserably hot. Even the gnats had gone to find shade. In between practices, I borrowed — or took, depending on your definition — Cletis's motorcycle, a Honda 175.

Every now and then he'd let me take it around the block, but on this particular day, I decided to drive it to Greenbo Lake with a friend. I didn't hang out much with this guy, since we came from different neighborhoods, but he'd invited me to go riding. So we motorcycled out to a place of true Appalachian beauty: lush, dense forest covering the hills, tons of deer, and picturesque views where the scenery would reflect off the water.

My papaw Casto used to take my brother Kebo and me fishing at Greenbo Lake when we were little. Susie and I also went there to "count the deer," and then we'd park under the moonlight. There was nothing like the feeling of our hearts beating together on a hot, humid summer night, with a thousand lightning bugs overhead giving off a fireworks show just for us.

My friend and I rode to the dam there. We parked our bikes and hiked on up to the top so we could see the entire lake.

Then he fished a pipe out of his pocket and placed some high-octane marijuana in the bowl. Back then, pot was as prevalent as the clouds rolling across the sky. You'd hear about Mexican this, Acapulco Gold, or Columbian Redbud, but the truth was, according to an article in *High Times* magazine, some of the best and most potent pot in the country was grown right in Kentucky's own Daniel Boone National Forest — and I think that's what we had, Homegrown Skunk.

We fired up the bowl and then a few minutes later, right in the midst of our conversation about how beautiful this place was, what a great day it was to be out riding our bikes, and wasn't everything in our lives perfect at that moment . . . just when we were nice and stoned and mellow, my hands were jerked behind my back, a pair of handcuffs was slapped on, and my hillbilly ass went rolling down the hard-packed trail we'd just hiked up. And I kept rolling until some burly sheriff grabbed my shirt and pulled me upright. Talk about a buzz kill.

Another sheriff led us to their car; I knew we were in trouble. Out of the corner of my eye, I saw Cletis's motorcycle getting loaded into a freakin' tow truck. They moved a chicken coop to make room for the bike. A sick feeling filled my stomach. I knew seeing Cletis's bike tossed up there was even worse than my ass getting hauled off to the sheriff's station.

The two of us ended up in jail. Someone from my friend's family got us out and gave me a ride home.

Telling my dad, the state representative, and my mom and Cletis what had happened was scary, and even scarier was telling Cletis about his motorcycle. But the worst part of all was Susie's parents finding out. If they heard that I'd been hauled in for marijuana use, Susie's and my relationship was over. Here's what happened.

My mom told my dad that he had to take me to court. "Ruthie, I'd be glad to . . . if I'm in town," he said. Miraculously (not), he was out of town when I was due in court, and so my mom took me (pissed off as hell, I might add). By then, Cletis's bike had been returned to 2317 Long Street, though I don't remember how. In court, I faced Judge James "Jimmy" Lyon, one of the area's great men.

He was the judge in Greenup County, Kentucky, for as long as I can remember. He was born without arms, worked his way through law school, and became one of the most respected men in the Kentucky judicial system. He'd handled my mom and dad's divorce and knew my family well.

I have a feeling Judge Lyon saw my mother's angry face and decided to cut me a break. He said the arrest would go away and not even appear on my record if I wrote a five-thousand-word essay on "da ebils (the evils) of mar-i-won-a" (a speech impediment made him sound like Elmer Fudd with a Cajun twist).

"Biway Cywus," he continued. "I know yo' family. I know yo' papaw Cywus. He da preacher man. I know yo' parents. Dey good people, too. You should be ashamed."

"And I am ashamed, sir," I said.

He was steamed.

When he said the word *marijuana* — "I want you to wight a five-thousand-wud essay on da ebils of mar-i-won-a" — he slammed his gavel down three times and seemed to gesture at me with his arms, though it looked to me, at that insensitive stage of my life, like his arms were flapping out of control. I got the message anyway.

I went to the library and researched marijuana . . . *in books.* Despite all my experience with pot, I needed actual facts to fill up twenty pages. From my reading, I learned that eastern Kentucky had some of the best and most fertile soil in the world for growing the plant. During the Civil War, the state had been the leading producer of hemp, which was used to make rope. The plant grew similar to tobacco.

Huh, I wondered, what would happen if the government taxed it like cigarettes and alcohol?

"Maybe they could pave roads and build schools with all that money," I wrote.

Susie proofed my essay before I turned it in. She believed that pot was the doorstep to the devil's living room, but dang if she didn't put down the last page and say, "Bo, I don't agree with you, but this kind of makes sense." Fortunately, Judge Lyon also thought I did a good job, and he told me so.

Once football season began, I put that ordeal behind me and played the best ball of my life. We won the Kentucky State AAA championship that year. It felt like we won the Super Bowl. A bunch of our wins came down to Robbie Tooley at center snapping the ball to me and Keeno, our kicker, putting the ball through the uprights.

Robbie was the team's star player. He had a cocky way of prancing from the huddle to the ball, which the local newspapers called the Tooley Trot. It got under the skin of opposing players, but our fans loved it. Robbie was our school's Burt Reynolds, the guy with the extra sparkle. Everyone loved him.

My best moment that year happened during Christmas break. One day, just before the holiday, I came home and found my mom very sad. The lady she cleaned for on Fridays was selling her piano. That was the only piano my mom had to play since selling her own piano to pay some bills when we were young.

For her, music was like breathing. She couldn't imagine not being able to play. Even that one time a week was like physical and emotional therapy for her, much like it is for me today.

I had saved nearly $2,000 from doing odd jobs and yard work over the years. Without telling my mom, I visited the lady she worked for and asked how much she wanted for the piano. Her price was way more than I could afford. Seeing my reaction, she asked why I wanted it. When I told her it was for my mom, she asked how much I could pay, and upon hearing the amount, she said, "It's yours for that price."

I shook her hand and wrote a check. Although I was now broke, I couldn't have been happier. My mom was going to have her own piano again.

Every year on Christmas we went to Cletis's mom and dad's, where Kebo and I would each get a pair of socks, eat dinner, and watch TV. It wasn't much, but it was our tradition. This year, however, I told my mom that I was going elsewhere. She was furious! I disappeared, and that made her even madder.

While she and Red and my little brother Mick were gone, my buddies and I loaded the piano in a truck and put it inside the new little room Cletis had made a while back by walling up the carport. We'd put a stereo in there, along with a potbellied stove. The piano fit perfectly.

Late that night, Ruthie and Cletis and Mick came home. My friends' cars were in the driveway, so I knew Ruthie would be pissed off, thinking I'd spent the night partying, and she was right. But when she came through the door, we all yelled surprise — and she saw the piano.

"Merry Christmas, Ma," I said.

She was speechless, which wasn't like Ruthie. She may have even wiped a tear from her eyes.

"Well, don't just stand there," I said. "How about a little 'Red Headed Stranger'?"

We put the song on the stereo, and she played along to the entire album. It was like she had joined Willie's band. And thanks to the way some of my friends enhanced the party atmosphere, it smelled like it too.

• • •

That spring, I took Susie to the school's Sweetheart Dance, where she was up for Sweetheart Queen. It was already a special night, but Robbie and I planned to make it even more special. We arranged to meet midway through the dance outside the back door, where we'd stashed a pint of Jim Beam and a big fat doobie. It was enough to get a buzz before the queen was announced.

As we slipped out, I used a brick to lodge the back door open a bit so we could get back in. Then we got pretty dang high. Unfortunately, when we tried to get back into the school, the door was closed and the brick was pushed to the side. I picked up the brick, smashed the window above the door, and reached through the glass for the doorknob. Genius.

As we reentered, we walked straight into Dick Baker, the school's principal and a deacon in Susie's church. The vice principal, Ronnie Back, the only person who'd busted my ass more times than Ruthie, was standing next to him.

Neither were the kind of man you said "Oh, shit" in front of. But in this situation, they were the most appropriate two words — and the first two that came to mind. Both men stared at Robbie and me, unflinching and stone-faced.

Robbie and I were both silent. I knew the best I could do was to anticipate the worst, and hopefully absorb the blow that was about to come from Mr. Baker. Silence filled the air. Then came the sound: *squirt . . . squirt . . . squirt.* I looked down and saw blood squirting from my thumb. It spurted all over my beige suit, reminding me of a scene from the movie *M*A*S*H.*

"Mr. Cyrus, it looks like you're bleeding," Mr. Back said. "That trail of blood leads right to that broken window. Huh? Ain't that something."

Then came what every student at Russell High School dreaded most — Mr. Baker saying, "Follow me."

He led Robbie and me into the office adjoining the Student Union, where the dance was taking place. The office was all windows, so when they flipped on the lights it couldn't have been brighter: there we were, in all our glory, for the whole school to see.

Susie bawled her eyes out. Robbie's date was none too pleased, either. Suddenly, the Sweetheart Dance wasn't so sweet anymore. Robbie and I knew what was coming: we were asked to leave.

I don't remember much of anything from the rest of that night, but in light of what happened, I do believe Mr. Baker let us off easy. He could've called the cops. He didn't. As a man of faith, he left the discipline to *a higher authority*.

CHAPTER 6

A College Education

I HAD NO REASON to be angry with Mr. Baker for what happened that night. But I did blame him for ruining the dance for Susie, and I wanted to get even with him. After we lost a baseball game one night, I got drunk with our baseball team's star pitcher and shortstop, Stewart Hensley, and then the two of us drove to Mr. Baker's house and pelted it with eggs. We hammered the place.

As soon as we ran out of eggs, we jumped in my Camaro and sped away. In less than a minute, a police car was behind me. It followed me down Dick Baker's road and into town, where I ran the one and only traffic light in Flatwoods. That caught the attention of another pair of cops sitting in their car outside Scott's Drugstore.

Suddenly I had two cars tailing me and a slow, sleepy night in Flatwoods turned into a scene from *Smokey and the Bandit*.

My plan was to beat them to 2317 Long Street and then duck in the back of the house. But they were right behind me as I circled my block, and I didn't have a backup plan. So I went around the block a few more times. On my third pass, my mom and Cletis were standing on the front porch and I could hear Cletis scream, "Get your dumb ass outta that car, boy! Stop now!"

On my next turn around the block, I noticed the neighbors stepping out to see what was going on. I looked over at Stewart for advice. "What do I do, man?" He shrugged. I turned up the stereo. I was blasting Earl Scruggs's "Dueling Banjos." How much more hillbilly can you get? I don't recall how many times I circled the block, but the cops waited me out and eventually hauled both me and Stewart to jail.

My mom made my dad go down there and get me. She actually drove to his house and said, "I'm not dealing with it. You've got to go get him."

My uncle Larry from Los Angeles was visiting my dad, and the two of them showed up at the station about 4 a.m. If Uncle Larry hadn't been there, my dad would've probably whipped me then and there. But my uncle jabbed my dad with his elbow and said, "Ron, we've done far worse — and you know it."

To make amends, my dad took me to Dick Baker's house the next morning with a bucket and a scrub brush, and the real punishment began. Stewart and his dad met us there, and we cleaned the principal's house from top to bottom. I also had to cut his grass for the rest of the summer.

Mr. Baker suspended both of us from the baseball team for two games. We lost both of them and it ended up costing us a regional tournament. I vowed that wasn't going to happen again, not under any circumstances. As a result, I skipped my high school graduation in order to play in an important game that same day. My mom was crushed, but the game was part of a state tournament.

It was also against Ashland, our biggest rival. If we lost, the season was over, and none of us was ready for the season to end. We had the better team and went ahead 9–0. We were one run away from a "mercy rule," meaning the game would stop if we went up ten to nothing. But all of a sudden my pitchers couldn't pitch. No one could throw a strike, and as every catcher knows, walks will kill you. Ashland came back to beat us 10–9.

We lost the game, and I missed my graduation. It was a double dose of punishment for breaking my mother's heart.

• • •

School wasn't out more than a week or two when Robbie Tooley and two other guys from Bellefonte, the rich part of town, talked me into going with them to Myrtle Beach, South Carolina. It was party central for high school and college kids, and most kids in Flatwoods made the trip down there at least once a summer. I agreed to make my maiden voyage with Robbie.

Susie did not want me to go; she was adamant about that. She was the one girl who wasn't captivated by Robbie's charisma, and she knew we'd be drinking a lot of alcohol and smoking a lot of pot down there. I went anyway.

Of course, Susie's predictions were right, and as a result, I don't remember much of what happened in Myrtle Beach. What I do remember is, on the car ride back, we were listening to a lot of country radio, and my three friends started singing along to Don Williams's hit "Tulsa Time." It had a catchy groove, no doubt why it had been a number one song. I started singing, too. I couldn't resist.

To be honest, I wasn't aware that I was singing out loud until Robbie turned around and said, "Damn, Cyrus, you're a good singer." He seemed surprised — almost as surprised as I was. I hadn't sung in front of people since I was a little kid with my dad, and he'd quit when Papaw Cyrus died. His gospel quartet had broken up then, too.

"Thanks, man," I said to Robbie, though I was too self-conscious to sing for the rest of the car ride.

Back home, Susie was upset with me for having gone to Myrtle Beach. I could tell something had gone down while I was away, and I was right. I picked her up the next day and drove someplace where we could talk. I'd barely finished parking when she dove in.

"Bo, my mom and dad won't let me see you anymore if you don't straighten up," she said. "Mr. Baker spoke with my parents about you. They're all worried about me being with you. My dad says you've got a chance to be a professional baseball player, maybe the next Johnny Bench. But they say you're blowing it and better get yourself together before it's too late."

I might've argued with her if deep down I hadn't known she was 100 percent right. I had just spent a few days doing nothing more than drinking beer and smoking pot. I couldn't muster a response right away. The truth is your strongest ally, but it can also scare the crap out of you, which was the way I felt at that moment.

"And what do you think?" I asked.

"I agree," she said. "And it's not just because I'm agreeing with my parents. I really think you're blowing it."

"What do you think I need to do?" I asked.

"Let me help you," she said. "I want to help you. Billy Ray Cyrus, my mission in life might be to save you."

Recognizing the possibility that she was right, I went with Susie on Sunday to the Russell Christian Church, her family's place of worship. The sermon that day was about getting a new chance in life, washing away your sins and starting fresh. Perfect. It couldn't have been more appropriate. Maybe Susie's mission was to save me. I leaned forward, taking in every word, and imagining what it would be like to be brand-new. The next thing I knew, I was in line to get baptized.

Susie sensed my nervousness.

She squeezed my hand and said, "You can do this."

"I know," I said. "I'm ready."

And I was. I genuinely believed I needed to be saved — not only my soul but also my life. I felt changed afterward. It was more inward than out, and I have to thank Susie for giving me that gift. She saw good things about me when others only saw trouble. She also saw what I lacked — faith in God and, more so, faith in myself.

That summer, my life was Susie, the church, and American Legion baseball for the Ashland Post 76 team. I tried not to think about the fall, when I would go away to Morehead State University. Even though I was excited about the next phase in my life, particularly the opportunity to be the starting catcher on the school's baseball team, it meant seeing Susie less. We talked about that, though.

By contrast, my friend Robbie continued on the downward path that I had been on until Susie wrangled me in a better direction. After graduating in May as the most popular guy in our class, maybe the most beloved student in the whole school, he received a scholarship to a technical school in Columbus, Ohio. Big things were expected from Robbie Tooley. But that summer, he began hanging out with a different crowd. They did a lot of drugs, including acid and something else called Crystal T, which I heard was an elephant tranquilizer.

One night that summer, Robbie took some acid and ended up at Russell High, where he busted all the school's windows with a hatchet. He went row by row, taking out every window on the ground floor. In the midst of that destructive frenzy, he cut his forearm on the glass. Whoever he was with dropped him at the hospital drenched in blood. He thought he was going to bleed to death.

By then, the police had been called to the school. They saw the blood and checked in with the hospital, where they found Robbie. People couldn't believe the news. Even I wondered why Robbie Tooley would do that. I also knew that if not for Susie and the church, I probably would have been with him that night.

Actually, it was more than Susie and the church. My turnaround began with Dick Baker telling Susie's parents that she shouldn't be dating me, and then Susie's parents talking to her, and so on, until finally I woke up. I listened to my inner voice, telling me to take a walk down that church aisle and save myself. I'm not proselytizing here. Ultimately, the decision to help myself was mine, and mine alone.

My buddy Robbie made the wrong decision. After busting those windows, his stock dropped among those in town who had always admired him. By the time the newspaper wrote up the story, his girlfriend had broken up with him and he'd lost all his friends. I'd never seen people turn so quickly on a human being. In the fall, he went to Columbus, where he mixed with the wrong people and his drug problem got worse.

I went off to Morehead and didn't hear about Robbie for a couple of months. Then one weekend I was home and heard a knock on my window late at night. It was Robbie, looking all wild-eyed and disheveled. "Hey, man, I'm sorry to come by this late," he said. "But I heard you started boxing, and I need you to teach me how to defend myself."

In fact, I had taken up boxing to stay in shape, but that was beside the point. I was shocked that Robbie Tooley needed *my* help defending himself.

I got up, made us some hot tea and asked what was going on. He explained that he was mixed up with some bad people in Columbus who were after him. He didn't offer many more details. We put on the gloves and sparred till the sun came up.

I looked to Susie for both counsel and comfort, which always made going back to Morehead hard. The space between us was more than I could handle. It drove me crazy. I spent most of my time thinking about Susie or waiting till I could call her from the pay phone in the dorm. Then one day while jogging through the woods near campus, I came upon a puppy shivering under some leaves. It looked half-starved and scared.

I guessed the poor thing had been tossed overboard from a car traveling down Interstate 64. I took him to my dorm room and, over the next few weeks, a couple of other guys helped me nurse him back to health. As he gained strength and trust, his spirit emerged, and he was a terrific companion.

My plan was to take him back to Flatwoods and give him to Ruthie, who'd never met a stray she didn't adore. But the day before I went back home, I returned to my dorm after class and found a crowd of students waiting for me in the lobby.

"They killed your dog," someone said.

"What? What are you talking about?" I said.

Someone had reported me for having a pet in my room, which was against school policy. Instead of coming to me for an explanation, the campus police had broken into my room, taken the puppy, and put it down. I immediately went to their headquarters, where I was directed to the head cop, who was expecting me.

"Rules are rules," he said. "We can't let you be an exception. If we did, what good is it having the rules in the first place?"

"So I'm an example?" I said, holding back my anger.

"That's one way to see it," he said. "Another way is that you broke the rules."

"So you killed the puppy?"

"Thank you, son," he said. "You're excused."

That night I made the rounds at all the fraternity parties on campus, and when I was good and soused, I got into my blue Camaro and headed for the dean's house. I drove right onto her perfectly manicured front lawn, gunned the gas pedal, and proceeded to execute a series of spectacular loop-de-loos. Let's just say that when I was finished, the dean's yard was no longer the garden spot of Morehead State University.

The following Monday morning, I was summoned to the dean's office. She was sitting behind a gleaming wood desk. Behind her was a wall of diplomas and awards. She motioned for me to sit and waited a moment or two before cutting to the chase.

"Mr. Cyrus, did you tear up my yard on Friday night?" she asked.

"Yes, I did," I said, calmly. "Did you kill my dog?"

"We had to," she said. "You broke our policy against keeping pets in the dorm."

"Killing that dog was against my policy, ma'am," I said.

She shook her head as if I didn't understand. But it was clear *she* didn't understand.

"Mr. Cyrus," she said, "on account of your actions you may no longer continue as a student here at Morehead State."

I stood up.

"That's fine with me," I said.

As I reached the door, I turned to her for one last jab. "I guess you're the reason they call this place 'moor head.' You earned that name, didn't you?" I had never said anything that harsh before. But she deserved it. Then I walked out, not knowing what was next but damn sure that I would find a better place.

CHAPTER 7

"My Buddy"

WITH MY NINETEENTH BIRTHDAY just around the corner, I was back in my old bedroom on Long Street and taking courses at Ashland Community College, a branch of the University of Kentucky. Susie was ten minutes down the road at Russell.

It was all good, I suppose. But things felt different. Not in a bad way. They were just different.

Just before spring, I got a job managing the campground at Greenbo Lake, one of the most picturesque spots in the area. To get there, you had to go up one Appalachian mountain, then down to the lake, around a half horseshoe-like shore, up another mountain, and then you dropped down to a little piece of land where there was a boat dock and the entrance to the campground.

Since not many people went camping before summer, I usually had the remote location to myself. I was stationed inside a ten-by-ten shack, a tiny wood building with a couple of small glass windows that let me deal with approaching cars. I also stored the clubs and balls for the miniature golf course, where I played whenever I had the chance.

Mostly it was too cold out there for anyone trying to keep warm. The wind would come howling off that lake. I kept a tiny electric heater going. Despite the chill, it was a cozy setup. It felt like my camp, and I liked being out there by myself.

I did have a phone in the station in case I needed to get in touch with someone or vice versa. It was old and black, government-issued from the '60s. An operator connected all calls in and out. Susie would call me every day around lunchtime from the pay phone at school. We would catch up and make plans to see each other later on.

One night I was running late, and I stopped at the state park's main lodge to turn in the money and receipts I'd collected from the miniature golf course. They had a small souvenir section inside, and on my way out, I picked up a stuffed bunny to give to Susie. Since the office was closed, I couldn't pay for it. I made a mental note to pay the next time I saw someone behind the counter.

I hurried to my car, which happened to be my dad's four-door Cadillac; I'd borrowed it that day. It was about 10 p.m., and Susie's parents wouldn't let me see her after eleven. I knew if I drove fast, I could make it to her house in about twenty minutes. So I went flying down the two-lane highway leading out of the area, and lo and behold, a drunk driver came down the road on the wrong side, headed straight for me. I swerved to the side and went spinning down a modest slope. My head when through the window and I got beat up pretty bad. I still have a scar on the middle of my hand where a vein was cut.

I staggered out of the wreckage, looked around and saw a trailer nearby. I knocked on the door and next thing I knew, I was in the back of an ambulance, heading to the hospital. As I lay on the gurney, with EMT workers cleaning my wounds and wrapping me in bandages, I heard a voice: "Cyrus, both of us know you stole the rabbit. But because you said you were going to pay for it later, it was a kind of gray area."

The circumstances were different the next time I was racing along those roads. It was April 1980, and the first blush of spring was evident across the landscape. I was late for work at the lake, hence the reason I was driving fast. I had turned from Route 207, a connector road that led from Flatwoods to Argillite, onto Route 1 and I was trying to make up time when I saw a nice car stopped on the side of the road. Standing next to it was an older man. He had white hair and was in a suit.

Despite my hurry, I stopped and rolled down my window. You never know on those country roads.

"Sir, are you OK?" I asked.

"Yes, I'm all right," he said.

He looked at me kind of funny.

"Say, ain't you that Cyrus boy?" he asked.

"Yes, sir," I said.

"It's unusual for a person your age to help a man in need, don't you think?" he asked.

I shrugged.

"Well, I find that's a unique quality in a human being," he continued.

"I just wanted to make sure you were OK," I said.

"Actually, I stopped to admire the cattle over there," he said, pointing off to a hilly pasture where a herd of cows were grazing on fresh spring grass. "I'd like to ask you something, son."

"Yes, sir?"

"You gave me something when you stopped here," he said. "You gave me your time. The fact that you cared whether I was OK speaks volumes about your character. That's a rare quality, son."

"I don't know," I said. "That's just how I was raised."

"Well, I've been around a little longer than you, and I think it is. And I want to give you something in return. How would you like to know the secret that could lead you to see, have, or do anything you want in this world?"

Inside, I was thinking *Hell yes! What's the catch?* Outwardly, I was more polite and restrained.

"I would love that, sir," I said. "It sounds incredibly exciting. What do I do?"

"Good, very good," he said, offering a hint of smile, before introducing himself as Dr. H. V. Bailey, a local chiropractor. "My office is right down on Argillite Road. As a matter of fact, I started renting the place in 1950 from your grandfather. You can't miss it. You come by next Wednesday at five p.m."

"I'll be there, sir," I said.

For some reason, I never doubted Dr. Bailey's credibility or intent. If the same thing happened to me today, I probably would have written him off. But something he said turned my brain on. For the first time in my life, I was hungry to learn. Basically, I was in from the start. And when I showed up at his office the following week, Dr. Bailey's last patient was on his way out. Dr. Bailey greeted me warmly, led me into his office, and presented me with a book, *Think and Grow Rich,* by Napoleon Hill. Hill was a newspaper reporter and motivational speaker from southwest Virginia who published his bestselling book in 1937. It went on to become one of the bestselling books of all time.

I stared at the cover almost as if it were a foreign object. Dr. Bailey was the first person who ever gave me a book. While I flipped through the pages, he explained the process of positive thinking and visualization that formed the basis of the book. He reiterated the message: I could achieve whatever I wanted with the techniques in the book. As we talked, I let him know I was ready. I kept waiting for Dr. Bailey to share some Yoda-type line that would instantly unlock the secret, but it turned out the wisdom was in learning the lessons and committing to them.

We started studying *Think and Grow Rich* together, as we would weekly for the next few months, reading each chapter together and discussing the passages we'd read. I copied key lines in a notebook and memorized important passages. Like "As ye sow, so shall ye reap." Or "What the mind of man can conceive and believe, it can achieve." Or "As a man thinks in his heart and in his soul, so is he." It all came down to this: thoughts are things. I had never been much of a reader, but this book obviously struck a nerve, as did Dr. Bailey. I had a pretty realistic view on my own life — the anger and shame I'd buried, having come from a family split by divorce — and I wanted, more than anything, to figure out a way to do better. According to Dr. Bailey, this book, *Think and Grow Rich,* was the way.

As I was studying, Robbie returned to Flatwoods, but he was extremely ill. He'd gotten into harder drugs and somehow contracted severe hepatitis. I was shocked when I saw him in the hospital. He was emaciated. He'd lost a ton of weight. His body mass was gone, and so was his passion for life. His latest girlfriend had left, he'd lost his scholarship, and he'd been expelled from school. Everything had crashed down around him, he said.

On my next visit, I brought him a *Playboy* magazine. I should have brought a Bible, or even *Think and Grow Rich.* But I didn't. I still regret that choice. I just thought the *Playboy* would lift his spirits. He loved girls. Oh man, did he love pretty women.

"Man, you're the only person who's visited me," he said. "The only one. When I get out of here, I'm going to go to church and get me a good girlfriend like you've got."

"You can do that," I said. "That'd be a good idea."

"When I get out of here, me and you will start working out again," he said. "We'll go back and hit the weights hard, like we used to."

"Definitely," I agreed.

I told him that I'd gotten into canoeing and had competed in a couple of contests. His face brightened. He wanted to go with me.

After he got out of the hospital, we canoed down the Little Sandy River and had a great time, even after it began to rain. It was a warm shower, the kind that feels good. We came upon a little bank where we found an old wooden swing attached to a tree. As we swung over the water and dropped in, a violent electrical storm filled the sky with thunder and lightning, and we laughed at it. We knew that we were flirting with danger, but we had been through worse. Plus, the risk made it fun.

We talked about God and what life was like without being all messed up. I said that I was really happy, and Robbie seemed genuinely happy to hear it.

We got back in the canoe and finished our trip. A ways down the river, Robbie spotted a glass pint of Jim Beam that someone had tossed into the shitty-ass mud of the bank. Who knows how long it had been there. The bottle was covered with moss. But there were a couple of swigs left in the bottle. Robbie held it up.

"Want a hit?" he asked.

"No," I laughed.

He cranked the lid off and slugged it down. I didn't know whether that was cool or desperate. But that was Robbie.

A couple of days later, I was in the middle of my shift at Greenbo Lake when the phone rang. It was Susie.

"Where are you?" she asked.

"At the campground," I said. "You just called me here."

I could hear people in the background screaming or crying. I couldn't tell which it was, but I could tell wherever she was it was pretty chaotic.

"What's wrong?" I asked.

"Are you sitting down?" she said.

"I can be. Do I need to?"

"Yes," she said, her voice sounding wobbly. "You need to sit down."

I pulled a little stool up close to the phone.

"Tell me what's wrong," I said. "You're scaring me."

"They just found Robbie Tooley dead in his basement," she said. "They say he killed himself."

"What? I don't think I heard you right. What'd you say?"

"Robbie," she said. "He committed suicide. They found him in the basement."

If Susie kept talking, I didn't hear her. I dropped the receiver, picked up a golf club and started swinging it against the shack. Glass shattered. I swung it again and more glass shattered. I did it again and the cash register exploded. Then I busted the phone. More glass broke, half a wall came down, and I was steadily beating that shack to the ground when I saw a car coming off the far hill.

Soon a state park ranger pulled up in front of the destroyed shack. I was standing in the middle of the rubble, holding a golf club.

"Cyrus?" he asked. "Are you OK?"

"Yeah," I said. But I wasn't OK.

"You have an emergency in Flatwoods," he said. "I need to take you home."

He loaded me into the back of his car and drove me straight to 2317 Long Street. My mom embraced me at the door, her eyes red from crying. Neighbors had gathered inside and on our front porch. I worked my way through the crowd, past the living room, and down the narrow hallway till I got to my room. I went in, locked the door, and fell face-first onto my bed.

I could have been like that for ten minutes, thirty minutes, or thirty seconds — I have no idea — when suddenly words came to me. Nothing like that had ever happened to me before. I didn't know what the words were, just that they were there and I had to get them out of me. I raised myself up, grabbed an old notebook and pen from the night table, and my hand started to move across the page.

I wasn't a writer. I had written a few school assignments but that was it, and I'd written them only because I had to. This was different. As far as I could tell, I was writing a poem. I'd titled it "My Buddy," but it wasn't like I'd made it up. Those words seemed to appear of their own accord, like I was possessed. They came so fast I could barely keep up. They just came. And that's all I know.

Robbie's funeral was three days later, April 28, 1980. The church was packed. It was standing room only. The entire town was there. Everyone from our football team was there. We all wore our jerseys. There were even some players from nearby high schools we'd played against. They wore their jerseys, too. People came from miles around to pay their respects to a great family who had lost a great son far too soon. His dad had read my poem about Robbie and asked if I would recite it at the service. So, despite being terribly nervous, and with Robbie's casket lying in front of me, I started to read:

Through all the years of growing up,
My best buddy's name was Rob,
We'd laugh, and we'd play and sometimes find trouble,
By throwing the corn from a cob,
We'd ride our bicycles and eat big icicles,
And set back without any thoughts,
And think of the things we'd had done that day,
And hope we'd never get caught.
One winter we decided to leave all our troubles,
And decided to go on a hike,
We left for the trail, the endless snow fell,
For three days we were both in a fright.
But we hung in there, my buddy and I,
Through temperatures of twenty below,
We worked together to stay alive,
To reach our strongly set goal.
We wanted to prove to the folks at home
That we both had the guts to survive,
So we toughed it out in the wilderness,
God, my buddy, and I.
My buddy once had a paper route,
And I helped whenever I could,
And people who didn't pay my buddy
Would often end up cleaning their wood.
There's so many times that I can remember,
From skinny-dipping to camping in a barn,
But one thing for sure, through all the years,
We never did no one no harm.
Long nights we'd spend, a pumping our weights,
And pushing each other real hard,
'Cause we both had a spot on the football team,
That our hearts had a longing from far.
We worked and we worked, and we reached our goals,
And we both got our names in the paper,
Me for the balls which I had caught,
And him for his world-known Tooley Trot.
Be we were not on a self-love trip,
We wanted to win a state championship.

So we fought and we scrapped as we followed the ball,
And in the end, we had conquered them all.
"But where does the time go?" we asked each other,
For now it was time to depart,
He went his way, and I went mine,
But we both made a deal from our hearts.
With a handshake we vowed, as we stared at each other,
To never forget all we'd been through,
And we vowed to stay the best of buddies,
No matter what else we would do.

At that point, I choked up and stopped. I stood uncomfortably in front of everyone, tears filling my eyes. I couldn't believe we were saying good-bye to Robbie Tooley, that he was gone. I wanted to leave, and I was about to fold up the paper and walk off when Robbie's father stood up.

"Keep readin', Bo," he shouted. "Keep readin'!"

I looked at him, nodded, unfolded the paper, and wiped my eyes.

So Robbie, my buddy, I hope you can hear me,
Wherever it is you may be,
I'll never forget you, ole buddy, ole pal,
And I know you'll never forget me.
I'll see you in heaven, I know that I will!
And you'll say, "Hey, God, here comes my friend Bill!"
But before I can come, there's work to be done,
And I know that you would be proud,
Just to help a kid, who seems to be lost,
Lost somewhere out in a crowd.
You'll always be with me, Robbie, my friend,
In my thoughts and all that I do,
And one thing I must say, before I do go,
Ole Buddy . . . I'll always . . . Love You.

So many times I've tried to make sense of Robbie's death. I've turned it around every which way and I can only say this: I've often prayed that God would somehow use my life to add a moral to the story as to why Robbie's life ended the way it did.

I look back at the words that came that day, and at this part in particular: "But before I can come, there's work to be done / And I know that you would be proud / Just to help a kid who seems to be lost / Lost somewhere out in a crowd." Robbie was lost. Like a lot of kids these days. But we should never allow kids to feel so alone, especially so alone that suicide becomes the answer.*

* For those needing help or wanting more information, call the National Suicide Prevention Lifeline: 1-800-273-8255, www.suicidepreventionlifeline.org.

PART II

Persistence

CHAPTER 8

"Buy a Guitar and Start a Band"

EVERYONE THOUGHT I WAS crazy. It was summer, and my baseball career was red-hot. I was playing for Ashland's team in the Stan Musial League. Teammates Cabot Keesey, Mark Moore, and Tim Holbrook had all been superstars for other schools, and I respected those guys. They dug the way I played, too.

I was all out, all the time. I would do anything to stop the ball. After practice, I had the coaches throw me extra wild pitches so I could practice knocking them down with my hands and body. At the plate, I had always hit around .300, which was decent, but thanks to my *Think and Grow Rich* studies with Dr. Bailey, I visualized myself hitting better and more powerfully, and it worked. I went on a home run tear.

My timing was perfect. Ashland hosted a Fourth of July tournament that was big among Stan Musial League teams, and our first game of the tournament was against Flatwoods-Russell. All my former teammates, the guys I'd played with from Little League through high school, were on that team, wanting to destroy me. In addition, scouts from the Dodgers and the Reds were in the stands, looking at me. Dr. Bailey was also at the game.

It was a big game to say the least — and I'm proud to say, I rose to the challenge. Flatwoods-Russell's leadoff man got on base. He was the fastest guy I'd ever known. I knew he was going to try to steal, and he did. After the first pitch, I popped up and threw him out at second. The next guy up chipped a pitch foul to my right. I dove and caught it — the best catch of my life. Then, in my first at-bat, I jacked the ball over the left field fence. It was probably the longest ball I'd hit in my entire baseball career.

My play stayed at that same level throughout the summer, and I heard the scouts were impressed and continuing to watch me, as they did serious prospects. I should have been thrilled.

But something odd happened in the weeks before that game and persisted through the summer. I heard a voice telling me to buy a guitar and start a band. I know it sounds crazy.

I know sane people don't hear voices — at least they aren't supposed to. But I did. It came to me the same way the words did to the poem I wrote about Robbie Tooley. I didn't hear it all the time. It was simply there, lodged in my brain, like a presence, and if I was driving or waiting for Susie or ready to go to sleep, I heard the words. *Buy a guitar and start a band.*

"You gotta get that out of your head," my teammate Cabot Keesey said. "You've got a chance to go to the big leagues. Focus on baseball. We're the best team in the tristate area."

"Yeah, I know," I said.

"Cyrus," another teammate chimed. "You don't even play guitar, do you?"

"No, I don't," I said, shaking my head and laughing uneasily.

I had certainly tried. My dad always had a guitar, and starting when I was a little kid, I would pick it up occasionally and try to play. It was futile. I was never able to put together the chords and a strum. I never found the rhythm, the feel.

I tried to ignore the voice. In the fall of 1980, I continued taking classes at Ashland Community College and got a job at Ashland Oil's cigarette warehouse, driving a forklift. I also delivered crates to the company's SuperAmerica gas stations. The following spring, Susie graduated high school, with plans to attend Kentucky's Georgetown College in the fall. Then, after a summer of standout baseball, Georgetown offered me an athletic scholarship. Although it was only a partial ride, requiring me to take out a student loan for the rest of the tuition, I was overjoyed. I'd be playing ball, Susie would be at the same school, and we'd be together. It would be like high school — only better.

What I didn't factor in was the voice telling me to buy a guitar and start a band. Susie was amused the first couple times I mentioned it. Then it became an irritant. Now, my girlfriend sent a very clear message. She was tired of hearing me talk about whether to buy a guitar and start a band, period.

"Bo, you need to quit smoking pot," she said.

"I'm serious," I said.

A few weeks later, I told her that I was thinking about not playing baseball. Then I admitted I wanted to quit school.

"What are you going to do?" she asked.

"Play music in bars," I said.

"Bo, let's be serious for a minute," she said. "You don't play an instrument. You're not a musician. You're a catcher. In college."

"I can't help it," I said. "I think this is what God wants me to do. I think it's my purpose. I'm being called."

"You're crazy," she said.

I dropped out of Georgetown just five weeks into the semester, and Susie and I didn't speak for a few days afterward. Going into damage-control mode, I waited till she went home for the weekend and then arranged to take her to Kings Island, an amusement park just outside Cincinnati. Going there was always a special event for us.

I picked Susie up at her house early in the morning and we drove to Kings Island in my red Chevy S-10. It was a little less than a three-hour trip. We got there early, hoping to be among the first through the gates, so we could go on all the rides before the lines got too long. We pulled into a parking space and leaped out of the car like superheroes. However, as I slammed the door shut, I realized that I had screwed up.

"Oh, shit!" I said.

"What?" Susie said, stopping in her tracks and turning around to see why I wasn't with her.

"I locked my keys in my truck."

Susie watched as I spent the next two hours trying to get the door open while people walked past us on their way to a good time. Eventually, someone helped me get the door open, and Susie and I managed to get on a couple of rides. But we never recovered from the strain and tension of my mistake.

We drove home in silence. I knew Susie and I were at the end of the line. She knew it, too. When I pulled up in front of her house, I told myself to take a long, intense look at her beautiful face and remember it forever in case I never saw her again. As it turned out, I didn't. We looked at each other. I said, "So this is it," and she nodded. She got out of the truck and that was it.

One morning I was at the cigarette warehouse, listening to the radio as I drove my forklift. It was September 1982, and the radio was tuned to WKEE, the pop station out of Huntington, West Virginia. Around eleven o'clock, I took a break, parked my lift, kicked back, and let the tunes wash over me. We liked to crank up the radio and let the music fill the vast space, especially when a song came on from a rocker like George Thorogood, whose song "Bad to the Bone" had come out earlier that year and was like a three-minute vacation from the boredom.

Between songs, I heard a promotion for a Neil Diamond concert. The station was giving away two tickets to the eighth person who called the station. They were going to continue giving away two tickets every hour till 9 p.m. that night. I had never once before thought about dialing in and trying to win — until now.

The reason? I heard that voice.

"OK, you've been wanting to know whether you're crazy or whether what I'm telling you to do is real," it said. "Call the station. You're going to win the tickets to see Neil Diamond."

"I've never won anything," I said to myself in response. "I don't know much about Neil Diamond, either. I don't even know why I'm talking to you."

At times like this, I really did think I was crazy.

"When you're at the concert," the voice continued, "you're going to see and hear why you're supposed to buy a guitar and start a band."

"OK," I said.

That was it: game on!

I ducked into the warehouse office, picked up the phone and dialed the radio station. I didn't get through. The line was busy.

"See," I said.

"Just play the game," the voice said. "If you don't win those tickets, game over. It's done. You're crazy, like you think, and you're going to need to get help. But if . . ."

I wasn't going to win. I was definitely going to need professional help. Nevertheless, I started to play the game. By 5 p.m., I was deep into it — more because I wanted clarification than the tickets. Later that night, at 8:55 p.m. to be more specific, I was in the weight room at the YMCA in Russell. I still had the radio on, and I knew WKEE had one last pair of tickets to give away.

I dialed the number, which I knew by heart, and this time, instead of a busy signal, someone at the station picked up.

"Hello, it's WKEE. You're caller number eight, and you are going to see Neil Diamond in concert!"

"Really?" I said. "OK."

"Caller eight, you don't sound very happy," he said.

"No, I'm just in shock," I said. "I've never won anything before."

"Not anymore. Hey, hang on and we'll get your information so you can get the tickets."

The concert was September 10. Unable to find someone to take, I drove to Charleston, West Virginia, by myself. It was a haul from Flatwoods, about seventy miles. My seat was way up in the rafters — beyond the nosebleed section. Neil's songs were classic, and he was a phenomenal showman. He could rock, slow it down, tell stories, and then pull out yet another humongous hit from his quiver, like "I Am . . . I Said" or "Sweet Caroline," and the entire place sang along with him.

At one point, he brought an orchestra and choir of gospel singers onstage and began singing "Holly Holy." His band and the orchestra played with one another, with a lush dynamic that I'd never heard on a stage before, and the singers carried on as if they were in church. Then suddenly, as if on cue, all of their voices dropped down to where the mood turned soft and spiritual and amazingly intimate considering there were probably twenty thousand people in the audience.

The multicolored lights dimmed, the stage darkened, and then Neil stepped forward into a solitary spotlight. In his low, slow, soulful voice, he spoke to the crowd, almost as if he were preaching. And who knows, maybe he was.

"I don't care if you're white or black," he said. "Rich or poor, man or woman . . ." He let those words simmer for a moment. "If you just believe in the power of love, you can reach your dreams and be all that you can be. If you just believe . . . and have faith."

As he said all that, I was swept away into some new place I had never felt before, not even in church. This was a church like no other: a church of music. It was either as if a hundred hands were upon me or I was being cradled in one giant hand. I had goose bumps. And then instead of hearing Neil Diamond, I heard another familiar voice: "That's it. That's why you're supposed to buy a guitar and start a band."

"But—"

"You can do it. You're going to do it. You're going to be a positive influence in people's lives. God is going to use you to share his light and love."

I wasn't the first person in my family to hear a voice. My papaw Cyrus had been told to become a preacher, and he did. And while my dad, who was currently in the seventh of what would eventually be twenty-one years in the Kentucky House of Representatives, never heard a voice telling him to help other people, he clearly answered a calling when he ran for office. Something motivated him.

Now the same was true of me. I drove home from that concert in a trance. Back at my mom's — where I was living at the ripe old age of twenty-one — I pulled my Chevy into the driveway, turned off the ignition, and sat there, trying to make sense of what was happening in my life.

Confused and a little scared, I looked up at the sky, a canvas of black, dotted with stars that seemed to stretch to infinity. Its vastness would have made me feel like an insignificant speck if not for what happened next. I pounded on the steering wheel and yelled, "I don't play guitar!"

"Buy a left-handed guitar." The voice was calm and direct.

I *was* left-handed, except for when I played baseball or threw a football. My dad's guitar, and every other one I'd ever tried to play, had been right-handed. Could it be that simple?

It was not so simple to find a left-handed guitar. Even in a big city, music stores don't keep them in stock. Finally, after numerous calls, I found a store in Portsmouth, Ohio, with a left-handed Fender F-3.

"Really?" I said to the guy on the phone.

"I just told you, man. We got one."

I said, "I'm coming to get it. My name is Cyrus . . ."

CHAPTER 9

Sly Dog

ALL THE WAY TO the music store, I kept telling myself that this was really happening to me. I was excited. I was barreling down the highway, literally and figuratively, which, I guess, is the very definition of faith. For the first time, I knew I was heading in the right direction.

The Fender F-3 cost me $225. I sped back home, sat down in the living room, took the guitar out of its case, and began to play. No, I didn't suddenly play like Jimi Hendrix or Stevie Ray Vaughan, but damn if holding that thing didn't just feel right. I had spent years mangling the songs in my dad's Glen Campbell songbook. Yet now I was making something that actually sounded like music.

I had never been able to play like this before but I didn't question it, either. It was clear my brain was just wired that way. The music all made sense, from my head to my heart to my fingers to my soul. It felt good and right, and I just went with it. I was going to start this band, right then and there, that night.

My brother Kebo had been laid off from the C&O Railroad and needed something to do, so he was thrilled when I called that night and invited him to join a band — my band. I also rounded up two guys from the warehouse — bass player Paul Rice and drummer Bob "Bubba" Wileman — and a guy named Pat Williams who played guitar. We met that night at 2317 Long Street, in our old converted carport.

I plugged into my dad's old PA from his gospel quartet days and taped one of his Elvis-era microphones to an old broom handle. For some reason, everyone just assumed I would be the lead singer. We jammed on Chuck Berry's "Johnny B. Goode"; Lynyrd Skynyrd's "Gimme Three Steps," "Sweet Home Alabama," and "Call Me the Breeze"; Hank Williams's "Blue Eyes Crying in the Rain"; George Jones's "He Stopped Loving Her Today"; and Kris Kristofferson's "Help Me Make It Through the Night."

All of a sudden, using my left hand — the same one I use to brush my teeth — the guitar made sense in a way it never had before. I watched my brother, copied the basic chords, and let the music I felt inside me come out. I credit Dr. Bailey and his book. Thanks to the powerful lessons of positive thinking, I put up no resistance to what I was trying to do. I pictured myself playing music, and I did.

The rest is history . . . only it took another decade to get there.

"Man, we're playing!" Bubba chortled after a Skynyrd song. "We've got a band. All we need is a name."

"Yeah, so what are we going to call ourselves?" someone else said. Good question. As we cooled off with some beers, Bubba knelt down and scratched Spike on his stomach. Spike was equal parts bulldog and scrappy mutt. He'd gotten in a scrape with another dog the previous Christmas and lost an eye, which the vet had sewed shut, giving him the look of an old pirate. I thought Bubba was brave to pet him on account of how ugly and unsavory he was, but my pal was amused by the way Spike immediately rolled over and opened himself up to the attention.

"Look at this guy," he said, laughing. "Yeah, you ol' sly dog."

"That's it," I said.

"What?" my brother asked.

"Our name. We'll call ourselves Sly Dog."

· · ·

Having music back in my life was a blessing. My dad was nothing but supportive. "If this is what you've decided to do, put your whole self into it," he said. My mom occasionally joined us during rehearsals in the converted carport, sitting at the piano in there and jamming on Bruce Springsteen's "Open All Night" and Bob Seger's "Turn the Page." If nothing else happened with my music other than seeing my mom going at the keys with a huge smile on her face, I would've thought the whole thing was worthwhile.

Playing brought out a feeling in me that had been locked away since I was a little kid. It released the joy I remembered as a five-year-old when the whole family made music together. I'd stashed that part of me in some distant corner for most of my growing up.

By day, I was a laid-back, introverted Kentucky boy (except when provoked), but once I picked up a guitar and stepped in front of a microphone, I turned into an uninhibited, balls-out rocker who couldn't wait to get onstage in front of people and share the good times.

We rehearsed as time permitted through the holidays and into the early part of 1983. I quit my job at the cigarette warehouse and prepared for stardom by investing twenty dollars in business cards featuring the band's name and a derby-wearing dog with long ears and a knowing grin.

BILLY RAY CYRUS
GUITAR-VOCALS

I loved whipping out that card. "Hi, I'm Billy Ray Cyrus of Sly Dog." Bam! The card didn't list a phone number, which defeated the whole purpose. But my ambition more than made up for my lack of polish (and common sense). I believed in aiming for the top, so one night I wrote down a bunch of goals, including one that set the bar really high: "Sly Dog will begin infiltrating the local tristate music scene and play at several venues whenever possible. In ten months, the band will land a house gig and begin building a local following."

I wrote a very personal goal, too.

"I will become a successful singer, songwriter, and entertainer. I will entertain around the world. God will use my music to touch people's lives and represent his light and love." And then, because everything I had ever read about setting a goal said to be specific, really specific, I added, "I will be known as the next Elvis Presley."

At the start of Sly Dog, I made a crucial decision about our music. We were only going to play cover songs until we had enough of our own original tunes. Every great band and artist played original material. That was the only way to go.

Had I ever written a song before? No. Was that a problem? Not for me. My first original tune was a country ballad about Robbie Tooley called "Suddenly," and the second was a barn burner called "What the Hell Is Goin' On." Both came quickly, as if they were hanging on an invisible clothesline, waiting for me to take them down. The third song also came easily, and made me certain I had chosen the right path.

Let me explain. In January 1983, I ran through the last of my savings and found a new job with Cravens Construction Company. I had met the owner, Ken Cravens, a year or two earlier in the weight room at the YMCA. We'd hit it off, and he remembered me when I knocked on his door looking for a job. He hired me to work on his construction crew even though I didn't have any experience and couldn't hammer a nail into a board if you held it for me.

"Don't worry about it," he said. "You've got good energy. You're fun to have around."

One of my jobs was to represent the company in court when they had problems with renters. They just needed a body from the company present; the lawyer handled everything else. One day I was there for a case against a renter who'd trashed his place, and during lunch I walked across the street to a restaurant. On the way, I passed the Greenup County Library, where I noticed the front page of an old newspaper displayed in the window. I don't know why I stopped to read it, but I did. The lead story described the death of an eight-year-old girl named Mary Magdalene Pitts. She'd been horribly abused — burned with a poker and mutilated — and then killed by her own father, Robert Pitts, and the woman he'd hired to watch his children. Her name was Marie Frazier. They had been on trial in the courthouse where I had just been a few minutes earlier. According to the story, Mary's little body had been placed in a glass coffin and displayed in front of the library where I now stood.

But weirdest of all was the description of the house where Mary had died. I realized it was the little shack beyond my dad's house in Argillite — the one where my friends Clyde and Jimmy had lived until it burned down.

I hadn't thought of that place in a long time. Suddenly, the tragic night came back to me: the commotion, the fear in Clyde's and Jimmy's eyes, the firemen unable to reach the house as it burned to the ground, and the sound I'd heard, a little girl's voice saying, "Help me. Help me, Mommy."

I knew what I had to do. After court wrapped that afternoon, I got in my truck and drove to the cemetery where Mary had been buried. I wanted to see her headstone. It was as if a force greater than me had propelled me there.

The place dated back to the 1700s and looked it. The grounds were unkempt and overgrown. I climbed up the side of a large hill, following the description of Mary's grave location in the old newspaper. I hiked through bushes and briars, my face and arms getting scratched. I stopped to pick some wild daisies, which I planned to put on Mary's grave.

I kept climbing and looking around, unsure of what exactly was driving this impassioned mission. Finally, I spotted Mary's tombstone, an angel with a broken wing. Sweating and bleeding, I scrambled over, knelt down, placed the flowers on her grave, and asked, "Why me? Why me?"

Honestly, I didn't expect an answer. But I heard a voice, that same voice I'd heard before.

"Someday you'll be able to tell my story." That's what I heard. Who or what or where that voice came from — your guess is as good as mine.

About ten years later, I wrote "Enough Is Enough," a song about child abuse that was meant to tell Mary's story, as well as put Mary's long-suffering soul to rest. But more immediately, I went home that very night and wrote a song called "Sunshine Girl." It was the third song I ever wrote, though I'm reluctant to claim credit since the words flowed right through me and out of my hand.

Summer comes, summer goes
Leaves will fall and the north wind blows
But your love makes the sun shine every day

Tears for you cloud my mind
Take my hand if you'd be so kind
Show me . . . that the sun shines anyway . . .

Sunshine Girl, keep me from cryin'
Sunshine Girl, teach me to smile
Sunshine Girl, when the rain has fallen
Open up your heart and let your sun shine down on me

Life's a game, I've been told
It's not fair, it can be so cold
But you always . . . find a way to . . .
Make me warm . . .

If everyone could be like you
Soft and gentle . . . yet so strong, too
Your sunshine, could be the lighthouse . . . through the storm

In February, Ken Cravens heard about my band and suggested we move our equipment into his spacious Bellefonte home and use it for rehearsals. He was a successful middle-aged man who had gone through a divorce and remarried a younger gal. Ken liked having us around to fire up the joint with some loud music. As for us, it was a sweet setup that beat the hell out of the measly carport at my mom's house. We jokingly referred to it as Sly Dog Lodge.

Beyond offering a place to rehearse, Ken became our manager. In April, he threw a birthday party for his wife and we provided the music. A month later, he arranged for us to play an assembly at

Summit Elementary School in Ashland and then for one thousand inmates at the nearby federal correctional institution. Both gigs were unpaid and arranged at the last minute, but I was desperate to play in front of people.

However, the day after we played the elementary school, I told Ken no more free gigs. I told him my goals. I wanted Sly Dog to become the house band at one of the local bars or clubs by my twenty-second birthday on August 25. I wanted to be signed to a major record label by my twenty-third birthday. I wanted my music to be heard around the world. And I wanted my music to share God's light and love.

Our first paying job was in the restaurant at the Jesse Stuart Lodge at Greenbo Lake State Park, the same place I'd worked a few years earlier. The lodge's clientele, mostly middle-aged folks looking for quiet in the woods and gentle country tunes at dinner, got a surprise when we served up a set peppered with the Allman Brothers Band and ZZ Top. No one complained, though, and Ken divided the night's pay: $150. Thrilled, we split it five ways, gave Ken a five-dollar commission, and spent the rest of the night celebrating.

"Thirty bucks apiece," I said, toasting the band. "We ain't rich. But we're on our way."

A week of playing in front of an audience taught us more than a month of rehearsals. We screwed around less and made fewer mistakes. We all played with more intensity and focus and we paid more attention to the way we blended with one another. When we were in front of people, there was no middle ground. It was all or nothing.

After the first few gigs, guitarist Pat Williams dropped out of the band, wanting a more stable life. I recruited my high school buddy and former baseball and football teammate J.R. Gullett as his replacement. J.R. was a genuine musician and country music authority who lent authenticity to our southern rock sound. Plus, he sounded great on those harmonies. Our voices blended really well together.

We played the lodge a few more times and also at several other similar venues, but each gig only made me hungrier to play more frequently. I was doing all I could do to get us booked in one of the numerous clubs in the area. I didn't care if it was the Catlettsburg Boat Club, the Auger Inn, the Red Fox Lounge, or one of the other rough-and-tumble watering holes where folks unwound after work. I wanted to take that next step, and the next one.

"Be patient," Ken advised.

"But my birthday's around the corner," I said. "Remember my goal is to be playing one of those places before August twenty-fifth."

"I know," he said. "You've told me. But as you can imagine, these people haven't even heard of you yet."

"They will," I said. "I believe if you build a place high enough on the mountain, then surround it with enough lights, and play really loud, I mean *really* loud, the world has to take notice." I smiled. "Either that, or they'll tell you to turn that shit down."

CHAPTER 10

Tarot Cards

EIGHT DAYS BEFORE MY birthday deadline, there was good news: Sly Dog had its first headlining gig at the Sand Bar, a popular club in Ironton, Ohio. The Sand Bar was located inside the Marting House Hotel, a place that dated back to the 1800s and was full of charm, if old and dilapidated was your style. J.R. described it as "clean but rough."

The place had been under water for a few days during the great flood of 1937, and on certain nights when the humidity was high, it felt like it had never thoroughly dried. As for rough, well, we could count on at least one fight breaking out before the night ended. Liquor, rock and roll, good-looking women . . . and somebody always had a knife or a gun . . . it was a recipe for trouble.

As such, I was uncharacteristically nervous before our first set. I placed a lot more significance on the show than anyone else. Once we began to play, though, those jitters disappeared and I turned into a party animal, easily winning over that night's crowd. As word spread, we drew bigger crowds on subsequent nights.

We played at the Sand Bar for the next seven weeks straight. Our sets included covers of songs by Billy Idol, George Jones, Lacy J. Dalton, Bruce Springsteen, Merle Haggard, Loverboy, the Eagles, Kenny Rogers, Bob Seger, ZZ Top, and Johnny Cash. We also pulled from my ever-expanding list of originals, including "Suddenly" and "What the Hell Is Goin' On," plus the fun honky-tonk rave-up "Mom Called Dad a Mother," "Take a Ride," "This Beer's for You," and "Babysitter."

My basic rule was if I liked it, I played it — and I played it loud. I took requests. If we didn't know the song, we learned it and played it another night. We never had a set list; I just tried to key in on the crowd's vibe. As a result, no night was the same other than the fact that we made a lot of new friends, including plenty of good-looking women.

One night in late September or early October, I was hanging out after the last set. We had played a packed house. In fact, we became so popular, the club was preparing to move us from the nightclub into the hotel's upstairs ballroom, a much larger room that must have been a jewel for the area's upper crust back in the 1930s. Now it needed refurbishing, and they were taking care of that before we plugged in. At any rate, it was closing in on 2 a.m., and I was cooling down from the night. The bartender and one of the waitresses were cleaning up, and I was staring off into space when a woman in her mid-fifties tapped me on the shoulder.

"Excuse me, Mr. Cyrus, but I was wondering if I could read your cards," she said.

I was confused.

"I don't have any cards with me," I said, thinking she meant business cards.

"No, no," she said, smiling. "Tarot cards."

"Huh?" I said.

"I don't want to call myself a fortuneteller, but I tell fortunes," she said. "It's kind of like a game. I lay down cards and tell you the things I see in your future and maybe some things about your past."

"Really?" I said. "Now? At what . . . nearly two in the morning?"

"I know," she said. "It sounds pretty weird. But something told me that I'm supposed to do this with you."

She sounded kind of kooky, but I was kind of kooky, too. I was half drunk and high as a kite. So why not?

We sat at a table in the corner. She reached into a large hippie-type canvas bag and took out a deck of cards. After a quick shuffle, she dealt several on the table.

"I see you have a brother," she said.

"Yes, ma'am," I said. "Two of them. And one's in the band."

"And your parents — "

"I have them, too," I cracked.

"They're divorced."

"How'd you — "

"Your mother . . . does she have an *R* in her name? A Ru . . . Ruth?"

"Ruthie," I said, warily. "How'd you know?"

When she had mentioned my brother, I thought, Lucky guess. I mean she had a fifty-fifty chance there. Or she could have said I didn't have any siblings, I suppose. But she didn't. Coming up with my mom's name? That was good. Then she laid down a few more cards and suddenly, out of nowhere, she jumped backward, startled. She looked straight into my eyes.

"I don't believe this," she said. "What I'm seeing . . . I don't believe it. I've never — "

"What?" I asked, leaning forward. "What are you seeing?"

Her voice dropped to a whisper.

"You have an inheritance," she said.

"*What?*" I said. "Nobody in my family has money. I don't know what you mean."

"No, not that kind of inheritance," she said without humor or irony.

She turned over a few more cards and started to cry. Now I was spooked.

"Your inheritance has something to do with someone who was here before," she said.

"Who?" I asked.

"I don't know," she said. "Every time the wind blows, you're going to get closer to finding your answers about who it is and what this means."

What? She was freaking me out. She also looked a little freaked out herself.

"A birthmark will confirm everything I've told you," she said.

"A birthmark?" I asked, not remembering my own birthmark at the time.

"There's a reason for everything I'm telling you," she said. "When you go to wherever this place is, you're going to see a man who is going to give you the information you need. He will confirm things."

With that, she was finished. She came out of the trancelike state, looking relieved and tired. My head was reeling. My nerves were jangled. And my buzz was ruined. This woman had gone to considerable trouble to tell me stuff, all motivated by her own need to inform me. Yet she didn't answer the one question I wanted answered. Was I going to make it?

I asked her.

"You're probably going to be a very famous person and your name is going to be known around the world," she said. "But it's not going to happen as quickly as you think."

"Next year? Two years?"

"I don't know," she said. "However . . . I see you playing in Las Vegas . . . and a lot of people dancing."

The Vegas reference made me smile. The rest was too weird even for me.

A new job did follow. One night, we auditioned at a newer, trendier, hipper place in Irontown, called Changes. Jimmy Getty, the club owner, offered us a gig, starting at $250 a week, an increase from what we were making at the Sand Bar. I liked Jimmy. He was a short, wiry man with curly hair, who bore an uncanny resemblance to exercise guru Richard Simmons. He promised good things would happen to us at Changes, and he was right.

We quickly became the club's unofficial house band. We still did shows at the Sand Bar and other places around Ironton, but Changes was our base, and our show turned into the city's biggest party. We played four forty-five-minute sets a night, and each night was like a powder keg with a slow-burning fuse.

We warmed up with what I called the dinner set, which I played sober. During the break, I asked the bartender for a cold beer and maybe had a shot or two of whiskey backstage and, possibly if not probably, a hit of some gangi, though I really can't remember. Some of my brain cells are gone . . . OK, maybe more than some. And by the third set, the party was on. Occasionally someone would send up one of those fancy flaming drinks, and I would make a show of drinking it. The fourth set was our zero-gravity show — no one was in their seat, everyone was flying.

At twenty-three, I felt certain that my life was headed in the right direction. On Thanksgiving, I thanked God for his blessings, and even though I still lived in my boyhood bedroom, I sincerely meant it. But as I settled in on the sofa for post-turkey football with Cletis, Kebo, and Mick, I had a sudden urge to get out and go for a drive. I needed air, and the wind was blowing. It reminded me of the night I met the fortuneteller.

When I got in my car, it was like I was on autopilot. I turned on US 23, took a right, and kept driving north along the Big Sandy River and eventually out to Louisa, Kentucky, the tiny burg where the Cyrus family had originally taken root. I'd been there as a kid, but I'd never driven there on my own. I drove past an old farmhouse and up a hill, following the road as far as it went. Then I parked, got out, and walked and walked.

Soon I found myself standing in the middle of the Cyrus family cemetery. I went to my mamaw and papaw Cyrus's grave. It was the only place I knew there. But every time the wind blew, my boots moved, leading me this way and that, until finally I found myself standing at the headstone belonging to Joe Cyrus, my great-grandfather. I knew a little something about old Joe, mainly that he had lost one arm in an accident. I remember my dad saying that he'd been scared of him.

I looked down and saw on the headstone that he had been born in 1872, on August 25. My birthday was also August 25.

"Oh my God!" I exclaimed. How did I not know that?

It was weird. Even weirder was the feeling I got as I stood there. It was like I was in the grasp of an enormous hand. This wasn't altogether unfamiliar. I'd experienced this sensation before, first at the Neil Diamond concert and then at Mary Magdalene Pitts's grave. I shut my eyes, breathed deeply, and looked heavenward.

"Why me?" I cried out.

I heard a reply immediately.

"Because you've been given all the things that I didn't have."

Who was talking to me? Was that voice coming from the grave in front of me?

There was more.

"I'm sorry to lay this burden upon you. But my soul and spirit depend on what you do with it. When you reach the end of your time it's going to be the end for both of us. The game is going to be over. You'd better be ready to meet your maker. I'm counting on you."

I knew this was weird. I was hearing voices. I felt like I was losing my mind, if I hadn't already lost it. However, it was really happening to me. Beyond that, I was at a loss for explanations. Now, looking back, I can say that I don't believe we walk through life alone. Maybe Robbie Tooley was still hanging with me. Maybe Mary Magdalene Pitts was with me. Maybe it was my grandfather. Or my great-grandfather. Heck, I don't know. Maybe all of the above. I don't claim to understand what was going on or why. I'm just telling you what happened.

I finally hiked back to my car and drove through the woods. As I passed an old farmhouse where Joe Cyrus had lived, I saw an older man stepping out of the front door. I slowed and recognized my uncle, so I stopped and rolled down my window.

"Billy Ray Cyrus, what are you doing up here?" he asked. "Does your dad know you're up here?"

"No, sir," I said. "I just drove up."

He invited me inside. I'd never been there without it being packed with fifty other Cyruses and people lined up for chicken and mashed potatoes in the backyard. I looked around and saw pictures of Joe Cyrus and his wife, Sarah, on the walls. My uncle said Joe was "a tough old bird." He told me a story about a time he got in a fight in a bar near the Big Sandy River and was stabbed.

"Where'd he get stabbed?" I asked.

My uncle pointed to a spot just to the side of my belly button, but a little lower.

"Right about there."

"Oh my God," I said to myself. "That's exactly where I have a birthmark."

A birthmark will confirm everything I'm telling you.

My uncle saw me freeze up and asked what was wrong. I had a sense deep down that not only was nothing wrong, but, in fact, everything in my new rock-and-roll life was unfolding exactly as it was meant to.

CHAPTER 11

———❖———

Too Rock for Country

W E PLAYED AT CHANGES virtually nonstop through the summer of 1984. The marquee out front rarely changed from TONIGHT: SLY DOG. With loyal fans coming every night, we needed a 45 to sell, so all of us chipped in $500 for a session at Barnhill Studios in Catlettsburg. "Suddenly" was our single, and "What the Hell Is Goin' On" was the B-side. We pressed fifteen hundred copies and sold them for $2 at our shows.

J.R. and I also went shopping at the Pied Piper music store, investing about five grand apiece in new equipment. We also spent an additional $105 each on insurance policies.

"Is he just trying to sell us something?" J.R. asked, as we stood outside in the parking lot.

"I think we have to get it," I said. "But that was every dollar I have."

"Me, too."

"Well, this is what I'm doing with my life," I said. "And if something happens, if some asshole breaks into the club and steals our shit, I'm in trouble."

I also made a few trips to Nashville, looking to take my career to the next level. I'd travel with my guitar and a bag full of our 45s. But I was naive about just how difficult it was to get noticed in Music

City. Take my visit to Music Mill Entertainment, an iconic Nashville recording studio. Nobody even came to the door. Instead, after I rang the buzzer, a woman spoke to me on the intercom.

"Do you have an appointment?" she asked.

"No ma'am," I said. "I just wanted to leave a tape."

"Sorry, no soliciting," she said.

As I turned to leave, a large tour bus pulled up in front. I looked up at the people taking pictures and craning their necks to see if I was someone they recognized. The driver provided narration: "This is the famous Music Mill, where the group Alabama recorded all of their hits." I thought, why doesn't he just go ahead and say, "And there's a bum with a guitar they won't even let inside"?

The few who did let me in either said I was too rock-and-roll for Nashville or else wanted money — lots of money. On one trip to Nashville, a buddy of mine named Jimmy McKnight and I met a "producer" at a Shoney's restaurant. He rolled up to the table in a wheelchair, wearing the worst toupee I'd ever seen. He gave us his pitch — "For ten thousand dollars, I can set us up with the best session players in town and make you sound like Alabama" — then set out a brochure and excused himself to go to the bathroom.

"I'll bet he's not even a cripple," Jimmy said.

A few minutes later, he returned and said, "Well? Are you ready to be the next Alabama?"

"I already have a band," I said, "and I want to make records like Bruce Springsteen does with his band. He makes 'em his way. I want to make records my own way."

"That's nice," he said.

Indeed. I stood up, patted him on the back, and thanked him for his time. I think he knew the jig was up. We left, and that day I realized what made Nashville's Music Row go 'round, and later that night Jimmy and I wrote a song about it called "Cashville." "I'm in Cashville, where money talks and bullshit walks and everybody's out for number one . . ."

. . .

A few months into the gig, the fortuneteller lady from the Sand Bar popped into the club. It was a rare slow night at Changes, with only a handful of people there, and she took a seat in the back. I recognized her immediately. She looked scared, almost sick. Her face was pale. I knew she needed to see me.

After my last set, I chatted with some of the guys in the band and walked up to the bar. I was doing my best to ignore her. It didn't matter. She found me. Her dark black eyes were locked on me when I turned and looked down at her.

"The girls with the Ouija board," she said. "Don't go around them no more."

"Huh?" I asked, startled. "How do you know about them?"

"I don't know nothing," she said, standing firm but looking even more frightened. "All I know is there's some girls with a Ouija board in a trailer, and don't you go around them no more, because there's something there that wants what you got."

With that, she walked out of the bar without saying another word or looking relieved for having talked to me.

I knew the girls she referred to. There were two of them, and they looked really good. I'd met them there at Changes, had some drinks and smokes, and they'd invited me back to their trailer, where they got out their Ouija board. The next time I went home with them, they got the board out again, and I was hooked.

I hadn't crossed a sexual line with them yet, but things were looking awfully tempting. One more trip over to their place, and I knew we were all going to be naked. That's when the fortuneteller showed up. Despite her warning, come Friday night, I set out for their trailer after I got off work at two fifteen in the morning.

I pulled in front of their place and noticed it was pretty damn dark and desolate. I thought, Shit, I wish they had some neighbors. This trailer was out in the woods. I saw a car . . . but it didn't look like the car I'd seen them drive. I paused before stumbling up the wood stairs that led to the front door.

Bam! Bam! Bam!

I knocked . . . and knocked again.

Bam! Bam! Bam!

Something didn't feel right.

"Cyrus, get the hell out of here," I said to myself.

As soon as I turned around, though, the door creaked open. It was pitch-black inside the trailer. Something was telling me to go inside. *Come in . . . come on in . . . come in . . .* I debated whether to go. But if those girls were inside, they would've turned on the light. And said something.

I was fairly convinced they weren't in there. So what was?

I remembered the fortuneteller lady said something in that trailer wanted what I had. What did she mean? My spirit? My life? I didn't wait to find out. I got the hell out of there.

In the middle of the night on August 15, 1984, Changes burned to the ground. The fire broke out hours after I'd gone home with my then-girlfriend, Charlotte. I didn't find out until I drove back to 2317 Long Street the next morning, walked in, and found my mom staring at the local news. From what I could see, the building and everything in it appeared to have been leveled by the blaze. I had to see for myself.

When I got there, the club was still wet and the smell of fire filled the damaged space. With a flashlight in my hand, I went straight toward the stage and saw that the drums looked like a melted candle. The rest of our equipment was burned nearly beyond recognition — J.R.'s classic Les Paul, all my guitars — everything except my guitar amp, a Bandit 65. It was charred but mostly intact.

I looked behind the amp where I kept boxes of our 45s and cash from our sales. There were four or five boxes altogether. The box with the cash was gone, burned. The 45s, it appeared, had all melted. When I opened the last box, though, I found a miniature book, a collection of twenty-five inspirational verses. I'd found it a few months earlier at the Brothers Four, a bar in Portsmouth.

Sometimes I would go outside between sets and read it and pray. I couldn't believe it had survived the fire intact. With the narrow beam of my flashlight, I saw it was open to a verse:

With every adversity lies the seed to something greater.

Once again I felt the hand of fate. Or the hands. I was sure this testament to faith was a sign to keep on keeping on, except to do it someplace else. Over and over again I'd heard I was too rock for country, and so I took this as a sign to take my rebel yell out west, to Los Angeles and rock and roll.

Right before the fire, we were booked to open for country legend George Jones when he played Melody Mountain, an outdoor festival in Ashland, at the end of September. It was our biggest show to date, in front of more than ten thousand, and though our equipment was borrowed from friends, we played like seasoned pros after George lived up to his nickname "No Show Jones." For nearly an hour, the promoter stood on the side of the stage and yelled at us to "play one more! Just one more!"

I was singing Billy Idol's "Rebel Yell" (perfect, right?) when I finally saw George's bus winding over the hill. By that point, I had nearly exhausted our repertoire, but I'd never had as much fun. Next, we opened for Dr. Hook at the Red Fox, another local venue. Then, after a two-week stint at the Roxy, a rock club in Ironton, I gathered Sly Dog together and announced that I was leaving the band and heading to Los Angeles.

I'd known I was going to leave since the fire at Changes, and the guys knew it, too. They understood I was going to head west after we made good on our bookings. I didn't want to abandon them, but my single-minded drive to make it, to reach my goal and most importantly to find my purpose, no matter what, was unmistakable, stronger than anything I'd ever known. It defined everything about me. Interestingly, as we stood backstage after the gig, what kept going through my mind was something I had memorized from the book *Think and Grow Rich* — a quote from Napoleon Hill: "Persistence is to the character of man as carbon is to steel."

This was the quote that had kept me going through tough times and self-doubt, and now it was motivating me to go for it, to go to Los Angeles, and, well . . . in short, to never give up.

CHAPTER 12

Baby Toys and New Cars

THE NOTECARD ON MY bedroom wall said everything about this next chapter in my life:

You will go to your cousin Saundra Sark's house in California, where you will set up camp and begin to infiltrate the Los Angeles music scene. Within a month, you will surround yourself with the best musicians you can find, start a band, land a house gig, and strike a deal within three months with Capitol Records.

My dad gave me his car, insisting I drive cross-country in a vehicle more reliable than my truck. I drove most of the way by myself, with only the radio for company. In Albuquerque, I stayed with a cousin who made weird special effects. One of his creations was a life-size skeleton with its own wardrobe and a place in the back where I could stick my hand and swivel its head, like a ventriloquist's dummy.

I called this character Charlie Ray, and stuck him in the passenger seat for the last leg of my drive to California. He was good company.

My cousin Saundra (she was my dad's sister's daughter) lived in

Long Beach, and after settling in and saying hello, I made a beeline for the beach, which I thought would look like a postcard straight out of a Beach Boys song. But instead of blond surfer chicks and golden sand, I found warehouses next to the beach and cargo ships idling offshore. The weather was cold and foggy — where was the fabled sunshine? I bought a bucket of Kentucky Fried Chicken, sat on a bench, and fended off hungry seagulls dive-bombing my chicken.

When I drove to Capitol Records — a round building designed to look like a stack of records — I couldn't even get in the front door. Nor could I get in anyplace else. No one cared about my demos, head shots, or pitches.

As my funds ran low, I landed a job as a forklift operator at Western Pacific Craft, a manufacturer of heavy-duty boxes that produce farmers used in the fields. The boxes were dipped in giant vats of hot wax and then I hauled them away. My coworkers were black and Hispanic men, many of whom were affiliated with Long Beach gangs that hated one another. The place was a cauldron of tension. One night a knife fight broke out and I almost got my throat slashed trying to break it up.

The funny thing about being there was that none of those guys knew my name. They heard my accent and called me "Country." It was so ironic. Here I'd come out to L.A. to rock and I was . . .

Well, it was a rough six months. After working all day, I was too tired to spend nights hustling my music and looking for gigs. Then my cousin Jerry (son of my uncle Larry, who had been with my dad the night he picked me up from jail) drove me to the Palomino Club, a North Hollywood club whose stage was a West Coast home away from home for Johnny Cash, Willie Nelson, Buck Owens, Patsy Cline, and Hoyt Axton.

It was Wednesday night — open mic night.

"Hold on," I said as we settled in at a table near the bar. "Where are we again?"

"The Palomino Club," he said.

"No, I mean what city?" I said. "Because this is where I belong. No offense to you, but where I've been staying is the wrong side of L.A."

I promptly moved from Saundra's to Van Nuys, a suburb in the middle of the sprawling San Fernando Valley, only ten minutes from the club. I rented a room in the back of a house owned by an older couple from England. On my first Wednesday night living in Van Nuys, I showed up at the Palomino, guitar in hand and a batch of songs in my head. Oh, man, getting back onstage in front of people rekindled the waning flame in my soul.

Unfortunately, open mic night didn't pay. Nor did I ever see any scouts from the record labels there looking for undiscovered talent.

I wrote a lot of songs in my room and answered ads for musicians in trade papers, but L.A. in the mid-'80s was all about heavy metal and hair bands. As soon as people heard my name and the twang in my voice, they gave me the usual thanks-but-no-thanks and advised me to go to Nashville.

I gave myself pep talk after pep talk. When I was a boy, my dad had frequently quoted Thomas Edison, who was once asked how it felt to have failed thousands of times to create the electric filament. "I have not failed, not once," he said. "I have discovered ten thousand ways that don't work."

I suppose I was making my own discoveries. Having quit my forklift driving job when I moved, I got a day job at Baby Toytown, a kids' store that sold strollers, bouncy seats, changing tables, and everything else new parents would need. It was near where I lived. I didn't know much of anything about stocking a nursery, but I tried to make up for it by being polite with a can-do attitude.

One day an expectant mom came into the store looking like she might have her baby any minute. I greeted her, and she turned out to be a talker. As I rang her up at the register, she declared that I was the best salesman she'd ever met.

"I didn't do anything, ma'am," I said.

"You were absolutely charming," she said. "And a help. I want you to meet my husband. He runs the Guy Martin Oldsmobile dealership in Woodland Hills."

"I appreciate the thought," I said. "But I wouldn't make a good car salesman. I don't even know how to change the oil in my own car — or even where to check for the oil."

"That doesn't matter," she said. "You go see my husband, Tim Richardson. He'll hire you."

Tim was from Alabama, and he liked my accent. It reminded him of home. But I imagine it was really his wife who had some powerful sway over him, because he hired me even though I didn't have experience or own a suit, or even a pair of pants that weren't blue jeans.

I was not a good car salesman. Just as I'd warned. In fact, the other guys in the showroom claimed that I actually drove customers away. One day, after I'd been there about two months without selling a car — without even getting a nibble — Tim Richardson called me into his office. I had a pretty good idea why.

"Bill, I love you as a human being," he said. "But we're losing a lot of customers who might buy a car. You gotta go."

"I'm sorry," I said. "I knew this was a bad idea coming into it."

"Well, you tried," he said. "Finish out the week and we'll settle up."

Fair enough. At least the pressure was off. As luck would have it, I showed up the next day and sold my first Oldsmobile. The day after that, I sold two cars; the following day, three more. All of a sudden it seemed like I only had to walk up to a customer and he'd open his wallet. I had no idea why, but I was making money, so I decided to stay, and Tim let me.

One Saturday I sold eight cars, a dealership record. The other salesmen continued to hate me, but now it was because I was the hottest car salesman in the Valley. In one month alone, I hauled in $20,000 in commissions. I rewarded myself with a couple of expensive new suits, and Tim Richardson thanked me with a new Cutlass Chalet, a sports car with a super-modified engine and tinted windows that branded me as a badass.

My luck took more than a professional turn the day Tim Richardson fired me. On the way home, I was stopped at a traffic light on Van Nuys Boulevard when a Camaro pulled up next to me with a drop-dead-gorgeous girl behind the wheel. She had strawberry-blond hair, a beautiful smile, and sparkling eyes. She was wearing a football jersey that said CALIFORNIA above the number. If anyone belonged on team California, she did.

I smiled at her, and she rolled down her window. When her hand rose, I saw she was holding a joint. "Do you smoke?" the girl asked.

I nodded and followed her to a nearby park, where we stood under a tree, talked, got high, and talked some more. There's the cliché love at first sight. For me, this was love at first hit.

I had a vague sense of having seen Lynne sometime before and, after a couple dates, I learned that she was an aspiring model who had once been a centerfold in one of my favorite magazines. When she told me, I blurted, "I *thought* I'd seen you." Maybe not the best thing to say to a beautiful young woman I was just getting to know, but she understood.

Soon we were living together in a tiny apartment in Van Nuys. We adopted a couple of kitties, including a scrawny black one we named Spooky. We had a brown plaid sofa and a large poster of Pat Benatar on the wall. Practically every morning I had to double-check my reflection in the bathroom mirror. Was that really me? I mean here was my hillbilly self living with a centerfold I had once fantasized about, and best of all, she was even nicer than she was sexy.

That was the thing about Lynne: the more I got to know her, the more I realized she was also pretty on the inside. New layers opened up all the time, like a flower unfolding slowly, and I would marvel at the quiet sensitivity she revealed. Her mother was homeless, which weighed on her daily. Lynne was determined not to end up living like that. She worked as a bartender and heard every line ever thought up by a guy. She learned to protect herself, and that gave her a bit of an edge. Yet she'd come home and share that big, soft heart.

For the next seven months, life was good. I was a top car salesman, confident, and in love. I continued to play music, mostly Wednesday-night freebies at the Palomino. I also wrote songs. They reminded me of what I was really about and, more important, that I wasn't alone no matter how much I felt like a fish out of water in L.A. Whether it was Robbie Tooley or someone else, I knew I had help from somewhere.

The only glitch was that I was still having trouble finding a way for people to hear my music. Near the end of 1985, a letter arrived from my dad. He knew I was struggling and said he wanted me to know that no matter what, he believed in me and was certain that I would do the right thing. He said something along the lines of, if I knew I was following my life's purpose, keep on doing it no matter how frustrated I got, because eventually I would get to where I was supposed to be. His love and encouragement, always beacons in my life, never shined brighter than when I read his letter that day. "Always know where you are and where you are going," he wrote, "but don't ever forget where you came from."

Those words went straight to my heart. I loved Lynne and appreciated my lucrative job, but I wasn't making any progress toward reaching my dreams. As I did daily, I repeated the goals I'd set for myself: to change my own life and the lives of others, and to share God's light and love, through my music.

Then Kebo called, explaining that Changes had been rebuilt and that the club's owner, Jimmy Getty, wanted me to fly in for an inaugural New Year's Eve show.

It took five seconds for me to make my decision, and back to Changes I went. During my absence, Kebo had been playing with a band called Main Street, and the marquee outside the rebuilt club said, NEW YEAR'S EVE PARTY WITH BILLY RAY CYRUS AND

MAIN STREET. The club sold out. The celebration overflowed into the parking lot. I saw familiar faces and made new friends.

Afterward, Jimmy and my brother both suggested I stick around and keep the party going. I'd been thinking the same thing. Lynne was disappointed that we'd be apart for longer than we'd planned, but she understood. About a week and a half later, I checked in with her. I was all jacked up: I'd played five nights in a row for the first time in nearly thirteen months.

"It's like I woke up from a nightmare," I explained to Lynne, "Changes burned down, and I ended up in California selling cars!"

"I wish I could've been there," Lynne said. "It sounds like a great time."

"I opened my eyes and was right back where I'd been," I said. "Thank God I woke up."

In early 1986, I returned to L.A. to tell Lynne that I was going to quit my job and go back to Appalachia for good. The problem was, I loved her and didn't want to see her upset. Then, before I had a chance to detonate my own bomb, Lynne told me that our little black kitty, Spooky, was gone.

I printed up fliers with Spooky's picture and our phone number and canvassed our neighborhood, knocking on doors in our apartment building and others' nearby. If people didn't answer, I left a flier under their door. I also tacked them up on telephone poles. At one place, an old lady answered the door. She was bawling her eyes out.

"Have you seen this kitty?" I asked.

"Have you seen what's happened?" she asked in response.

She opened her front door wider and motioned toward the TV across the room. To me, the screen looked blue, almost blank. From where I stood, I thought maybe there was a dot in the middle of it, maybe a dot with smoke coming out. But I couldn't tell.

"The space shuttle blew up. With Christa McAuliffe on it," she said, weeping. "It just blew up. They're all gone."

"What?" I exclaimed.

"Just after takeoff," she said. "Come in; watch the report."

With this old lady sobbing next to me, I realized the irrelevance of my problems: Where was my kitty? How would I break the news of my departure to Lynne?

Still, Lynne didn't take the news well when I finally worked up my nerve to break it to her. She cried her eyes out for days. I kept telling her that I'd get my feet on the ground and then maybe she could visit — or even stay. I described the woods, the rivers, my people. Even though I knew she was a full-blooded California girl, I said, "Maybe you'll like it there."

To Lynne's credit, she understood why I was going back to my roots. Although my heart was committed to her, I had to follow my gut. I was a musician. I didn't belong out in L.A. wearing Florsheim shoes and selling Oldsmobiles. The next few weeks were painfully sad. At the end of February, my brother Kebo flew out and helped me load my stuff into a U-Haul, which we hooked up to the back of my car.

"I'm going to come see you," Lynne said as we hugged one last time. "A lot!"

I headed east, picked up Interstate 40 around Barstow, and never looked back.

CHAPTER 13

"Roses in the Winter"

I'D BEEN HOME A little more than a month when Lynne came to visit. Excited, I picked her up at the Cincinnati airport and drove her down the Appalachian highway, a brand-new stretch of road. Accustomed to multilane freeways in L.A., she was amused as I explained this was progress over the two-lane road we'd had before.

For the next two weeks, I showed her my old life before I moved to California. We hiked in the woods and boated on Greenbo Lake. She watched me play at Changes. She saw the way the crowd multiplied between the first show and the fourth, when the whiskey flowed and the dance floor was packed. Lynne had fun, but she was smart and could read between the lines. Night after night the bar was packed with beautiful women. It was a nonstop party, and I loved being part of it.

Both of us were sad when she had to go back home. Our drive to the airport was quiet, painfully so, and when we said good-bye at the gate, we knew it was really good-bye to something special.

I stayed in party mode. The band — Kebo, Mark Carlisle, and Bobby Phillips on guitar, Joey Adkins on bass, and big Bob Anders on drums — was pretty dang tight. I was jubilant that I'd found my way back home, literally and figuratively, and turned back into a big fish in a little pond. By summer, Changes continued to rock even harder and so did we. Booze, weed, music, women; it all flowed nightly and mightily.

Our set list was a high-octane mix of outlaw country (Willie, Waylon, Merle), southern rock (Skynyrd, Molly Hatchet, Charlie Daniels), straight-ahead rock (ZZ Top, Bob Seger), and a bunch of originals I'd written, including "Snooze You Lose," "Appalachian Lady," and "What the Hell Is Goin' On." People knew when I hit high gear. I stood front and center, my shirt ripped or completely off, and leaned out over the dance floor singing Billy Idol's "Rebel Yell."

As the nights got hotter and stickier, I noticed this pretty blonde in the bar. The first night I remember seeing Cindy, she was wearing a small halter top and very short shorts. It was probably about twelve fifteen on a Friday or Saturday, and with her sweet little face, greenish blue eyes, and that outfit, Cindy stood out among the crowd on the packed dance floor.

She was with an older man, who also stood out for being smaller and better dressed than all the rednecks. I wondered about her, but she disappeared after a few songs.

The next week and the week after that, Cindy continued to come to Changes. We played a game where we didn't speak. The stage was elevated about three feet above the dance floor, and I noticed each time she came in she got closer and our eye contact became more direct. I think she tried to dress a little more provocatively each time, if that was even possible.

The tension between me and Cindy was a battle between willpower and desire. It was like Eve tempting Adam all over again. I sang about it, too — the song "Pink Cadillac" was on the set list nightly. Then one night she sent me a drink onstage — and yeah, I gave in. I bit the proverbial apple.

Over the next month, I would step outside during breaks with Cindy and her friend Johnny. She and I would smoke a joint as Johnny, a nonsmoker, kept the conversation going. He was the first openly gay man I'd met, the first who became a close friend. As he heard me talk about my career, he was impressed with my positive approach, and he arranged for me to speak to his students about setting and achieving goals.

Eventually I asked Cindy out to dinner and then took her to Greenbo Lake, where, with the addition of various substances, our unbridled lust careened out of control, and our relationship took off from there. I remember it being like a nonstop party.

In December, Cindy took a few days off from her job to accompany me on one of my periodic trips to Nashville where I hoped to persuade someone to listen to my songs and sign me to a deal. I had a meeting or two, but neither was a for-sure appointment. It was an unusually warm day, though, perfect for a pretty drive. We took Cindy's convertible and started the good times immediately. By the time we got to Lexington, the top was down and Cindy was riding shotgun without her shirt (she liked to get the sun). Between there and Morehead, we had finished our first joint, and I turned to her and said, "You know what? Nashville's nice . . . but it'll wait."

"Huh?" she said. "What're you talking about?"

"If I go down there, somebody is just going to turn me down. Or they're going to tell me I suck. I'm feeling too good for that. Why don't I hang a left on Interstate Seventy-five and go to the Smoky Mountains instead?"

Cindy's smile said it all.

We might've reached behind us into a cooler and pulled out a couple of cold beers; I can picture us doing that. I know it's terrible to drink and drive; I don't do it now, ever. But I certainly did it back when I was a twenty-five-year-old dumbass. Cindy and I drove to Gatlinburg, Tennessee, a well-known getaway in the mountains, and got a tiny cabin room in the primitive section.

All we wanted was to find a waterfall. That's how simple life was back then. Giddy and laughing, we hiked up into the mountains and found a beautiful spot on the Little Pigeon River. I knew this once had been sacred ground for the Cherokee, and I could feel that spirit in the scenery.

We got fired up with beer and some vodka and OJ. Back at the cabin we added shots of tequila. Then we threw a little lightning on top of that cocktail, and well, all I can say is that we got every nickel we could out of that hotel room that night and the next day. Before leaving, Cindy said, "I got an idea. Let's go to the courthouse and get a blood test, and then we'll go to the little white chapel in the middle of town and —"

"Oh my God," I said, without letting her finish, "that's a fantastic idea! And that Merle Haggard song I play when I'm real drunk, 'Roses in the Winter'? We'll get some rings, I'll play that song, and we'll be husband and wife."

And that's how our drunk asses came to exchange rings and vows a short time later in front of a justice of the peace. Afterward, through the fog in my head, I remembered that I had band practice that night. With no way of making the six-hour drive in time, I called bassist Joey Adkins and told him that I had just gotten married.

"You did what?" he exclaimed.

"I married Cindy," I said. "In Gatlinburg. So I can't make it tonight."

"Holy shit," he said.

"Man, it really was some holy shit," I said, laughing.

Looking back, the funniest part of the whole thing — hard as it is to believe — is that I wasn't certain about Cindy's last name. I'd heard her use Smith or Lewis; but now she was officially and legally Cindy Cyrus. My brother, who had married the first girl he kissed, Missy, thought I was crazy to have exchanged vows with a woman I'd known only three months. "Brother, you don't know what you just did to yourself," he said. The other guys were fine as long as it didn't interfere with our music.

My female fans were not so open-minded. Early in 1987, I was onstage, in the midst of the night's third or fourth set, when a waitress brought me one of those fancy flaming drinks and motioned to a couple of women who'd bought it for me. They were standing behind Cindy. Smiling, I blew out the flame and was about to take a sip when I heard my wife's voice rise above the din of the crowd and the buzz of our amps: "That bitch set my hair on fire!"

When I found her in the crowd, her friend Johnny was smothering her head with a wet towel as Cindy whipped around and confronted the two women. Fortunately, a couple of bouncers intervened. Cindy wasn't hurt, but we agreed it was safer if she didn't come to the club anymore.

Folks in the tristate area were passionate about the band. We might as well have been REO Speedwagon. The setup couldn't have been better. Jimmy Getty paid us well. Cindy and I lived in an apartment at the end of Long Street, in the area I'd tried to save from developers as a kid. I wrote about my life, which was good.

I still recorded my songs on a little Fostex recorder — just a guitar and vocals, plus a guitar track or two — and then I'd drive to Nashville, hoping to get someone interested. It was the same old same old, with no payoff. But I was a determined SOB and held tight to my belief that I was pursuing something greater than a whole industry of people saying no. They were merely making a decision. I was chasing destiny, even if I was the only one who believed it.

But I wasn't the only one. My dad urged me to enter a battle of the bands contest he'd heard advertised in Winchester, Kentucky. For some reason, he badgered me until I thought, What the hell. He went along with me and watched as I played a couple of songs. Afterward, a man approached me, saying he wanted to invest money in me. I'd heard that a hundred times before. I pointed out my dad across the room and said, "Go tell him."

In the meantime, I got a beer and watched them talk. But damn if that guy, Jim Green, and his wife weren't telling the truth. They put up $10,000, and together with my dad and I, we started a company called Gold Line. The money we brought in was mine to do with whichever way I thought would get my career going.

The irony was, this relative largesse left me nearly paralyzed with fear. I ran every idea that came to mind by my dad. I tried not to spend a penny because I thought I'd be dead in the water once I ran out of funds. Eventually, though, I went to Nashville and spent $7,000 recording two songs for a 45, "All Night Love" and "Remember," a song I'd written about Lynne. Recording was a fantastic experience. But afterward, the producers sat me down in a coffee shop where we were celebrating a job well done and said they'd need another fifty grand if I wanted to get it on the charts.

"Top thirty," one of them said.

"And for another fifty thousand," his partner added, "we can probably get it in the top five, maybe the top three or four."

I shook my head in amazement.

I think they thought they had a fish on the hook. But I was genuinely amazed that (a) they thought I had that kind of money; and (b) they thought I was that gullible.

"If we get another ten, maybe we could get it to number one," the first guy said.

"Number one," I said in a Jed Clampett–like, gee-whiz tone. "This almost sounds illegal. What kind of chart are you talking about?"

"*Cashbox*," one of them said. Once again, I thought of that song I'd written, the one titled "Cashville."

I pressed up that record, thinking that if I played enough gigs and hustled the 45 to local radio stations, it would take off — and, like Loretta Lynn in *Coal Miner's Daughter,* so would I. But the band was unable to push to the next level. We were all drinking and partying way too hard. Way too many of our friends were doing the same thing. And we had way too many women coming at us from all angles.

We were like a train going way too fast around sharp curves. Something that was supposed to be pure — music — became the right hand of the devil. Unfortunately, my brother Kebo and I were at the center of the flame. Stuff was going on, onstage and off.

Finally, after one show where things got way too crazy, a couple of the guys cornered me and said they didn't want to play with my brother any longer. It may have been a situation where they couldn't play with him. It didn't matter. We were at a point of no return.

I heard what they said, but I stuck up for my brother. Blood was thicker than water. As a result, some of the guys left, some stayed, and we kept going. But pretty soon we were confronted with the same situation.

Soon I was out of options. I had played with nearly every musician in the tristate area. Now I had to face facts. I couldn't defend Kebo anymore. Maybe it wasn't about defending him, though. Maybe it was that I was trying to save him from himself, and no one could do that but him.

I wanted to save his family from the heartache and pain that he and I had witnessed as little boys. Forces of evil were crashing around him and me, around both of us, but the fact is, he was married to Missy and had a little girl, and there were more than a few occasions when things got ugly. Finally, it was obvious, he and I needed to talk. And we did. Our conversation was painful and awkward; I said it seemed apparent that he needed a break, and so did I. It was time for us to go our separate ways.

Saying that to my brother was one of the hardest things I've ever done. We'd been partners since childhood. Kebo and I went through a few years of estrangement before we could repair our relationship. But it wasn't just us. The whole band was busting up. The wheels were coming off the bus for all of us, not just me and Kebo. It was for all the usual reasons: too much sex, drugs, and rock and roll.

Indeed, in September 1987, about a month after Kebo and I had our talk, the entire band threw in the towel. I was stunned. I shouldn't have been, but I was. Then things settled down and began to make sense. I was going to have to stretch outside my comfort zone. It was time for me to move on to plan B or C or D . . . or L, M, N, O, P. Whatever plan was next in line. I didn't know, or couldn't remember.

CHAPTER 14

—◆•❉•◆—

"King of the Ragtime Lounge"

I WAS BACKSTAGE IN a club in a Beckley, West Virginia, hotel, asking myself what the hell I was doing playing a Top 40 club in a Beckley, West Virginia, hotel. It was nearly winter 1987, and I had joined the Players, a band led by Harold Cole, a talented, hard-working bass player I'd known casually for a few years. He and another guy from the band, guitarist Terry Shelton, had come to my house from Charleston and asked me to join their group.

Next thing I knew, I was in Beckley. And then Richmond. And then Myrtle Beach. And then other towns in Virginia, Tennessee, Texas, and Georgia — my second exit from the tristate area. I thought it was a graceful way for me to bow out before any more feelings got hurt. But the setup was what had me scratching my head backstage in clubs. The Players had an agent out of Roanoke who booked them into little dance clubs in small southern hotels. They played disco / Top 40 songs and had a singer, Robbie Ernst, who did the first half of every show. Then I came out for a second half, which consisted of country and rock and roll. I kicked into Skynyrd, Bob Seger, Johnny Cash, and my originals — which the crowds hated. They'd come to dance! Not just dance: they'd come to *disco* dance.

I struggled for a while before loosening up and not worrying so much about whether they liked me or wanted to rock. I came out and did the only thing I could do, which was be myself. Once I did that, I learned I could teach any room to party. I also learned how to perform. No, I learned how to *entertain* — and crowds reacted.

The show changed. Robbie and I traded off on lead arrangements. When I backed him up, I focused on harmonies, something I'd always loved. The best part was that Harold took care of the business side. For the first time in my musical career, I wasn't saddled with the responsibilities of contracts or handing out paychecks on Saturday nights.

These guys were good. In addition to Harold, Robbie, and Terry, the lineup included Doug Fraley on drums and David Baxley on keyboards. The Players were very polished and professional. They worked hard. Their repertoire forced me to adapt to new musical styles and stretch, say, on more intricate rock songs with keyboards and synths, like Def Leppard's "Animal" and Whitesnake's "Is This Love."

The best part was, I hit it off musically with these guys. Although our tastes differed, we shared a mutual appreciation of one another's abilities. Terry's guitar playing knocked me out. He could play rock, country steel, or pop and sound exactly like the licks on records; even better, he added perfect licks on my originals. I knew to keep someone that good by my side — and I did. We're still friends, and that says something.

The schedule Harold booked could be exhausting. It never stopped, and that took a toll. After one long stretch on the road, we were supposed to have a week off and then double back through Georgia. But when everyone bitched about the long drive, Harold, in an uncharacteristic move, canceled the shows.

A few days later, he presented a better offer anyway. He'd spoken with Bud Waugh, the owner of the Ragtime Lounge in Huntington, West Virginia. Bud offered a monthlong gig at $1,325 a week. It sounded perfect. The club was a fifteen-minute drive from the little house Cindy and I had bought in Ironton. But there was one condition: "Cyrus, he wants *you* to sing . . . a lot," Harold said. "If you'll sing most of the songs, he'll agree to the house gig."

I said, "Hell, yes" — and our month-long gig turned into the next three and a half years.

April 13, 1988, was our first night at the Ragtime, and it was memorable for how *not* memorable it was. The crowd for our first forty-minute set was enthusiastic but small, and it got only smaller as the night progressed. By the last set, we might as well have been playing for friends and family.

But three days later, we got a break: Richard Marx came to town needing an opening act after his bowed out at the last minute. We eagerly trucked our gear over to the Huntington Civic Center and played our asses off the next night. The next day, the newspaper singled us out as a local band that delivered a smoking half hour of kick-ass country and rock — good, party-time, get-down music.

And guess what? The next night, a Saturday, the Ragtime Lounge was packed. The cozy honky-tonk didn't hold many people to begin with, a dozen or so more than two fifty, but we played and people partied with an energy that made it feel like ten times that number.

In June, Robbie left the band, and Harold rechristened it Billy Ray and the Players. Three months later, we opened for REO Speedwagon. Imagine doing that at eight o'clock and then two hours later being back onstage at the Ragtime. The good times there just got louder and wilder. I couldn't be on that stage without someone calling out for my originals, like "Mom Called Dad a Mother," a funny bar song I wrote, or "Whiskey, Wine, and Beer." I also played a rocking cover of Nancy Sinatra's "These Boots Are Made for Walkin'."

Other popular songs were "Milkman's Eyes," "All Night Love," "I Think About You Day and Night," and "Remember." I had about thirty-two originals at that time, and I tried to play six to eight every set. A bunch of them were genuine hits with the crowd. I looked the part of a bad boy. I wore wristbands, necklaces, T-shirts with the neck and sleeves ripped out, a bandana tied just below my knee, and buckskin boots. All of us sported mullets except for Terry Shelton, who'd be the first to tell you his was a skullet. Our philosophy was simple: if you ain't coming to party, you might want to stay home.

My marriage was similar. I think both Cindy and I would agree that our relationship at this point was more of a party than a traditional partnership. Playing that bar night after night was a different kind of lifestyle. There were girls who liked to hang out, and Cindy gave me the OK as long as I didn't get too crazy with it.

Once that happened, though, the sanctity of our circle, if you will, was broken. As a result, we'd have to deal with the hurt feelings and consequences of those entanglements. But it was pretty good fodder for a songwriter — and I wrote a ton.

Nearly every day on the stretch of US 52 between Cindy's and my place on South Sixth Street and the Ragtime, I dreamed up songs, singing lyrics into a microcassette recorder I kept in the glove box. At home, I would finish them off on my crude four-track, which I referred to as my laboratory of music. Then, on Mondays and Tuesdays, my days off, I tried to pedal them in Nashville.

It was a six-hour drive there, and I would walk up and down Music Row, holding my satchel of songs and photos in one hand and my guitar in the other. I'd knock on the door of Tom T. Hall Publishing, Conway Twitty's Twitty Bird Productions, and other similar businesses. I canvassed Chet Atkins Boulevard. I ignored the signs that said NO SOLICITORS. If I got inside, I talked fast.

Each week, I felt the sting of rejection, but giving up was never an option. I had burned all bridges that led anywhere other than becoming a successful singer-songwriter.

Then a door opened. In November 1988, Kari Reeves, the daughter of singer-songwriter Del Reeves, welcomed me into the publishing office she managed for her father. They had a considerable business. In a refreshing change from the usual chorus of thanks-but-no-thanks, she wanted to hear my music — and she was also gorgeous.

I gave her a cassette of "All Night Love" and "Remember" and watched as she put it in the stereo system next to her desk and pressed PLAY. After listening to the songs, she asked if I would play another on my guitar. She watched me intently. Our eyes never moved from each other's. Afterward, she smiled.

"I like you, Billy Ray Cyrus," she said.

I just stared back at her.

For a little while, I wasn't sure if she was talking about my music or something else, or both.

We talked about music that afternoon, that night, and for days afterward. We spoke on the phone frequently and at length. Always about music — my shows, my songs, other people's songs, the business. My favorite thing about Kari was that she really loved music. She knew every Grand Ole Opry star; she knew Nashville. She knew the performers onstage and the power brokers behind the scenes. She knew bands and songwriters. She knew talent.

As the daughter of a certified country music legend, she was on the inside — or at least she had access to the inside — and that impressed me. I was both intrigued and intoxicated when Kari said she thought I had talent and charisma and said she wanted to help me become a star.

"You want to help?" I said.

"Yes," she said, smiling.

"No one's ever said that to me in this business," I said. "Maybe not ever."

"Then I'm glad we met," she said.

Kari had a little cabin on her dad's farm and also a funky old house on Belmont Boulevard, just off Music Row. One night she invited me to her house. Kari lit candles, opened a bottle of wine, and we played songs all night long. She told me how my songs made her feel. We bared our souls to each other, and then things started getting a little crazy.

CHAPTER 15

"Opening Doors"

I NEVER CLAIMED TO be perfect. I knew what happened with Kari was wrong in the context of my marriage, but the sanctity of those vows had been broken long ago and I couldn't tear myself away from Kari. She wrote about me in a Nashville music magazine, arranged for me to record my songs "Baby Sitter" and "Whiskey, Wine, and Beer," and before the year was over, she persuaded her father to see me at the Ragtime.

That was a big deal. By then, Terry Shelton and I had written and recorded the song "It Ain't Over Till It's Over." (I gave Cindy writer's credit on it, because why not? I gave her credit on a lot of songs in those days, figuring if I ever made it big and they earned some money, she would deserve it for putting up with me.) Two local radio stations — WTCR out of Catlettsburg and the WLGC out of Ashland — played that single (it was actually a demo) and announced that Del Reeves was going to check me out at the Ragtime.

Back then, the radio stations were part of the whole thing. They were plugged into whatever was happening. The people at the Ragtime were their fan base, and they were digging the songs. They played the hell out of "All Night Love," "Remember," and "It Ain't Over," which became a hit in Huntington, West Virginia.

That was the first time I started hearing one of my songs on the radio, and it was cool, way cool. It made me feel like I was getting somewhere.

That night Del came to the Ragtime, the place was on fire. Packed to the walls. People waiting to get in. The dance floor overflowed when I segued into "Whiskey, Wine, and Beer" and "Snooze You Lose." Then every BIC lighter in the room was lit when we played "It Ain't Over Till It's Over." My opening set was nearly all originals, with maybe a couple of cover tunes at most, like Restless Heart's "Fast Movin' Train."

Del was unmistakable — a very tall man with a head of silver curls. He saw two sets and stayed until about midnight. Before leaving, he shook my hand and said, "You got something, kid."

Then, with the pressure off, I let loose in the third and final set of the night. "Send me up one of those drinks on fire," I said. "We are going to party down." And we did. By then, that drink wasn't the only thing burning.

Del wasted no time signing me to a standard production agreement. Under the terms of the contract, he provided interim management duties in exchange for a percentage of my earnings. Then he produced a more polished version of "It Ain't Over" at his Allisongs Studio in Nashville.

For all the excitement, though, nothing happened for a few months. The holidays and New Year's passed. In February 1989, drummer Steve French, an old classmate of mine in Flatwoods, and keyboardist Barton Stevens joined the band after David Baxley and Doug Fraley went their own way. I kept hammering away at the doors on Music Row with nothing to show but black-and-blue knuckles.

I was ready to bust down a few of Nashville's locked doors when Del arranged for me to meet Buddy Killen. The head of Tree Publishing, at that time the largest in Nashville's history, Buddy was a musician, songwriter, and executive. And most of all, he was a legendary song man.

Out of respect to Del, Buddy let me play a couple of songs and then gave me his feedback. Later on, I told Del and Kari that nothing had happened. In retrospect, that wasn't true. First, he allowed me into his office and listened to me play. What can you give someone that's more valuable than your time?

He also gave me advice that I use to this day. After I finished playing, we talked about the songs and songwriting in general, and then he said, "When you're writing a hit song, say as much as you can say in as few words as you can say it. If you don't need a word, take it out."

Brevity required the strength of a lumberjack, the detachment of a surgeon, and the gentle touch of a poet.

Del also connected me to heavyweight manager Jack McFadden, who was famous for guiding Del's career as well as the careers of Buck Owens, Merle Haggard, Lorrie Morgan, and Keith Whitley. Like Buddy, Jack met with me as a favor to Del. Afterward, he agreed to help. But to say he was my comanager would have been a stretch. He never came to see my show, didn't listen to my music, and didn't understand what I did. He hardly returned my phone calls. But his wife, Jo, kind of took me under her wing. "You just keep gettin' in front of him," she told me. "Sooner or later he'll get it."

I once stopped by Jack's office, hoping to get a word with him. His office door was open a crack, and as I peeked through, I saw a couple standing in front of his desk, talking. The guy turned around. It was Keith Whitley. He was with his wife, Lorrie Morgan. Jack regarded Keith as his surrogate son. The brief look Keith gave me seemed to say, "Sorry, brother, I have a feeling I'm blowing your moment, your chance to meet Jack."

I turned around and began to walk out, disappointed. Jo caught me before I reached the door and promised to speak with Jack. She listened to my songs, liked 'em a whole lot, and told her husband that he needed to meet with me.

And he did. Jack called me in and agreed to help me navigate Nashville's tricky waters. He even arranged to take me to a meeting at CBS Records. I circled the date on my calendar: May 9, 1989. It was the biggest day of my life.

• • •

I woke up early that morning with Kari in the cabin on her father's farm. I left the house eager and hopeful. I wanted to get to the parking lot about thirty minutes before Jack. Unfortunately, as I drove to our meeting spot, I turned on the radio and heard that Keith Whitley had died.

"Oh my God! This can't be!"

As I recall, the DJ was careful to say the report was not yet confirmed but it appeared to be accurate. I drove to Jack's office, where I found Jo, in tears. Stan Barnett, another agent there, was also crying over the tragedy. A moment later, Kari arrived. She'd tried to catch me on the road.

All of Nashville and country music fans around the world cried a river of tears that day. A great talent had left the world, and needless to say, the meeting never happened.

I was due onstage at the Ragtime at 8 p.m., and I had a six-hour drive ahead of me.

By noon, I was in my car, heading north. I drove in a trance. When I got to Morehead, Kentucky, close to Keith Whitley's hometown of Sandy Hook, I tuned the radio to WCTR, and through the static of the signal coming in, I heard their tribute to Keith. When they played "I'm No Stranger to the Rain," I shed a tear. How could I not?

As I went along, I gave myself a talking-to. Though, to be honest, what I was hearing was that voice within. But since I had just passed the Sandy Hook exit, I imagined Keith was talking to me: "Hope I didn't mess you up, hillbilly. I just want to tell you that you're out of control. You don't need that whiskey tonight. Don't be like me. Pull yourself together." I wish I could tell you that I'd imagined that voice. But I knew it was for real when I heard one more thing: "You got to be there for Jack. Jack's going to need you."

Holy shit, I thought I was done hearing voices. I guess not.

I didn't stop drinking or partying that night or anytime soon, but at the Ragtime, where the smell of beer and whiskey greeted me like a somber handshake, I opened my set with "I'm No Stranger to the Rain" — and boy, those words never rang more true.

CHAPTER 16

✦•✦•✦

"Some Gave All"

TALK ABOUT A HELL of a week. It was early summer, and after my fourth set on Wednesday night I lingered at the club and partied all night. It was still early when I got to *my* house; the sun was just starting to crack the morning sky.

As I pulled into the driveway, I saw a bunch of stuff piled up in the front. It looked like Cindy was preparing for a garage sale, until I looked closer and saw that all my worldly possessions were on the grass. I guessed Cindy was pissed. OK, more than pissed. As I stared at the pile, I saw my neighbor leave his house and walk to his car, heading for work. He was wearing a suit, and I was in the clothes I'd worn onstage the night before, reeking of alcohol and whatever else.

Our cat, Mr. Sly, was also watching me from the front window. He seemed to be saying, "Man, you really blew it this time."

This wasn't my first time rolling in late. Cindy and I had different schedules. I'd sleep in the morning and get up around three or four in the afternoon. Then I'd hit the gym and wait for Cindy, who got home around 5:30. She'd make dinner, we'd eat, then she got in bed, and I'd go to the Ragtime.

It was complicated, and now, with my belongings on the front lawn, my life was even more complicated.

I sat in my car wondering where I was going to live. Two seconds later, I grabbed my microcassette recorder and began to sing:

> Wher'm I gonna live when I get home?
> My old lady's thrown out everything I own.
> She meant what she said
> When she wished I was dead
> So wher'm I gonna live when I get home?

I continued to sing and went into a verse.

> I knew our road was gettin' kind of rocky
> She said I was gettin' way too cocky
> She waited till I was gone
> She packed from dusk till dawn
> So wher'm I gonna live when I get home?

I grabbed my guitar and strolled into the house as if nothing had changed. I sat beside my cat, Mr. Sly, and pulled out my recorder and wrote the last verse.

> She decided she would keep my cat
> My transportation, I wouldn't be needin' that
> She kept my TV, the bills she gave to me
> So wher'm I gonna live when I get home?

After playing the song from front to end, I pleaded with Cindy to let me stay and promised we'd deal with the situation later. I also gave her half writer's credit for settin' my stuff out in the yard. "If you hadn't a done that, I wouldn't have wrote this song," I said. She liked that, but still cussed me out before getting ready for work, which seemed to make her and me feel a little better.

Then I carried my stuff back inside, took a bath, and slept until later that afternoon.

When Cindy came home that night, I was waiting with burgers on the grill for dinner. I told her that she was right. No doubt about it, I was an asshole. She smiled, and for a moment things seemed a little better.

• • •

I was mad at myself and depressed when I got to the gig. It was Thursday, and I was still mildly hungover from the previous night, or rather earlier that morning. As I sat in my dressing room (which was really a closet for kitchen and cleaning supplies), I had to decide whether to power up to the next level or deal with feeling miserable. I had a guitar in my hand, as usual, and began to play; I also began to sing, and within a few minutes I had written the song "She's Not Cryin' Anymore."

> *She used to cry when I'd come home late*
> *She couldn't buy the lies I told*
> *All she wanted was to be needed*
> *Someone that she could call her own*
> *The love I know I took for granted*
> *Until she walked out of my door*
> *Too little too late to say I'm sorry*
> *'Cause she's not cryin' anymore.*
> *She's not cryin' anymore*
> *She ain't lonely any longer*
> *There's a smile upon her face*
> *A new love takes my place*
> *She's not cryin' anymore.*

Between sets, Terry Shelton, my guitarist, followed me back into my dressing room and we had something good rolled up, which was always a ripe time for me to let things hang out. I told him what had happened between Cindy and me and then sang what I'd written. He loved it. Me, him, and Buddy Cannon wrote another verse and it would become another hit off that first album.

Both Friday and Saturday went by without me writing anything. In lieu of songs, I sobered up. On Sunday, I was between the third and fourth sets when I saw a stranger at the bar. Sunday night crowds tended to be light, and I usually recognized everyone there for the late shows. Hell, from playing there five nights a week, I pretty much knew everyone who set foot in the place. But this night was one of the sparest I'd seen. In fact, I saw an empty stool at the bar next to this stranger, and I couldn't recall ever seeing an empty barstool. Or that guy.

Intrigued, I walked up to the bar for the first and only time since plugging in at the Ragtime that evening. I ordered a cold beer and said, "How you doing, sir? I'm Billy Ray Cyrus."

He stuck out his hand: "I'm Sandy Kane."

"I don't believe I've seen you here before," I said.

He told me he was from Sandy Hook, Kentucky.

"I know Sandy Hook," I said, immediately thinking back to Keith Whitley. After a moment, I asked, "You're a Vietnam veteran, aren't you?"

I had a feeling. Something about the way he looked. His eyes said the most. He opened up and talked about it a little, and I listened intently.

As he finished, the bartender gave me the sign. My break was up.

"I got one more set," I said. "You got any songs you want to hear?"

He thought for a moment.

"Man, you know any Skynyrd?"

"Oh yeah," I said.

"Bob Seger?"

"Uh-huh."

"Credence?"

"Yes, sir."

"Well, that'd be perfect for me."

After rounding up the band, I explained what was what and led them through a superset of Skynyrd, Seger, and Credence. We ended on a powerful version of "Call Me the Breeze." When I came offstage, Sandy Kane was at the bar, still sitting on his stool, only this time he had a big old smile in the middle of his grizzled face.

"Thank you," he said. "That was a gift."

"Hey, thanks for your service," I said. "Thanks for going to Vietnam. I knew a guy who came back and didn't have any legs. He was a schoolteacher from our area."

Sandy nodded.

"You know what they say. All gave some, and some gave all."

He shook my hand again and walked away.

Instead of partying that night, I got in my Chevy Beretta and drove home, feeling a bit mellow and kind of sad. US 52 was empty. It was like a dark asphalt snake running parallel to the Ohio River illuminated under a sliver of silver moon.

If I hadn't reached into the glove compartment for my recorder, I probably would've completely forgotten that I was in a car, that's how far away my head was as I told myself the story of meeting Sandy Kane.

"He wanted to hear Credence, Seger, and Skynyrd," I said, speaking into the recorder. We gave him a double shot of our southern best, and when he left, he said, "All gave some, and some gave all."

The recorder was going, so I just started singing to the melody I heard in my head. I thought back to a statue I used to see when I was a kid, somewhere we used to travel to when we played football. It was a monument to veterans. I could still see it in my mind. It read: *All Gave Some, Some Gave All.*

> *I knew a man called him Sandy Kane*
> *Few folks even knew his name*
> *But a hero yes was he*
> *Left a boy, came back a man*
> *Still many just don't understand*
> *About the reasons we are free*
>
> *I can't forget the look in his eyes*
> *Or the tears he cried*
> *As he said these words to me*
>
> *All gave some, and some gave all*
> *Some stood through for the red, white, and blue*
> *And some had to fall*
> *And if you ever think of me*

Think of all your liberties and recall
Some gave all

Now Sandy Kane is no longer here
But his words are oh so clear
As they echo throughout our land
For all his friends who gave us all
Who stood the ground and took the fall
To help their fellow man

Love your country and live with pride
And don't forget those who died
America, can't you see

All gave some, and some gave all
And some stood through for the red, white, and blue
And some had to fall
And if you ever think of me
Think of all your liberties and recall
Some gave all

And if you ever think of me
Think of all your liberties and recall,
Yes recall
Some gave all
Some gave all.

I finished without pausing. I never wrote a word on paper. All of it came out as a piece. I was so freaked out that I woke up Cindy. Breathless, I sat on the side of the bed with my guitar in my lap. "You're not going to believe this," I said.

Instead of telling her what had happened, I sang her the song. When I finished, I asked what she thought of it. She wiped her eyes.

"Yeah," I said. "Me, too."

I knew "Some Gave All" was different from my other songs. From that night on, it felt like it was my child. It was part of me. It became my mantra and my attitude toward life. I knew the song was special, so the next day I drove to Flatwoods to play it for my mom, who had the best set of ears of anybody I knew.

After playing "Some Gave All" for her and seeing her reaction, I was even more confident about the song. I knew what I had to do: give it to Charlie Daniels. He was such a big supporter of Vietnam veterans I thought it was a natural for him, and he might even make it a hit.

My mom said, "That song is going to change your life." I told her about my Charlie Daniels idea. "He'll record it and I'll be a songwriter," I said.

"Oh no, Billy," she replied. "I love Charlie. But that's your song." She shook her head. "That song is meant for you."

"But—" I started to say.

"No, you are not giving it to him," she interrupted. "Do not give it to him. That is your song. I have a feeling about it."

A couple of weeks later, my mom ended up riding with me to Charlie's concert in Beckley. She hadn't seen me perform in a long time, and she really did love Charlie Daniels and his sound. She said the way he played the fiddle reminded her of her dad, my papaw Casto. What she didn't know, though, was that I had made a demo of "Some Gave All" on my four-track and, despite her "feeling," planned to give it to Charlie. I was obsessed with that; the song was going to bust me through the doors in Nashville.

In the backstage area at the festival, I met Charlie's longtime keyboard player, Taz DiGregorio. Taz had cowritten Charlie's massive 1979 hit "The Devil Went Down to Georgia." I showed him my tape and asked if there was any way to get it to Charlie. He pointed out the window to their tour manager and nodded.

"Let's go," he said.

I held my cassette but let Taz talk to the tour manager.

"Mr. Daniels is in a meeting," he said.

"No, man, you don't have to be like that," Taz said, clearly knowing better. "This is my friend."

I ended up handing the cassette to the tour manager, hoping

he would follow through and get it to Charlie. Years later, after the song and the album carrying the same title had been out for a while, I met up with Charlie, who told me "Some Gave All" was one of his favorite songs of mine. He swore he'd never heard it back in the day.

"Well, I gave it to you first," I said. "That's the truth."

"I didn't hear it or else I would've cut it," he said. "Fate must've been on your side."

And he was right.

CHAPTER 17

A Big "Little Deal"

NIGHT AFTER NIGHT, WHEN I went home from the Ragtime, I watched CNN and recorded the bleakest stories on my VCR as if I was documenting the end of the world. I taped 'em all: wars, earthquakes, the depletion of the ozone layer, the slaughter of wild animals, world hunger. If there was a catastrophe someplace, anyplace, I found a way to relate to it.

Sometimes Cindy woke up, came downstairs, and got mad at me. She thought I might be losing my mind and perhaps she was right. But I felt like I needed to feel. For some reason, there was an awakening inside me. The world was spinning fast and I was running out of time.

In July of the previous year, 1989, I'd finally signed a management contract with Jack McFadden, who seemed ready to get back to work after losing Keith Whitley. But nothing happened.

Though I was becoming impatient, I had to think back to earlier years when I was frustrated and anxious to get something going. I almost made a big mistake. I nearly signed with Bernie Faulkner, an independent songwriter and producer out of Hazard, Kentucky. His label was called BFI Records. He'd seen me play at a talent contest sponsored by Wrangler jeans. But I didn't want to sign just because I was desperate. I spoke with my dad, who advised me to do what felt right and not to settle just because I was in a hurry. I did have other options. In fact, I was leaving a meeting on Music Row, between 16th and 17th Avenues, when I walked out a back door and into an alley, where I said, "God, tell me what to do. Should I sign with BFI Records, Lord? Show me a sign. Amen." When I opened my eyes, I noticed a blue dumpster in front of me, and stenciled on the side in big white letters it read, BFI."

"Wait a minute," I said out loud. "Wait a minute! I've come too far and put too much into this to sign with the garbage man."

In January 1990, Jack convinced Buddy Cannon, a talent executive with Mercury Records, to see us play at the Ragtime. The audience response that night was so overwhelming that Cannon told his boss at Mercury, Harold Shedd, that it must've been cooked up to impress him. A nobody couldn't be *that* popular. They concocted a scheme to sneak into a gig I had in Huntington, and they saw me again in May when I opened for Reba McEntire at Louisville's Freedom Hall, where fifteen thousand fans whooped and hollered like crazy for me to continue my short set. Some of them actually followed me back to the Ragtime, where I played three sets that same night.

For the next two months I waited for a phone call that didn't come, for reasons I didn't understand. I had a big fan base, a great band, songs that were on local radio, a powerful manager, and I was writing some of the best songs of my career. What was it going to take for something to happen? Jack took my demos to numerous labels, and all of them turned me down, including Mercury.

I was frustrated, depressed, and desperate. My marriage — what was left of it — skidded to a halt.

"Billy, you might never make it, and I can't keep going through this," Cindy said.

I needed help or guidance, and one day my inner voice told me to go back to Flatwoods, back to the church where Papaw Cyrus had preached. Although I hadn't been there for years, I figured it couldn't hurt. So the next Sunday I showed up and took a seat in the back row. Some folks recognized me as the honky-tonk singer, and others knew that the church had once been my papaw's. As the preacher began his sermon, I flashed back to the way my brother and I used to kneel at the altar and say the Lord's Prayer.

Minutes later, I snapped to attention when the preacher, his voice rising with the sharpness of a pushpin, said, "God loves a desperate man! God loves a desperate man! When you are desperate, you don't get down on your knees and say, 'Now I lay me down to sleep, I pray the Lord my soul to keep.' No, you get down on your knees and you pray, 'God, I'm desperate!'"

I stood up, walked to the front, and dropped to my knees. A few others joined me. I bowed my head and prayed, "God, I'm as desperate as they come. If you're ever going to help, please help me now."

That night, I drove to the Ragtime and did my sets. The Devil threw everything he had at me, too. But I went home after that fourth set. On the way home, I spoke into my recorder. "I will call Harold Shedd at Mercury Records first thing in the morning. I will tell him that I need to see him for five minutes and play him my best. If it ain't good enough, then I should probably do something else."

The next morning I woke up early, dialed Mercury Records, and asked for Harold Shedd. Harold's secretary, Joyce, answered the phone. I'd met her several times. She wouldn't put Harold on the line, but she did listen to me say that I was coming to Nashville the next day and wanted five minutes of his time.

"Just five minutes," I said. "Then I'll leave and never bother either of you again."

The line went quiet. I thought I heard the ruffling of paper. Maybe she was checking Harold's appointment book. She came back to the phone.

"Five minutes is all you're going to get, Billy," she said.

"That's all I'll need," I said.

I drove down that night, and early the next morning I walked into Harold Shedd's office. I had five minutes for the biggest audition of my life. I sat on a chair in front of Harold's desk. There was no time to waste. I pulled out my guitar and said, "Mr. Shedd, this is the best thing I got. If it ain't good enough, I won't bother you anymore." I began to play "Some Gave All." After the last note, I looked at Harold expectantly, eager for a reaction. He'd sat with a poker face through the whole song, and his expression didn't change when I finished.

Finally, he nodded and said, "I'm going to structure you a little deal." Then he got up and walked out of the room. I sat there and thought, what did he mean by that? What's he going to do, have me cut the grass here at the record company?

When he returned, a small man in a suit was with him. His name was Paul Lucks. He was the president of the label. He shook my hand and said, "Mr. Cyrus, welcome to Mercury Records. I'll get hold of your manager, Jack McFadden."

I put up my guitar and got out of there as quick as I could, before anyone could change their mind.

After leaving Harold's office, my first stop was Jack's. I couldn't wait to tell him the good news and burst through the big hickory door that had once been closed to me. When I did, he looked up from behind his desk, startled.

"Jack, I did it!" I said, pumping my first into the air. "I got a deal with Mercury Records."

He lifted his head and stared at me. Just then, his secretary came on his speaker and said, "Jack, line one. It's Paul Lucks." He continued to stare at me while I heard him say, "Yep . . . yep. OK, Paul . . ." By that point, his dark eyes looked like Daffy Duck's when he lands in the pot of gold. He said, "Congratulations, my boy. You did it."

On January 3, 1991, I officially signed my contract with Mercury Records. Jack arranged a press event at Ashland's Paramount Arts Center, in the same theater where I'd watched Disney movies as a kid. My parents, Mercury executive Paul Lucks, a handful of reporters, and about three hundred fans applauded as I put my signature at the bottom of the contract. Jack boldly predicted I was "Nashville's next big superstar."

Less than two weeks later, I recorded "Some Gave All," the song most people, including me, expected to be my first single. That day was special for a number of reasons. It was January 16, the first day of Operation Desert Storm, and when I laid down the vocals I wasn't singing just for Sandy Kane and other Vietnam vets. I was also singing for all the US soldiers in the Gulf, providing a sendoff and a foreshadowing of what some of them would face later. It was very emotional.

The session was held in Nashville's Music Mill, the legendary log structure where I wasn't exactly welcomed when I first showed up in town to peddle my songs. Now I was in the ten-thousand-square-foot state-of-the-art recording studio. It felt right, like I belonged.

We recorded, mixed, and put the final tweaks on "Some Gave All" in one marathon session. Late that night something weird happened. The Mill's lobby had high-vaulted ceilings and walls decorated with dozens of photos and gold records showcasing the stars and legends who'd walked through the doors and made music that changed their lives. At the top of one wall was a large, framed picture of Keith Whitley's album with two platinum records inside. During a break, Jack and I walked into the lobby and suddenly the large framed plaque basically sprang from the wall and crashed to the ground right in front of Jack's feet. Glass shattered. I saw the color drain from Jack's face.

"Cyrus, I have to go home now," he said, choking up.

"No problem," I said. "I got this."

Mercury had assigned veteran producers Joe Scaife and Jim Cotton to my album. They were forthright in telling me the label wanted to see if what I did onstage translated to a record. I asked to use my band, Sly Dog, instead of studio musicians. We'd gone through more personnel changes after Harold Cole departed at the end of 1990, but I believed Terry Shelton (guitar), Greg Fletcher (drums), Barton Stevens (keyboard), and Corky Holbrook (bass) were as tight as any guys they could assemble — plus, we'd added Keith Hinton on guitar — and they were *my* guys.

"I'm not going after the Nashville sound," I said. "I want my sound. That's what got me here."

I wouldn't have felt like a real artist if I'd gotten to that point and then surrendered. I wanted to make my record the way Bruce Springsteen made his: work up the songs with my band and then go cut the tracks.

Explaining that every new artist made the same request, Jim, Joe, and Harold Shedd said they'd give the band one trial, and only one. Nearly twenty-four hours later, when we listened to the final version of "Some Gave All," everyone knew . . . they passed the test.

"You can use your band on the album," Harold said.

It was a special moment, at a special time, in a special place, with a special song . . . where music changed everything.

CHAPTER 18

————◆•◆•◆————

"Don't Tell My Heart"

F OR THE NEXT SIX MONTHS, I tried to survive while the label's brain trust ostensibly decided on the songs for my debut album. In reality, I don't think they knew exactly what I was or how to package me, so even though I was on their official roster of artists, they kept me on the sidelines.

I thought they were missing a huge opportunity. The United States was fully engaged in the Gulf War, and CNN was broadcasting the play-by-play live on television. I thought they should release "Some Gave All" right then. People went nuts every time I played the song at the Ragtime or at any of the other clubs and venues in the tristate area. Fans held their BIC lighters high in the air. I pleaded with Jack to get the label to release the song.

"We're missing out, Jack," I said, with a huge sense of urgency. "Tell 'em this is big. The song has to be out now!"

I was freaking out pretty hard.

One person who agreed with me was Leticia Finley, a stunning blonde who everyone called Tish. She was a former model, and her best friend first brought her to the Ragtime to see me. Then she and some of her other girlfriends came more regularly, enough that I recognized her. How could I not? She turned every head in the joint.

Every once in a while we talked, until we had a little friendship going. She had two beautiful small children, Brandi, four, and Trace, two. She knew about my record deal. One night I asked if I could drive her home and she said yes. We sat out front of her house and talked till the sun came up. I played her "Some Gave All" on my car stereo.

"That might be your best song," she said.

"I think so, too."

"With the Gulf War going on, you ought to get your record company to put it out soon," she said.

"That's what I keep telling 'em," I said. "I think I'm going to die before it ever comes out."

And I meant it. The club was so full of wild girls and drunken guys, so crowded, and there was so little oxygen and so much craziness, I felt like I was suffocating. I couldn't even go on a break without everyone trying to make me happy in some way. I knew if something didn't happen to get me out of there, someone was going to kill me. It was like a premonition. Something bad was going to happen if something else didn't happen first.

In early June, I finally went back into the studio. Joe and Jim and Harold and me and Buddy Cannon, the head of A&R, picked out nine songs: "Could've Been Me," "She's Not Cryin' Anymore," "Wher'm I Going to Live?" "These Boots Are Made for Walkin'," "Someday, Somewhere, Somehow," "Never Thought I'd Fall in Love with You," "Ain't No Good Goodbye," "I'm So Miserable," and "Some Gave All," which was already done. They wanted one more song.

My producers played humongous roles in shaping the album. Jim was from Memphis and had a résumé of feel-good music, and Joe was a good ol' boy from Tennessee who had a good set of ears for a hit song. Right before we began to record, they came to the Ragtime one night to hear us. It had been awhile since they'd seen me live, and to capture the right feel on the album, they had to see me play there.

Joe drove up to Huntington one day to rehearse me and the band, and on a break we all walked to Terry Shelton's apartment. On the way there, Joe said he had a song he wanted me to hear.

At Terry's, we sat down at the kitchen table. Joe took out a tape and put it in Terry's boom box. Right before pressing PLAY, he said, "You might think I'm crazy, but I think this thing's a hit."

"Let's hear it," I said.

After a few guitar licks, a voice started to sing:

> *You can tell the world, you never was my girl*
> *You can burn my clothes up when I'm gone . . .*

After two more lines I jumped out of my chair, raised my arms in the air, and exclaimed, "That's me! That's me! I love it!" It was pure bar-band southern rock-stompin' fun, a good time waiting to happen, and I knew people would want to dance to it. I could hardly sit still myself. Nor could I resist singing along to the chorus:

> *Don't tell my heart, my achy breaky heart*
> *I just don't think it'd understand*
> *And if you tell my heart, my achy breaky heart,*
> *He might blow up and kill this man.*

The song, a sad but whimsical take on love, was called "Don't Tell My Heart." Don Von Tress, a Vietnam veteran who'd been making his living hanging wallpaper, was the songwriter. We found out the Oak Ridge Boys and Ronnie Milsap had both thought about recording the song but then passed. The Marcy Brothers, a trio from Northern California, did record a version earlier that year, but they changed some of the words. I thank God I didn't hear any version other than the demo of Don banging it out on his flattop guitar.

That's what I heard, that's what I loved, that's what I built off of. Once I got a hold of it, I never let that song out of my grasp.

I loved it.

And I knew Joe was right. It was going to be a hit.

We went back to the bar, worked it up right there and then, and played the song that night. Actually, we played it in every set because people kept wanting to hear it. It was fun.

• • •

Working on a budget of less than six figures — $92,000 to be exact — we spent two weeks recording the rest of the songs. We started at nine in the morning and quit between eleven and midnight. Every day was a marathon. I didn't know any other way. There'd been so much press in the tristate area about my signing and the album that I was already a big star, but I knew if I didn't execute the album I was going to look like a fool.

What's the saying? A man's big chance is only as great as his preparation.

I thought about that constantly.

I'd cut a track, sing, do overdubs with different instruments, then sing, get a good vocal, and then do harmonies. I wouldn't leave at night unless we had a good rough mix. That was the way I had done it for years: marathons, focus, staying in the moment, capturing the music while it was hot.

Harold Shedd was the boss, the overseer of the songs, the final word. But he had good instincts, and his instincts were to let me follow my gut. There weren't any rules for an artist like me, because I didn't fit into any specific mold. Periodically, Harold brought someone in and played them "Don't Tell My Heart," and the reaction was always the same: they'd say, "This is going to be big. This is huge."

During the recording, I literally lived in my car — my Chevy Beretta. We had Shoney's Inn to shit, shower, and shave, but my car was my office, closet, and home base. On the day of the photo session for the album cover, I parked it down by the Cumberland River in downtown Nashville. Photographer Peter Nash, who'd worked with Alabama, Emmylou Harris, and Waylon Jennings, liked that location and had planned a bunch of different setups and wardrobe changes near there. However, as I got out of my car, in the clothes that I had put on that morning, I said, "Hey, why don't you just shoot me here?"

He snapped away, and those shots — basically the moment I stepped out of my car to do the session — turned out to be the ones everyone wanted for the cover. I was glad, too, because there was no phoniness about 'em. That was the guy who was following his dream, the guy who was making music.

Soon after we finished recording the album, I lost my longtime house gig at the Ragtime. It happened on a Sunday night during the peak of summer. By then, people were coming from all around, from as far away as the Carolinas. The little club was packed. During the intensity of our last set of the night, a fight broke out. There were always fights, but this one had guys waving guns and knives. People were flying over tables.

"Holy shit," I said to Terry Shelton (we were still playing at the time — well, barely playing). "Someone's going to die."

Terry nodded, stopped playing, unplugged his guitar, and headed offstage. He had a scar across his throat from where he'd been slashed years earlier during a brawl in another club. "I'm out of here," he said.

"Bud's going to fire us," I said, referring to the Ragtime's owner, Bud Waugh, who was drunk as hell and already screaming at us to get back onstage and play.

"The hell with that shit," he said.

All of us followed him. The last one off the stage, I looked around and saw blood everywhere. The cops were already on their way, and Bud was going ape-shit.

When we returned on Monday to inspect the damage, he was waiting for us. He had moved most of our equipment outside the club.

"You guys are fired," he said. "You let me down last night."

There went my steady gig.

Gradually we picked up a club in Knoxville; another place on the Tennessee–North Carolina line; a Cowboys in Fayetteville, North Carolina; Miss Kitty's in Marietta, Georgia; another Cowboys in Myrtle Beach, South Carolina; Bronco's Lounge in Richmond, Virginia; and the Executive Inn in Paducah, Kentucky.

The gigs earned new fans, like Raymond Bullock, a Vietnam vet who came into Bronco's almost every night just to hear "Some Gave All." His mission in life was to find homeless veterans and drive them to the VA hospital or wherever they needed to go. He drove an old limo—and I mean old—but he wanted the vets to feel like they were going first class. One night he piled me in the back of his limo with about eight other vets who weren't able to or didn't want to go into the bar. I pulled out a cassette with a rough mix of "Some Gave All" and gave it to Raymond.

"This is the song I told you guys about," he said, sliding the tape into the stereo. Then he turned to me. "Is it a hit yet?"

"It's not out yet," I said.

"Well, get it out, man. It's the best song I've ever heard." Then he cranked it up.

I knew something big was going to happen once that album was released. I felt it in my bones. But I was worried. As crazy as my world had been a few months or even weeks earlier, it was getting even crazier. It was like the ground was shaking and the sky was filling with thunder. Something was going to happen. I called Jack daily. "You gotta call the label and get them to move on this record," I implored. "It's time. It's past time. We're losing time. I might die here if I don't get out of here right now," I said in a voice that was as close to screaming as I got. "I'm going to die here."

"Patience, my boy," he said. "Harold takes his time and thinks these things out."

"But I don't *have* time," I said. "You don't understand what it's like for me. If I stay here, I'm gonna run out of air. It's like I'm a big fish in a tiny bowl. There's not enough oxygen in the water."

In October, Cindy filed for divorce. There were no hard feelings. Both of us recognized our marriage was a relic from another time. I gave her half of my share of the royalties on the six songs on *Some Gave All* that I'd written while we were together. I wanted to give her something that no one could ever take away—a thank-you for all she'd endured while we were together.

· · ·

In December 1991, Mercury finally came up with a plan to release *Some Gave All*. Jack McFadden and I sat down with Harold Shedd, Buddy Cannon, and other executives in the label's conference room. They explained they were going to put my album out early the next year. I clenched my fist and thought, *finally*. It was about time.

As we dug into the details, I shared my thoughts on artwork, song sequence, song titles, and the most important part of all, the first single.

I told them how the crowds where I played all had the same re-action to my songs. They come in used to cover bands that play boot-scootin', line-dancin' cowboy music, so the first time they hear my Appalachian swamp rock, they hate me. They wanted to hear straight-up, boot-shuffling country music, and I don't really do that. "But as soon as I played 'Don't Tell My Heart,' they hit the dance floor and the rest of the night was a flat-out good time."

Everyone at the table nodded.

"I'll tell you something, though," I continued. "The name of that song is wrong. Everyone calls it the Achy Breaky song. They yell it all night long. 'Play that Achy Breaky song.' I hear it every night, all night long. 'Play that Achy Breaky song.' I could probably just play it over and over. I think it should be called 'Achy Breaky Heart.'"

Harold leaned halfway across the conference table, nodding as though he'd found where the treasure was buried.

"I think you're right," he said.

After agreeing that "Achy Breaky Heart" would be the single, we made plans to shoot a video of me performing the song live. One of the promotion people suggested a dance contest, too. A couple of weeks later, we met with choreographer Melanie Greenwood, singer Lee Greenwood's ex-wife. She got up and did a few line-dancing moves for me.

"Yeah, that looks cool," I said. "That's exactly what I see a lot of them doing in the club. But it needs a hook, like the Twist — something that connects the dancers to the singer."

"What do you do when you sing it?" she asked.

"Uh, I don't really move," I said. "I'm the singer . . . If I do move, it's probably something like this — " I got up and kinda moved my hips from side to side.

She froze her discerning eye on me for a moment, then smiled. "I got it." And she did. She showed me a small move, which I tried, and suddenly everyone at the table began high-fiving each other.

The dance created in that conference room soon became known around the world as the Achy Breaky. We made an eleven-minute instructional line-dance video and later shipped it to cowboy bars and dance clubs across the country. Mercury sponsored a nationwide dance contest. Suddenly everybody was doing the Achy Breaky and the record wasn't even shipped yet. The stage was set.

PART III

Be Careful What You Wish For

CHAPTER 19

Don't Tell My Heart

O N JANUARY 20, 1992, we shot the video for "Achy Breaky Heart" at Ashland's majestic, old Paramount Arts Center. Although it required eighteen takes and we worked late into the night, the final version was perfect. I was really happy with it, and also with everyone who was in it. If you watch closely, you will see that the crowd included Tish, Brandi, my ex-wife, Cindy, and my sister, Angie. It might be the only music video ever made with both an ex-wife and a future wife in it.

In early March, the video came out. On the day it aired, I was playing — and living — at the Executive Inn in Paducah. Harold Shedd drove up from Nashville, and during a break between my first and second sets, we walked outside and he pointed up to the sky.

It was a starry night and we were out on the banks of the Ohio River, the backdrop for many of my life's more significant moments. Harold looked up at the sky.

"You see all them stars up there?" he said. I stared up at the Milky Way, too.

"Yeah," I replied.

"Well, you may not realize it, but you're gonna be right up there with all them real soon . . . starting tonight."

"Really? You think so?"

"Oh yeah," he said, confidently. "A big star."

But my reality was still inside that club. I did another two sets that night. Between them, I went back to my room and saw the video for "Achy Breaky Heart" on TV for the first time. It should've given me goose bumps, but the volume on my video sounded about 10 percent lower than it did in the other videos, and that upset me. This was my one chance, and I'd fought for it.

It turned out, my ears were correct. Joe and Jim and the others figured out that one of the dubs they'd sent to CMT did contain an error and wasn't playing as hot as other videos.

Luckily, everyone who could hear loved what they heard. The moment Melanie Greenwood's dance video reached clubs across the country, millions of people embraced "Achy Breaky Heart." It hadn't even made it to the radio yet! By the end of March, the song hit the *Billboard*'s Hot Country Songs singles chart — still without the single having been officially released yet. It was happening. All of us knew it. The fuse was lit and inching toward the TNT.

On April 3, I performed "Achy Breaky Heart" on *Nashville Now*, Ralph Emery's prime-time show on TNN. Emery, the Country Hall of Fame TV host, provided the most important platform for country music, especially for a new artist. Like an unknown comic going on *The Tonight Show Starring Johnny Carson*, it either launched your career or got you a pat on the back and a "Nice try, kid."

From the moment I signed with Jack, and even back with Del Reeves, I badgered them about getting me on Ralph Emery's show. "Just get me on," I said. Now that it was going to happen, I obsessed about it. I talked about it with my mom and dad, Jack, and the guys in Sly Dog right up until the moment the director cued us to start playing, and then it was as if I had visualized the whole thing.

During those three and a half minutes, I felt the world shift under my feet. My dad had come to the show, and we talked in the parking lot afterward. He asked me what I thought. Grinning, I said, "Dad, I think the teeter just went to totter."

• • •

The next day I played a show at the Paramount in Ashland. Before the show, I ran around out front and posed for a photo with the marquee over my shoulder in the background. It read: SOLD OUT. It might as well have said BLAST OFF. "Achy Breaky Heart" had all the magic I'd anticipated, and then some. In the weeks following the dance video, we had harnessed a perfect wave of momentum. It was No. 1 on *Billboard*'s Hot Country Songs for five weeks. It spent twenty weeks on the chart overall. It also went to No. 4 on *Billboard*'s Hot 100 and became the first country single to go platinum since Kenny Rogers and Dolly Parton's 1983 smash, "Islands in the Stream."

The record company was deluged with calls, including one from someone at CMT in a happy panic. "What in the world have you done to us? The phones are ringing off the hook." Another came from an angry plant foreman in Dothan, Alabama. "You're going to have to tell us when this video airs because I can't get my ladies out of the break room!"

That reaction was just the start. On May 19, *Some Gave All* was released and it was like the burning fuse had finally reached the dynamite. The album debuted at No. 1 on both *Billboard*'s country and pop album charts; within a week, more than a million copies were sold. The numbers it put up were not only impressive, they were, as Harold Shedd and Jack McFadden both told me, unprecedented. The album spent seventeen consecutive weeks at the top, went platinum nine times over, eventually sold more than twenty million copies worldwide, and became the biggest-selling debut album by a male artist ever.

And where was I when all this happened?

Hangin' on, workin' and runnin' just as hard as I could to keep up with this rocket.

We were flooded with offers and deals, some for huge amounts of money. I only said yes to one concert right away, and I agreed to do it for free. It was the fifth annual Rolling Thunder motorcycle rally in Washington, DC, an event to honor prisoners of war and those labeled missing in action — in other words, those who gave all. I considered their logo and flag — "You are not forgotten" — the very embodiment of "Some Gave All."

The concert was at the foot of the Lincoln Memorial. Nearby was the Vietnam Memorial Wall. People and motorcycles, vets and their families, filled the National Mall. It was an amazing sight, thick with emotion. Rain came down steadily as I took the stage. I was bummed, thinking this moment could've been great if not for the rain; then I looked up and imagined those drops were tears cried for all the names etched on the wall.

"Cyrus," I said to myself, "forget the rain. You get up there and give it everything you got."

Don Von Tress, the writer of "Achy Breaky Heart," joined me onstage, for the first of many times we played together. He was a two-tour Vietnam vet who'd served with the 101st Airborne and been part of more than 140 helicopter missions. Having him sing "Some Gave All" with me that day only made it more poignant.

My mom and Cletis stood in the wings. I remembered when she'd told me not to give "Some Gave All" to Charlie Daniels because it was my song. But as I watched the crowd, I realized it wasn't my song. It was *their* song — and always would be.

Backstage, I was rehashing the set with Don when my mom appeared and gave me a hug.

"Billy, did you see it?" she asked.

"What?"

"During 'Some Gave All,' right at the last chorus, a bald eagle swooped down in front of the stage, then flew across the sky and over the Capitol."

"Ruthie, I hate to burst your bubble," Don said, "but that was a seagull."

My mom shook her head.

"It might've been a seagull to you," she said, "but it was an eagle to me." We shared a laugh. It was a special moment and a special time.

. . .

I went back to Bronco's Lounge for one last stand. My manager thought I was crazy to give up a week, when I could be making five figures or more, for a gig in a bar where I was likely to spend more buying drinks for old friends than I'd get paid. But I honored every commitment I had made before the record broke, and Bronco's was one of them.

The *Toronto Sun,* of all places, loved that angle. The paper's editor was a big Elvis Presley fan, and he sent a reporter to find out about this hillbilly who was being called the new Elvis. The reporter found me in a crappy hotel in Richmond, Virginia, saw what was going on, and busted the thing wide open. In fact, he coined the phrase "Cyrus Virus."

But what's great is all the different and surprising ways music touches people, all kinds of people, everywhere. There are no boundaries. And one night I heard a knock on my hotel room door. I looked out the peephole and saw this big old veteran standing outside. It was Raymond Bullock, the guy who would bring a limo-load of vets to the bar every night and have me play "Some Gave All." I'd never seen him without his green beret on. Now he was holding it, along with his dog tags. After I said "Hi, what's up," he solemnly extended his hand and offered me both his beret and tags.

"Mr. Cyrus, I want to give you these," he said.

"I can't take those from you," I replied.

"No, they're yours," he insisted. "The first night I heard you sing 'Some Gave All' was the first night since returning from Vietnam that I felt like I was home. I don't need this stuff anymore."

After Bronco's, I knew it was time to climb into the rocket. I was ready. I rented a small apartment in Nashville so I'd have a place to dump all my stuff, but I barely remembered the address. The road became my home. I said yes to practically everything. In the last six months of 1992, I did at least two hundred dates . . . and probably more. *Good Morning America*? Sure thing. *Top of the Pops* in London? I'll be there. A club in Fort Knox? No problem. Alabama, you want me to play at your June Jam in Fort Payne? Sure, tell me what time I go on.

In fact, it was in June, while I was on my way to that annual country music extravaganza, that a little controversy arose. Travis Tritt told some folks in the media that he thought "Achy Breaky Heart" was "frivolous" and he hated to see country music devolve into an "ass-wiggling contest."

Trust me, I knew with "Achy Breaky Heart" it was either love it or hate it. There was no middle ground, not with a song that big. And I knew the media loves a good fight more than anything. I considered responding but my dad, who knew a thing or two or twelve about critics from being in politics, had his own suggestion. "Son, you take it as a compliment that you made someone so upset. You know every action has an opposite and equal reaction. You can't have so many people out there love that thang without having someone hate it. So you don't say nothin'. You just go about your business."

Good advice. Then, without me even knowing beforehand, none other than Bruce Springsteen — the Boss himself — played "Achy Breaky Heart" at one of his shows and said, "I don't care what anybody says. It's a damn good little rock song." You can only imagine how much that meant to me at the time.

And then Jack McFadden called to tell me that I'd received a letter from another supporter, a man whose gravelly voice and black boots carried a lot of weight: Johnny Cash.

The Johnny Cash.

Here's what the letter said:

Billy Ray,

I was very impressed recently to hear you give God the credit for your success. It's good to be reminded where all goodness comes from.

Thirty-six years ago I was working with Elvis and saw him take the same kind of flak you're taking now.

Congratulations on the way you're handling it all. In your case, as in Elvis', the good outweighs the bad.

Let 'em have it. I'm in your corner.

Johnny Cash

On my pony, Dusty, at my grandparents' house in Flatwoods, Kentucky.

Papaw Cyrus, my paternal grandfather, holds his Bible proudly in the foothills of Appalachia.

My paternal grandparents, Mamaw and Papaw Cyrus.

Left to right: Mary Guila Casto; my mother, Ruthie; and my dad, Ron. Those were very happy times.

The early years of my dad's quartet, the Crownsmen.

With my maternal grandfather, Papaw Casto, and brother Kebo in Russell, Kentucky.

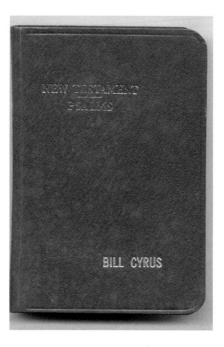

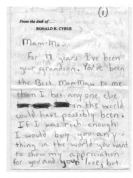

My childhood Bible.

A letter I wrote to Mamaw Cyrus before the Kentucky State high school football championship game, which my team won.

I was the lead vocalist, rhythm guitarist, and songwriter in my first band, Sly Dog. One of our first recordings was a country ballad called "Suddenly."

A River Cities newspaper review of Sly Dog: "A man of many moves, Ray and his counterparts possess the willingness and determination necessary to make it to the top."

Me and Terry Shelton onstage at the Ragtime.

Me and the Players, rocking the Ragtime in the late 1980s.

A ticket for my August 1985 performance in Los Angeles.

An early 1980s performance at Changes.

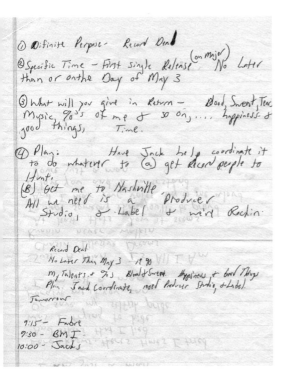

A list of my early personal goals, including "Record deal no later than May 3, 1990."

Wearing my favorite boots onstage at the Ragtime in Huntington, West Virginia.

The copyright certificate for "Some Gave All."

With my sister Angie *(top)* and my brother Kebo *(bottom)*.

Opening up for Lee Greenwood before I even had a record deal.

My first royalty check from BMI, issued on November 12, 1990—for $5.95.

At Gulf Shores, Alabama, in the mid-1990s.

A day I will always remember: my last fishing expedition with my dad on Lake Ontario in summer 1991.

Performing on the *Some Gave All* Tour.

Holding my daughter Miley after a concert at Fan Fare in Nashville, surrounded by a crush of people. I captured this memory in the poem "The Moment."

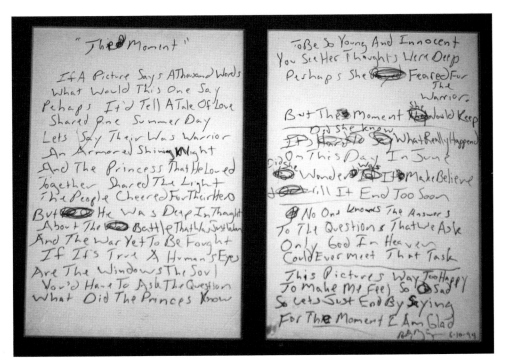

"The Moment"

If A Picture Says A Thousand Words
What Would This One Say
Perhaps It'd Tell A Tale Of Love
Shared One Summer Day
Lets Say Their Was Warrior
An Armored Shining Night
And The Princess That He Loved
Together Shared The Light
The People Cheered For That Hero
But He Was Deep In Thought
About The Battle That Was Just Won
And The War Yet To Be Fought
If It's True A Human's Eyes
Are The Windows The Soul
I'd Have To Ask The Question
What Did The Princess Know

To Be So Young And Innocent
You See Her Thoughts Were Deep
Perhaps She Feared For
The Warrior
But This Moment she Would Keep
Did she know
What Really Happened
On This Day In June
Did she Wonder Was It Make Believe
Will It End Too Soon
No One Knows The Answers
To The Questions That We Ask
Only God In Heaven
Could Ever meet That Task
This Pictures Way Too Happy
To Make Me Feel So Sad
So Lets Just End By Saying
For The Moment I Am Glad

6-10-94

Me and Miley, 1993. Sitting up in the woods, the best of times.

With Miley in my Nashville driveway, before taking a spinner on my Harley. (I promise we put on our helmets after this photo was taken.)

With legendary rockabilly musician Carl Perkins in 1993.

At Myrtle Beach with Cody and Miley.

Onstage with Braison during the 1996 *Trail of Tears* tour.

Onstage with Miley in 1996, passing her the microphone to sing "Hound Dog." I call this picture *The Passing of the Torch*.

Jamming out with Bryan Adams in the mid-1990s.

With Tish in 1997.

The family in 2001. Back row, left to right: Brandy and Trace. Front row, *left to right:* Braison, Tish, Noah (on Tish's lap), and Miley.

Tish and me with *(from left to right)* Braison, Noah, and Miley, taken while I was filming the television show *Doc* in 2002.

Left to right: Miley *(front),* Tish, Gretchen Wilson, me, Noah *(front),* Braison, and Trace.

Miley and Ron Cyrus—her "Pappy." Miley launched the Pappy Cyrus Family Foundation after he passed away in 2006.

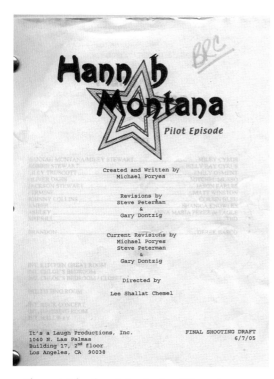

The script for the pilot episode of *Hannah Montana.*

Building a snowman in Nashville with Noah.

Welcome to my office: my teepee, on top of Spirit Mountain.

The medals that soldiers gave to me during my visits to Iraq and Afghanistan.

With President Bill Clinton at the Starkey Hearing Foundation's twelfth annual So the World May Hear gala on August 4, 2012.

Courtesy of Starkey Hearing Foundation

Here I am enjoying a moment of peace in one of my favorite thinking spots.

© *Nancy Lee Andrews*

Nashville insiders were always reluctant to let new people into their circle, and I wasn't much on schmoozin'. Some of them didn't know what to make of a guy who was more comfortable in tennis shoes and cut-up T-shirts than black boots and a Stetson.

The tabloids got on my butt, too. One of them claimed I'd been a Chippendales dancer when I lived in California. Then, right after I signed up to open several dates for Dolly Parton, the *Globe* put the two of us on their cover, claiming we were lovers. That was funny. I hadn't even met Dolly yet.

Before the first show, I asked Jack if he could arrange for me to meet her. I showed up at her dressing room with the tabloid in my hand. Dolly was wearing a beautiful blue dress that looked like it was made out of diamonds.

"Hi, I'm Billy Ray Cyrus," I stammered. "I wanted to come say hi and apologize for this."

I handed her the tabloid.

"Honey, don't you apologize for that." Dolly laughed. "That shit sells records."

The tabloids did get one story right: On April 8, I became the father of Christopher Cody Cyrus. His mother was Kristen Luckey, a twenty-three-year-old waitress I met the previous summer when we performed at Cowboys in Myrtle Beach. They also reported Tish was pregnant, too. It was a double bubble of trouble.

The timing was not ideal. But the only plan that mattered was God's plan, and I accepted that.

I was on the road through midsummer. In July, my second single, "Could've Been Me," began its climb to No. 1. I spent the last three weeks of that month recording songs for my second album at Nashville's Music Mill. Then I was back on the road.

In August, upon receiving my first substantial check, I immediately paid off my twelve-year-old student loan from Morehead (it's the only debt I've ever had in my life — and it bugged the crap out of me) and then got my mom to a dentist. Poor Ruth had spent years trying not to smile because she hated her teeth. Her smile was the best investment I ever made. I also purchased my first home, a log house on seven acres about thirty minutes outside Nashville. Jack had found it for me.

"I think you'll like this, my boy," he said as we drove there.

He was right.

"Do I have the money to pay for this?" I asked.

"I think you do," he said.

The owner was a quiet man who had served in Vietnam and let me know he appreciated my song about veterans. As he showed us around, I saw the property also included a barn. Inside was a horse, an Appaloosa named Roam. I rubbed his face.

"Does the horse come with the house?" I asked.

"I hadn't planned on it," he said. "But something tells me you and that horse are going to get along."

He was right. When I moved in, he left me a housewarming gift — an old piece of wood for over the fireplace onto which he'd carved SOME GAVE ALL. It was beautiful. With my own home, a barn, and a horse, I felt blessed. Then I bought a fully loaded Corvette and a truck. The funny part was that I was never around to enjoy any of it.

During one stretch, I went to twelve countries in ten days. I saw both the Grand Canyon *and* the Eiffel Tower from the window of a plane. On another stretch, I appeared on *The Arsenio Hall Show*, performed in Bakersfield, and sang the national anthem at Game One of the World Series in Atlanta.

I remember getting calls from Tish and my mom and my dad wanting to know where I was. I just said, "On a different planet." It was true. I would wake up going, "What day is this? Where am I?"

Truth was, I was where I was supposed to be. After a show in Dayton, Ohio, I was signing autographs when a woman with a young boy in tow grabbed a hold of me. "My seven-year-old boy is autistic and never spoke a word until a couple of months ago," she said. "Then I heard him singing 'Achy Breaky Heart' in the living room!"

I felt my heart fill with joy. Hearing this kind of thing put me in a place where I knew I was part of a larger purpose.

"What's his name?" I asked.

"Randy," his mother said. "He's started to talk all the time. But the first words out of his mouth were *achy breaky heart.*"

Then there was Heaven Leigh Yarborough, an eighteen-month-old girl with cerebral palsy from Cleveland, Tennessee, who I'll never forget. Doctors said she'd never walk, but Heaven took her first steps after watching the video for "Achy Breaky Heart." As her mother, Marjorie, told me, her doctors thought it was a fluke. Then she bought the video and Heaven stood up and walked again.

Throughout the rest of the year, I scheduled a special meet and greet at each show. Sometimes there were hundreds and hundreds of people, and within each group there was always someone with a special story — a miracle if you will — about someone who'd found a connection to a higher power through the music. As much as it affected their lives, it also left a permanent impression on me, one I carry with me to this day. It's part of who I am.

By the end of 1992, I had put out two more singles, "Could've Been Me" and "Wher'm I Gonna Live." I felt like I might never get off my tour bus. In fact, on the back was a mural of my red truck parked at home, and beneath it were the words "Where'm I Gonna Live When I Get Home?" But I'll tell you what I realized as I criss-crossed the country, singing my songs and hearing people's stories. I *was* home.

CHAPTER 20

Good Advice

I N NOVEMBER 1992, I was on a sold-out tour in the United States and Europe. I was scheduled to take a break in the middle of December so I could be with Tish when she was due to give birth to our child. I wanted to be at the hospital with her even though she kept saying she only wanted her mom, Loretta, and would call me when it was time. "I've been through this before," she said. "There are just too many nasty things going on in that room for me to want anyone but my mother with me."

Fine with me. We talked multiple times a day while I was on the road. But as soon as my plane touched down in Nashville, on November 23, I received a fax from Jack McFadden. It said, "Baby girl Cyrus born." Shocked, I called Tish and instead got a hold of her mother, who told me that while I was in the air Tish's doctor had decided to induce her. He'd feared some complications and, to be completely forthcoming, there were some. But the net result was that Tish and I had a baby girl.

When Tish got on the phone, she said she'd been through so much, I should go straight home and come to the hospital the next day. I said, "Are you crazy? I'm on my way. I'm coming to see you guys. I'll be right there." And that's just what I did. I went straight to the hospital.

Tish was weak and our baby was in an incubator on 100 percent oxygen, but I'll tell you, both of them were beautiful, and their spirits were strong, and after about eight days, both of them were able to go home with me to the log cabin, where we celebrated Thanksgiving, albeit a few days late. There was no question we had a lot to be thankful for.

Despite arriving three weeks early, our little girl was perfect. She had ten fingers, ten toes, and eyes that were brighter than all the stars in the sky combined.

As for her name, I'd had sensed early in Tish's pregnancy we were going to have a baby girl, and I'd said, "It's going to be that child's destiny to bring hope into the world." Once my premonition proved correct, I knew only one name fit her, and that was Destiny Hope. I had no doubt it was the perfect name — that is, until I saw her for the first time.

"Look at her!" I said. "She's smiling!"

She was always smiling. No newborn that I knew of had ever seemed so happy to have arrived in this world. Every time I held her, I seemed to say, "Oh look, she's smiling." Then I came up with this little rhyme: "Smiley Miley, puddin' piley, kissed the boys and made 'em miley." I don't know what it meant. But soon I called her "Smiley." Then we dropped the "S" and called her Miley. Before we knew it, that's all anyone called her, Miley . . . Miley Cyrus.

It's funny — and I'm going to jump ahead here — but one day, after she started first grade, she came home with a note from the teacher. It read, "Destiny Hope will only sign her name as Miley. Is that what you call her? If so, is that OK?" We replied, "Yes, we call her Miley." And that's when it became official.

Anyway, after she was born, I moved Tish and Miley, and Brandi and Trace from her mom's house into my log home. I wanted everyone to be comfortable. As for me, going from bachelor to chief bottle-warmer was an easier transition than I would have imagined. From the get-go, I embraced daddy duties. Not only did I change her diapers, I took the responsibility to an extreme. One night, after coming in from the road, with my hours screwed up and unable to sleep, I drove my Corvette to the Kroger and bought every baby diaper they had in the store. I got every size, too, from newborn, to three to six months, to those for a year old. Whatever they had, I bought it.

Then, because my Corvette had no backseat or trunk space, I made a bunch of trips back and forth between the store and our house. By the time I had finished stacking them in the garage, I had built an impressive wall, the best defense against baby poop in Tennessee. Tish was wide-eyed when she saw it the next morning.

"What the hell?" she said.

"Look," I said, grinning, as I pointed to a row. "These are for six-month-olds."

"But Miley's barely two months," Tish said.

"She'll grow into 'em," I said.

Fatherhood shaped all aspects of my life. On the road, I was the lucky recipient of much affection from fans. At shows, they threw flowers and stuffed animals onstage. Afterward, I gathered them up, massive amounts, and I dropped them off at whatever children's hospital was nearby. My tour bus rolled up on our way out of town. I did this for years. If my life was about sharing God's light and love, this was the icing on the cake. Those nights I stopped at the children's hospital were some of the most gratifying of my life.

When I came off the road, I craved solitude, a place to recharge and be alone with Tish and the kids, and live the normal life that gave rise to my songs. I had some money coming in and, of course, more than a few advisors telling me what I should do with it. But as a guy who grew up with nothing, I didn't trust anyone with my money. The only thing I trusted was land. I could see it. I could stand on it. And, since I consider myself part Indian, I figured I'd notice if someone tried to steal it.

So when two homes next to mine went up for sale, both of them A-frames, I bought them, along with another thirty-two adjacent acres on a hill overlooking Franklin and Nashville.

The setup was perfect. Tish, the kids, and I moved into the larger of the two A-frames, Tish's mom moved into the other, and I turned the log house into a gym/office/recording studio.

My spending spree didn't end there. The record company had given me a Harley with all the bells and whistles; I turned around and bought the same bike, dressed to the nines, for every member in my band. I also paid off my mom and Cletis's house at 2317 Long Street. Then I paid off my dad and Joan's house.

Many of these stories were told when *People* magazine named me one of their 50 Most Intriguing People of the Year, and ABC followed me at home for a TV special that aired the following February. One story that wasn't told: On New Year's Eve, I headlined Bally's in Las Vegas, and during the day, the world record for the longest line dance ever was set as part of a radio promotion. I witnessed it. Afterward, I remembered that the fortuneteller at the Sand Bar had envisioned me in Vegas with "many people dancing." Here it was, happening right in front of me. I felt a chill.

In January 1993 — the same month Mercury released "She's Not Cryin' Anymore," the fourth single off my album — I attended the American Music Awards in Los Angeles. I was nominated in four categories and went home with awards for Favorite Country Single and Favorite Country New Artist. It was unbelievable.

One month later, I was seated behind Michael Jackson and Elizabeth Taylor at the Grammys. Michael was receiving the Grammy Legend Award. Even though I had several nominations, I was too tongue-tied to say anything to the King of Pop. During the show, though, I heard something hit the floor and roll to a stop. I looked down and saw a dime by my shoe. I ignored it until I noticed Michael going through his pockets. I picked up the dime and held it over his shoulder.

"Are you looking for this?" I asked.

Damned if he wasn't.

"Thank you," he said, taking the dime in his ungloved hand.

I looked at Jack McFadden, who was next to me.

"Why does Michael Jackson have a dime in his pocket?" I asked. Jack shrugged. Who knew?

To be honest, I thought it was even weirder for me to be included in a show with Eric Clapton, Celine Dion, and other superstars. A year earlier, I had begged Mercury to release my album. Eight months earlier, I had been playing the Executive Inn, keeping one eye on the TV above the bar so I could see if my video played. Now I was seated among Elton John, Mariah Carey, Don Henley, and Tina Turner.

Like everyone else, I knew Eric Clapton was going to sweep the Grammys that year. I understood. He was up for "Tears in Heaven" and *Unplugged,* both masterpieces.

I knew I wasn't going to win a Grammy. But what the heck? A year before, I'd been living out of my car. I wanted to give thanks to God for allowing me to live this dream — and part of that dream was just having my name in the same sentence with Eric Clapton's.

I'd be the first to applaud the deep emotions of love and loss that "Tears in Heaven" evoked in people, including me. I love the song and even recorded it. I said my thanks by wearing a T-shirt that had JOHN 3:16 written across the front.

The next day I got on an airplane whose first-class section included Tina Turner and Bob Seger. Before I buckled my seat belt, I unfolded my newspaper. The headline read CYRUS BIG LOSER. I stared at that paper, stunned and embarrassed. I felt a hand upon my shoulder. My first thought was, it was God. It wasn't. But it was close. It was Bob Seger. "Put that thing underneath your seat where it belongs," he said.

I thanked him and then turned into a fan, letting him know how much his song "Turn the Page" meant to me. It was one of the most influential songs in my life.

"Hang in there, man," he said. "Play your music. Don't let the bastards get you down."

Good advice.

· · ·

Between tour dates, I poured myself into finishing my second album, *It Won't Be the Last*. Studio days were precious, and Seger's advice stayed in my head. Producers Jim Cotton and Joe Scaife and the guys in Sly Dog often stayed with me in the Music Mill for days at a time, through marathon sessions. We knew there was pressure, that people were going to judge this second album, but we tried to keep that out of mind. Every day when we came into the studio, we high-fived each other and said, "Keep the music first."

That was our slogan: Keep the music first. I loved the album we made, especially when you consider that the days I wasn't in the studio, my ass was strapped to a rocket, going around the world at the speed of sound and also trying to get to know my new baby girl. I thought the album reflected my diverse interests, especially songs such as "Throwing Stones," which I'd written after "Some Gave All," and the title track, "It Won't Be the Last." The highlight was bringing in the Jordanaires, the vocal quartet that had backed Elvis Presley, to sing harmonies on the song "When I'm Gone." I felt shivers when I looked up and saw Ray Walker and the others and felt their history.

My dad was a devout fan of the Jordanaires and drove in from Frankfort just to watch the session. At one point, I glanced at him in the control room and saw him gasp in amazement. Success brought a lot of privileges and opportunities like this, and the best part was being able to share it with my dad.

In June, my album was released. I refused to let the label put my picture on the cover, insisting they use a silhouette of my profile instead. The record company wanted to see my face. "I'm tired of my face," I told 'em. We had a pretty heated argument, but I wanted the attention to be about my music, not my looks or my hair or anything else, and in the end, though they weren't happy, I prevailed.

It Won't Be the Last debuted at No. 1 on the country charts and No. 2 on the *Billboard* 100. Once again, the critics weren't impressed, but the fans were; by the fall, it had gone platinum and produced four hit singles: "In the Heart of a Woman," "Somebody New," "Words by Heart," and "Talk Some."

Jack put me on the road for the rest of the year, starting with the annual CMA Fan Fair where I invited Bryan Adams to join me onstage for a few songs. It didn't help me fit into Nashville's idea of a country music star, but what the hell. I had been a big fan of his for a long time, and it turned out he liked me. Before the show, I received a note inviting me to jam. I thought it sounded too good to be true, but I decided to call the bluff. Only it wasn't bluff. I looked up and here he came. I didn't give a shit if some people had a problem with that, which they did. I wanted to be known for playing all styles of music, not just one kind of music.

Let me just say, Bryan came out and we rocked 'em hard. We did a rock-stomp version of "Achy Breaky Heart" and Sly Dog kicked straight into "They Call Me the Breeze."

Bryan had one of my favorite producers in the world with him — and also one of the best — Mutt Lange. He'd produced some bands, including AC/DC, Def Leppard, and Foreigner. Before the show, we were hanging out in my tour bus and Mutt was staring out the front window, toward the audience. He spotted a beautiful, dark-haired young woman. She stood out in the sea of people. "Who's that girl out there?" he asked. "I gotta meet her. I'm gonna marry that woman."

"That's Shania Twain," I said. "Harold Shedd just signed her. She's really talented."

Moments later, Mutt was off the bus and on his way. Not long after that, Shania and Mutt got married.

Meanwhile, my tour bus crisscrossed the county. In this world before BlackBerrys and cell phones, I was in the bubble, isolated from everything but music. It was a gratifying, lonely, strange world of songs, shows, fans, and the double yellow line of highway. One night, somewhere out west, my bus pulled into the back of an arena. It was about 1 a.m. and I walked inside to look around and get the vibe of the place.

The backstage area was crowded with roadies loading gear into semis. My rigs were backing in as the rigs belonging to whichever band had played there that night were backing out. Suddenly, a figure emerged from the shadows. I heard him say my name. At first, I couldn't see him. Then I recognized Kurt Cobain from Nirvana.

"Hey, man," he said. "Congratulations. You pissed off the whole world."

We shook hands.

"Thanks, man," I said. "I guess I did. I really appreciate you saying that." And we both laughed a little.

We chatted briefly and realized we both had daughters around the same time. His little one, Frances Bean, was a few months older than Miley. I also told him that my drummer, Greg Fletcher, was his biggest fan.

"He'd freak out if he knew you were here," I said.

"Then don't fuckin' tell him," Kurt muttered.

We looked at each other. There was an awkward silence as we realized what he had just said and how he had said it. Then we both laughed.

I shared two laughs and one F-bomb with Kurt Cobain that night. I'll always cherish that moment.

Laughter's a good thing. This one time I bought an old John Deere tractor just because I wanted an old John Deere tractor. I liked the way it looked. I had a ton of fun climbing up on that beautiful piece of machinery. I had no idea what I was doing, but I loved to take it places that had never been mowed. Plowing over virgin ground reminded me of the good old days. Tish would listen to me brag about my tractor-driving skills and laugh at me as I'd get in predicaments, as I was always driving it into places where I got stuck. "One day you're going to turn that over and cut your arms off," she warned. She thought I was weird. Can you imagine?

One afternoon, I was on my way to *Crook & Chase*, the long-running talk show hosted by Lorianne Crook and Charlie Chase. I drove myself in my front-wheel-drive Cadillac. As I started down the driveway, I decided to check on my horse, Roam. Suddenly I was driving that Caddy on my four-wheel paths, and I got too close to the pond near where I kept the horse.

Next thing I knew, the front half of my car had slipped into the water. I barely made the show. Tish didn't stop laughing at me until I got home that night. We had fun just living and loving each other. The simple days were the best. Here's a typical example: While on a walk through the woods one day, we started to monkey around, one thing led to another, and we got all fired up and made love, or something like it.

A month or so later, we found out that Tish was pregnant with our son, Braison. He wasn't planned, but I welcomed the news. I liked the idea of being a daddy again. I was planning my schedule, as was always the case back then, adding tour dates and TV shows. I remember looking across the room and seeing Tish playing with Miley. I loved her and wanted to be with her forever.

What did forever mean? Well, I had to make a decision. Either I married her soon or I would go on tour, make another album, and she would get frustrated, rightly so, give up on me, and move back to Kentucky. The truth was, she had given me an ultimatum. I had till the end of the year to marry her. Or else.

I knew what day it was and how much time I had. It was now December 28, three days after Christmas, and I had to make a choice. On the one hand, Tish and Mammy had already planned the wedding. They had booked the preacher from Mammy's Methodist church. And Tish had bought fake glasses and a mustache from a costume shop for me to wear into the courthouse so we could get the license before the media found out and the circus hit. We would recite the vows in our family room — our house was an A-frame with a two-story cathedral ceiling, so, in a way, it was like a church. Tish had the whole thing worked out.

On the other hand, right after the first of the year, I was supposed to start a new leg of my world tour, including a performance for the Queen of England. It was going to be big. I'd heard Princess Diana was even supposed to be there. That excited me. I thought she was so beautiful and graceful, and I half-jokingly told my manager that they wouldn't have to pay me if I could meet her.

But something about being gone for such a long time didn't feel right. I have to tell you the God's honest truth. Instead of wanting to go on tour, I could feel myself being drawn in another direction, and I knew why. I had a chance to have the one thing I had always wanted, the one thing I'd never had: a home where the mom and dad live together with their children in happiness and love.

Now I had toys, homes, cars, trucks, horses, and land. I even traveled by Lear jet. I had everything that money could buy. But money couldn't buy family. Not a happy, loving family. And here it was, right in front of me. Why was I hesitating?

I'll tell you why. Because it meant I had to get married.

So, here's what happened. That morning of the twenty-eighth, with the clock ticking and Tish waiting, I went to the place where I did all my serious thinking, the highest peak on my thirty-two acres. There, I crawled into my Apache Nest, a little shelter I'd built out of roots and sticks and mud. I lit a fire and I tried to imagine what the future looked like, how it would roll out if I went on tour, what I might say to Princess Diana if I got to meet her, and how it might feel to stand next to Tish and say, "I do . . ." And of course the look in the kids' eyes as they realized Daddy was here to stay.

It didn't take long before I said to myself, "You know what? I'm going to trade the Queen for the King, and the King is Almighty God . . . and I'm going to marry Tish. I'm going to be a good husband and a good daddy. I'm going to do what my family needs."

I walked back to the house, and when I went inside, Tish was in the kitchen with Brandi, Trace, Miley, and Loretta. They all had the same look on their face — annoyed. They couldn't wait for me to come down off that hill. I walked straight to Tish and stood in front of her.

"You still wanna get married?" I asked.

"Are you serious?" she said.

"Yeah," I said. "Let's go."

Just recently Tish reminded me that after the big wedding, the two of us went out to dinner. "Do you remember where we went?" she asked.

"I'm sure I thought you deserved the best," I said.

"You sure did." She laughed. "We went to Burger King. Do you remember what we got?"

"Of course. We both got the chicken sandwich."

CHAPTER 21

Storm in the Heartland

FOUR MONTHS LATER I was in a room at the Regal River-front Hotel in St. Louis when I turned on the news and heard that Kurt Cobain was dead. The news devastated me. We had crossed paths several times since our first meeting, and each time we exchanged greetings. Under different circumstances, we might've been friends. I could also close my eyes and see myself three years earlier listening to *Nevermind* in my Chevy Beretta as I was getting a divorce, losing my home and my cat.

I knew the circus had overwhelmed him. I feared it could get like that for me, too, if I didn't cool my jets. As a result, the following month, after Tish gave birth to our son, Braison, whose name was inspired by all the brazen chances I'd taken, I finished my tour and hunkered down at home. I needed to step away and focus on family and the things that mattered.

My dad used to say nothing is as good for the inside of a man as the outside of a horse, and he was right. I woke up, saddled Roam, and rode for five miles. I saw deer, quail, rabbits, and a flock of wild turkeys. A double shot of Mother Nature was what I needed, and I made those rides part of my daily routine.

One day I took Miley for a ride on my four-wheeler. She was around two years old and game for anything. "Let's go for a spinner," I said, using her term for ride. Her eyes lit up as I strapped her into a baby-toter on my back and zoomed across the large, flat fields and up the hill into the woods. Every time I stopped to check on her, she was all smiles, Smiley Miley. She loved to go fast.

On the way back, I sped over a spot where some trees had fallen during a recent storm. In that instant, I had to make a quick decision: duck or stop. I ducked and made it. But I forgot I had a baby on my back. I heard a *thwack* — and stopped.

"Oh my God," I exclaimed.

I knew without looking that Miley's head had hit a branch. Blood flowed from a gash in her head. I raced home and Tish helped me wash her down. I thought the worst, like possibly I'd broken her neck. Fortunately, she was laughing by the time Tish swaddled her in a fluffy towel. But I still remember this with a shudder as the day I almost took her head off.

The mishap did nothing to dim my passion for the outdoors. Nor Miley's. The land touched my soul in a special way. It was the freedom that came with it. There was no end to its beauty. I had recently tried to purchase twelve additional acres next to my property, which would have given me about fifty in total. But when the sellers found out I was the buyer, they doubled the price. I was insulted. I walked away and put out word that I wanted to move.

The next day my real estate agent found a house she described as "perfect." It was the former residence of architect William B. Cambron, who had lived there from 1972 until his recent death. The house was a replica of Andrew Jackson's Nashville mansion, the Hermitage. But it wasn't so much the house that made it perfect for me as it was the land, 212 acres of rolling hills and woods, which she described as unbelievable.

"The house even has an indoor pool," the realtor said enthusiastically.

"Sounds like I've got to see it," I replied.

The next morning I rode my motorcycle to the house. I was in the country when I came upon the driveway, which snaked up past fenced pastures and tree-covered hills. It was green for as far as I could see. The actual house was still up ahead, well out of sight, yet what I could see gave such an instant sense of calm and comfort that I said to myself, "Cyrus, you're home."

My real estate agent and Mrs. Cambron were waiting for me when I coasted up to the front of the house. They invited me inside for a look around.

"I don't need to," I said. "I already love it."

A gravel road went past the house and disappeared into the woods. Mrs. Cambron said I was welcome to explore it. I said thanks and roared off. About twenty minutes later, I returned, grinning as if I had found the pot of gold at the end of the rainbow. The women wanted to know what I thought.

"I'm in," I said. "Let's work it out."

The real negotiation was with my wife. As far as Tish was concerned, the Federal-style mansion was too far out in the country. She also thought that it needed a ton of renovation, and she hated the indoor pool. That crushed me. I thought that was the coolest part. It kind of made us like the Beverly Hillbillies. I was already practicing hollering, "Hey Miley, get the monkey and meet me at the cee-ment pond."

Tish had no desire to be like the Beverly Hillbillies. I don't think she watched that show.

Still, I couldn't resist the temptation and bought the home and all 212 acres that came with it.

However, by the fall of '94, we still hadn't moved in and the house sat empty. We even talked of selling it since it seemed like I might be too busy to generate enough enthusiasm and energy for the family to make the move. I was getting ready to release my *Storm in the Heartland* album. The fourteen songs covered social issues like the struggle of America's farmers ("Storm in the Heartland"), appreciation of the earth ("Geronimo"), intensely personal topics like child abuse ("Enough Is Enough"), and the trials of raising a family ("I Ain't Even Left and It Already Don't Feel Right").

We shot the video for the first single, "Storm in the Heartland," at my farm. The footage included my neighbors and their kids, all farmers, doing the work their families had done for generations. At the center was Mr. Harris, a proud, lifelong farmer who cut my hay. He was straight out of Central Casting: big and strong, with sun-weathered skin and eyes that reflected the wisdom of an eighty-year-old man who'd worked the soil his whole life.

The first day of shooting was wonderful, but we didn't finish until late at night. I had a call for sun-up the next morning, so instead of going home, I called Tish and said, "You know what? I'm just going to stay out here in this house."

"But it's empty," she said. "There's nothing in it."

"I got me a little food from the caterer," I said. "I'll borrow a coffeemaker. I'll be fine."

I woke up the next morning, put on some coffee, and walked out the front door, where I came face-to-face with a rising sun, a blanket of fog lifting off the field, and the diamond-like shimmer of morning dew. It looked like heaven. I walked slowly off the porch and into the field, and took a leak. Why not? There were no paparazzi, no tabloid reporters or snoops of any kind.

"Freedom," I thought. "Here it is."

Later that day, I spoke with Tish and told her that she and the kids had to come out and stay just one night. She did, and we never left.

I was devastated when the single "Storm in the Heartland" stalled at No. 39 on the radio chart. Though I did all the press I could to ensure its success, the song fell off the charts as quickly as it appeared, and the album itself just missed the top 10. It hurt. I loved that album; I'd poured my soul into every song, and so I'd expected more enthusiasm. I didn't get it, though, and there was plenty of blame to go around. But it didn't matter. I knew I'd hit the flip side of having so much success. The song "Throwing Stones" from the previous year said what I had already known: "What goes up, must come down." And I was on my way. Upset, frustrated, and hurt, I called Jack McFadden and said, "I ain't going to the CMAs. If they're going to allow 'Storm in the Heartland' to disappear, the hell with it. I don't care. If it ain't about the music, then I don't care."

On the evening of the CMAs, I rode my Harley to the highest part of my land and was sitting there when I spotted Mr. Harris in the field, cutting the hay. The sun was about to go down, the shadows were stretched across the ground, and I said to myself, "Cyrus, you know what? I bet Mr. Harris ain't going to be around here that much longer. He's probably never been to the CMA Awards. Why don't you go down there and ask him if he wants to go tonight." And I was just crazy enough to do it.

I zipped down the hill and invited Mr. Harris to the show. He took off his hat and thought about it a moment.

"Is there time for me to throw on a pair of jeans?" he asked.

He was wearing overalls.

"Sure," I said. "I'll pick you up in a half hour."

Tish looked at me like I'd lost my mind when I told her that I'd changed my mind and was going to the awards show with Mr. Harris. But soon Jack McFadden had a car picking us up and my farmer neighbor and I were cutting through the star-studded crowd inside the Grand Ole Opry. When we arrived, Mr. Harris turned heads. Wynonna Judd said, "That's the man in your 'Storm' video, right?" George Jones stopped him and asked, "Don't I know you?"

"No, sir," Mr. Harris said. "I cut hay for Billy Ray Cyrus."

"Oh my God," George said. "You're in his video. I know who you are. Let me shake your hand."

And Mr. Harris lit up when the Oak Ridge Boys, who'd also joined me on "Storm in the Heartland," had a photo made with him.

Storm in the Heartland ended up selling more than 500,000 copies, enough for gold-record status. However, I still think of it as one of the tragedies of my career. I battled with the label over song selection, sequencing, and the cover photo, which I hated. None of the singles went top ten. "The Fastest Horse in a One-Horse Town" died at the starting line.

All of a sudden I couldn't buy a hit. I was no longer Mercury's favorite son.

My family kept me focused on what was really important, and

my friends provided much-needed support that kept me believing in myself as an artist. Ray Walker from the Jordanaires, guitarist-songwriter Ed King from Lynyrd Skynyrd (he cowrote "Sweet Home Alabama" and "Saturday Night Special," among other classics), and Carl Perkins, the Sun Records rockabilly legend who wrote "Blue Suede Shoes," were among those who visited me at the farm.

None were more supportive than Perkins, who became a close friend and confidant. We had met a few years earlier on Ralph Emery's *Nashville Now*. We clicked on the air, and during a commercial break, Carl leaned close to me and said, "I really like the way you approach things, hoss. You don't fit the mold, and I like that."

"Thank you," I said.

"You see all these cats in Nashville, and they're just chasing each other's tail," he continued. "They all want to know what the other guy's doing and then they go do that. But I don't see that in you. That's never been my thing, either. Or Sun Records'. The history of this town is about artists who live the music and keep it real and do what they're doing because they love it."

After the taping of *Nashville Now*, Carl said he wanted to hang out some more. I was getting set to do the video for "Talk Some" off my second album, *It Won't Be the Last*. The shoot was in Memphis.

"Is there any way you'd want to come over?" I asked.

"Oh, man, just let me know when and where," Carl said. "I'd be honored." Then he added, "And you know what else? I want to write a song with you."

Carl Perkins, with his hall of fame history, wanted to write with me? I composed myself real quick.

"It's funny you say that," I replied. "On the way here I thought of a good hook — 'Truth is I lied.'"

"Truth is I lied," he said, trying out the words on his tongue. "Truth is I lied . . . huh, I like it."

A few weeks later, Carl joined me in Memphis on the set of the video for "Talk Some." The centerpiece of the video was a live performance of the song, but it was bookended by Carl and me arriving in a black '56 Chrysler and me leaving in a private jet at the end.

As soon as Carl saw the old car, which had been trucked in from a junkyard, he turned to his wife and exclaimed, "That's Judy! By God, that's Judy!"

Evidently, back in the '50s, after getting some money, he had bought a car like that Chrysler and named it Judy. In fact, he thought this exact car *was* Judy.

"You have to give it to me," he said.

"Give it to you?" I asked, confused.

"Yes," he said. "You give it to me. Then I'll give it to you. I want to give you *my* Judy."

Lo and behold, I ended up with Judy at my house. I also ended up with a good friend in Carl. He enjoyed coming out to my farm and walking the trails, letting his dogs run and chase rabbits. It cleared his mind and helped mine when I began to doubt myself after *Storm in the Heartland.*

"Cyrus, just do one thing and you'll be all right," he said.

"What's that?" I asked.

"Stay true to your music," he said. "And be real. Be who you are. Don't be chasing trends. Don't be chasing the next thing. Don't be trying to win the favor of whoever is in the big chair. Just write what's in your heart. Write what's you."

I never got around to working with Carl on "Truth Is I Lied." I still gave him partial writer's credit, if only for his enthusiasm and friendship. But Don Von Tress and I wrote the song and put it on my next album, *Trail of Tears.* For that album, I started going to my guitarist Terry Shelton's house and working there.

He understood where I was emotionally. He also knew the antidote for what ailed me.

"Come on, man," he said. "Let's just make some music."

Terry was always on the cutting edge of technology. Years earlier, when we were on the road, he would disappear into his hotel room, set up his computer — the first one I'd seen — and look for ways to get on this new thing called "the Internet." Now, in his log cabin, he had what passed for the primo home recording studio. It was perfect for a rock-and-bluegrass album — what I thought of as homegrown music.

Michael Joe Sagraves joined us on guitar, mandolin, and harmonica, and step-by-step we discovered a sound. We began with what would become the title track, "Trail of Tears," and added "Tenntucky," "Truth Is I Lied," and "Call Me Daddy," my most personal song to date.

I'd written it in August 1994, between shows in Myrtle Beach, where my son Cody lived with his mom, and Virginia Beach, where I taped my second ABC TV special. My dad had been with me in both places. Filled with the conflicting emotions of trying to be a good father one day and leaving my son the next, I basically wrote the story of my life . . .

Little boy running through the yard
Fell and skinned his heart
And later climbed up in a tree

As he looked into the sky
He began to cry
And said, "Daddy, why'd you leave?"

Call me daddy, I'm feelin' blue
Call me daddy, I need to talk to you
Call me daddy, help me through
And then he bowed his head to pray
Call me dad

The little boy became a man
Found a bride and took her hand
And made a baby all their own

As he looked in that baby's eyes
As the baby cried
He swore, "You'll never be alone."

Call me daddy, when you're feelin' blue
Call me daddy, and I'll talk to you
Call me daddy, and I'll help you through

And then he bowed his head to pray
Call me dad

Another life has come and gone
Another baby's grown
And stands alone against the world

As he looks into the sky
He begins to cry
And says, "Daddy, I miss you."

Call me daddy, I'm feelin' blue
Call me daddy, I need to talk to you
Call me daddy, help me through
And then he bowed his head to pray
Call me dad.

Terry and I referred to the album as Project MDSSE — or Most Disrespected Singer-Songwriter Since Elvis. Jack McFadden and I split up over the album. He couldn't understand why I was "wasting time on that bluegrass thing." After hearing of Jack's and my falling out, the record company wanted to know what was going on with me, and one day Luke Lewis drove out to Terry's. He wanted to hear the album.

"It's homegrown," I said as a prelude before playing him several songs.

Afterward, he kept nodding his head as if the music was still coming out of the speakers.

"Oh, man, keep doing this," he said. "This is so refreshing. Nobody is ever going to think that Billy Ray Cyrus is out here making these rootsy-bluegrass-rock records. It's cool."

"So you like it?"

"It sounds great," he said. "You're probably not going to get a lot of airplay with this. You're probably not going to sell a lot of albums. But you will get the acclaim you deserve. The critics will love it."

I understood, and I was relieved the boss had just given me the go-ahead to make the music I was feeling.

CHAPTER 22

————◆◆◆————

"It's About the Chase"

I T WAS DECEMBER 13, 1994, and I was all geared up and excited for a big night of strange happenings and weird stuff. Tish was making fun of me, an easy and popular pastime in our house. She and our nanny A.J. had put the kids to bed upstairs and the three of us were sitting at the kitchen table. I was venting my frustrations. My single "Trail of Tears" had been released and peaked at No. 39, the same exact spot where "Some Gave All" and "Storm in the Heartland" got to before they reversed course.

"What is it with me and the number thirty-nine?" I said.

Knowing my obsession with numbers and my efforts to find connections between the twists and turns of my life and various dates — like May 9, the day of Keith Whitley's death and also the day Braison was born — Tish wondered if I might be a little OCD. As she said that, I noticed the calendar and exclaimed, "Oh my God!"

"What?" she asked.

"Do you know what date it is today?"

"December 13," she said.

"Exactly!"

Exactly a year earlier, on December 13, 1994, the very same day, I had been in my teepee on top of the hill late at night and seen the lights outside the house go on and off about a dozen times. When I told Tish about it the next morning, she'd asked, "What were you smoking in that peace pipe of yours?"

Now, I reminded her of what had happened.

"So?" she said.

"You just wait," I said.

She laughed and looked around the room. "Yeah, where's your ghost? Where's your poltergeist?"

As soon as she said that, the kitchen lights blinked on and off several times, before the whole frickin' house went dark. The temperature dropped until we could see our breath. Spooked, Tish and A.J. woke the kids, loaded them in the car, and checked into the nearby Best Western.

I stayed at the house that night. I lit candles and went around and checked on things. It was cold, but I loved it.

It took three days to get the power back on. It turned out that Bill Cambron had buried all the power lines underground so they wouldn't spoil his views of the land. One of them had snapped halfway between the road and the house.

The next year, on December 13, 1995, I decided to take Judy, my old Chrysler, out for a drive at about eleven o'clock at night. My brother Mick had gotten her engine running, but this was the first time I'd tried to take her for a drive. After some priming, I got the engine to turn over and started down the driveway. Soon my farm disappeared in my rearview mirror and I found myself crossing some old train tracks at Thompson's Station, within sight of the actual old train station dating back to the Civil War that gave the town its name.

Once I crossed the tracks, Judy died, leaving me stuck surrounded by darkness in the middle of nowhere. I got out and did all the things you're supposed to do when your car stops. I opened the hood, fiddled around with this and that, kicked the tires, and finally cursed out that old machine. It turned out, the fault was mine: I was out of gas.

I started to shiver. I needed more protection from the cold than the flannel shirt I was wearing. A fog set in. It began to look as though Dracula might jump out of the woods. By now it was about midnight, and I was debating whether to jog back to my place when I saw a car winding down the road toward me. When it was close enough, I waved and the driver stopped.

"Aren't you Billy Ray Cyrus?" he asked.

"Yeah, I am," I said. "My car's out of gas, I think."

He gave me a lift to my house, where I had a gas pump and a can I could fill up and take back to get Judy running again.

"You bought Bill Cambron's place, right?" he asked.

"Yes, sir," I said.

"I'm the preacher that Bill came to when he had the vision."

"I heard about that," I replied. "Is it true he saw an angel?"

The preacher nodded. Apparently, Bill Cambron, whose designs had helped shape the look of downtown Nashville, including the original Country Music Hall of Fame, was enjoying life at the place I now owned. That is, until a fateful day in December 1991 when an angel came to him and said he needed to get saved because he was going to die.

"Then what happened?" I asked.

"Bill died a year later."

A few minutes later, he dropped me off next to Judy. As I filled her up with gas, I wondered what were the chances of that preacher having picked me up in the middle of the night. I realized how everything is connected in some strange way or another. Either that or Tish had been right: I needed to lay off the peace pipe.

Well, life went on and soon after that my *Trail of Tears* album, released on January 1, 1996, debuted at No. 20 on the country charts, 125 on *Billboard*'s album chart, and sold only 125,000 copies, making it my lowest-selling album yet. Ordinarily I would've been crushed by disappointment, but *Trail of Tears* earned me the one thing my platinum and gold albums hadn't: recognition from critics. Good reviews streamed in from *People, USA Today, Entertainment Weekly*, newspapers in Dallas, Miami, and Memphis, as well as *Music City News* and *Billboard,* whose headline declared, BILLY RAY DESERVES RESPECT.

With a renewed sense of confidence, as well as a new manager (Al Schiltz, my road manager since 1992), I embarked on an acoustic tour. Instead of the lights and special effects of previous tours, my show was toned down.

My next album, *The Best of Billy Ray Cyrus: Cover to Cover* completed my contractual obligation with the record company and showed the evolution of my songwriting. I also laid the foundation for the future by including three new tunes, "Cover to Cover," "Bluegrass State of Mind," and "It's All the Same to Me," which became a surprise hit on country radio. "It's good to see Billy Ray Cyrus back in country music, where I think he belongs," the esteemed critic Chet Flippo wrote.

Others agreed with him. In June, I was the big winner at the TNN Music City News Country Awards, which were voted on by fans. So it meant even more when I accepted trophies for Best Song, Best Single, Best Video, Best Album, and Male Artist of the Year.

But not all the news was happy. Jack McFadden had died the day before the awards show, from cirrhosis of the liver, following a long decline.

I saw him for the last time about a week before the awards show. I showed him a video of a new song called "Under the Hood" from my next album, *Shot Full of Love.* After, he pounded his fist on the bed and insisted on seeing it again and again. Even in the best of health, Jack wasn't a demonstrative person, and now he was frail and weak, so his reaction was really something.

I tried to reminisce about old times, but Jack wanted to talk about my future, knowing full well he wouldn't be around to see it. Both of us had tears in our eyes. Before I left, Jack reached out his hand and asked if we could pray. He was not much of a religious man, but that was OK. You find it when you need it. As I held his hand, I felt the power of a pioneer, a man who'd had the vision and the wisdom and pure love of country music, which he'd shared with the world. He'd worked with Buck Owens, Merle Haggard, and Keith Whitley, and I had been fortunate to have him take me under his wing at a time when I needed his guidance. I squeezed his hand and let him know he'd been essential in my rise. Then, the following week, at the awards show, I thanked the fans over and over again, and I thanked Jack, and Carl Perkins, who'd passed away six months earlier after losing his battle with cancer.

That was a lot of loss to deal with all at once, but Carl's death was something of a relief from the suffering he'd endured at the end. Even so, I missed our friendship, those walks and our talks when he taught me so much. He'd even passed some of his wisdom on to Miley.

Once, when she was five years old, we were walking with Carl through the field. His dogs were out in front of us and they had lit onto the trail of a rabbit. As they began to yap, Carl noticed Miley's concern for the bunnies and told her she needn't worry.

"Honey, you see me and your daddy don't carry guns," he said. "We aren't going to kill the rabbits. Hunting isn't about killing anything. It's about the chase."

About twelve years later, Miley would have a massive hit song called "The Climb," and it was basically about what Carl had said to her out in the field — namely, life is more about the adventure you have while living it than it is about getting any one place.

Merle Haggard once told me the same. I asked him if getting to the top was the best part of his career, and he said, "Hell no. Once you get to the top of the mountain, there's only one way to go." He smiled and pointed down. "Gettin' there's the best part."

At Carl's funeral, I sang an original song called "Goodbye," which I'd written for him. Ricky Skaggs joined me on the mandolin. We rehearsed in the church with Carl lying right in front of us, and we sounded great.

When we performed it for real, though, in front of Carl's family, George Harrison, Garth Brooks, Jerry Lee Lewis, Wynonna Judd, and Sam Phillips, among others in the standing-room-only church, Ricky's amplifier broke and he spent the whole time messing with the knobs. I was playing with the greatest picker in the world, only his gear didn't work.

I thought, Man, Carl wanted one more joke, didn't he? It was his last chance to remind me not to take myself too seriously. And I didn't. Because really it was about sharing that song. This was the one and only time I'd sung "Goodbye." I wanted it to belong to Carl, to be his, and to be my way of saying a final thank-you for being my friend.

CHAPTER 23

What's Meant to Be Will Be

I THOUGHT MERCURY BLEW a major opportunity to capitalize on my big night at the TNN Awards by waiting almost six months to release my next album, *Shot Full of Love*. With my contract up and our relationship all but officially over, I'd made the album their way. The executives wanted me to toss aside my original songs and use "radio friendly" material from Nashville's top songwriters, with the town's No. 1 hit-maker, Keith Stegall, pulling it all together as the producer. I even had Sly Dog sit it out in favor of session musicians.

Although I made no secret that I was fulfilling a contract and trying to make everyone happy, I have to say, I loved the finished product. I had a blast making the title track, "Shot Full of Love," a remake of Juice Newton's 1981 song, though my version was inspired by the Nitty Gritty Dirt Band's killer take.

In the studio, Keith paired me with guitarist Dann Huff, who tore it up and became integral to my next album as well as a good friend. I thought the song "American Dream" should've been a hit, and I have no doubt "Under the Hood," a groovy barn burner released as the first single, would've been a No. 1 if someone other than me would've cut it. Disappointingly, it failed to even chart.

We made a video and it went to No. 1 at CMT. But that wasn't the single for radio. The single was a song called "Busy Man," and it became a hit. The song was about a father who is too busy working and keeping up with his job and neglecting his family, until one day he wakes up and realizes what's really important.

At concerts, I could see the looks on the faces of the dads in the audience as they sang along. That said it all. It was great to have a song out again that was touching people's lives.

If it had sold only two copies, though, I would've considered it a success on account of a little girl named Jenny. Before we started, I came across a fan letter from her. Written in the flowing script of a young girl, she explained that she was a cancer patient and she'd always dreamed of meeting me. I made some calls. On the first night we were in the studio, I came out of the booth after singing "Give My Heart to You," and Jenny was there in a wheelchair, waiting.

Her face lit up; so did mine. We visited, took photos, and had a good time. Her friendly spirit and love of music stayed with me throughout the recording of the album.

In the spring, Jenny's grandmother sent me a letter saying that Jenny had passed away. At her funeral, the kids from her school said a prayer, and then, per Jenny's own brave instructions, her friends and classmates played "Achy Breaky Heart" and danced and released hundreds of butterflies.

After reading that letter, I sat still for a long while in the workroom where I made my music. I pictured that brave little girl whose eyes had been filled with God's light and love. Those are the special moments of being a recording star — and they are equal parts gift and responsibility.

I also heard from Raymond Bullock, the former Green Beret who used to come into Bronco's Lounge to hear me play "Some Gave All." Those days felt like ancient history. Now Raymond had heard I was hanging out in Tennessee, and he wondered if he could come by with his buddies.

So Raymond and a bunch of fellow veterans got in a van and

drove to my place. I took them to the top of the hill where my tee-pee was and we prayed for one of their guys who wasn't doing well. We sat around, talked, and walked some of the trails.

I told them how the hill where we sat had been a sacred place for the Chickasaw tribe. At another point, I gestured to the south so we were looking toward Columbia and Spring Hill, where Civil War troops had massed before the bloody Battle of Franklin. The ground echoed with footsteps from the past. We could almost feel them. As the sun went down, we built a fire and talked more.

A few months later, I found a note on my gate from Raymond. It said, "Mr. Cyrus" — he always called me Mr. Cyrus — "It's Raymond. I hate to bother you. I'm in town and I have a gift from the guys. I'd leave it by the gate if I could. But I can't. I want to drop by if anyone is home." He left a phone number.

He was at a little hotel nearby, the Goosecreek Inn. My brother Mick and I laugh about that place because the C in the sign often burns out so that it reads Goose reek Inn. Raymond came over shortly after I called him. I met him and his friends at the gate on my dirt bike, trailed by my one-eyed German shepherd, Spirit.

"Can we go back to the top of your hill?" Raymond asked. "I got something in the back and can't really get it out here."

I tried to look in the back of his van. What was back there — a live animal or something?

He followed me to the top of the hill, where he got out and pulled open the van's side door, revealing a massive totem pole. It must've weighed four hundred pounds. The guys wrestled that thing out of there, dug a hole, and planted it. I thought it was pretty great. Then Raymond walked me around the back and pointed to where they had carved a message:

> Thank you for the night we spent on Spirit Mountain. It may have been an evening for you, but it was a lifetime for us.

I was humbled and at a loss for words, which is pretty unusual for me.

"I feel inadequate," I finally said, "compared to the gift you've given me. The freedom to have a dream, to be a kid that dreamed of being the next Elvis: buy a guitar, start a band, go rock-and-roll. How come I can do that? Because you guys, and men like you and your dads and grandfathers, made a sacrifice so we can live in the greatest country in the world where freedom is the priority . . ."

Given experiences like that, my dad wondered why I beat myself up so badly over whether a song was No. 1, 3, or 39.

"Look around, Bo," he'd say. "It's all good."

It was. It was better than good.

I knew that to be true. Like a lot of people, though, I had trouble remembering that life, as Carl Perkins had told me, was about the chase, not the chart. As I'd said numerous times, "Achy Breaky Heart" had been both a blessing and a curse. It had put me on top of a mountain *and* at the same time in a deep hole. With every album, I was trying to prove myself. Did I have to? Probably not.

But I did.

I tortured myself. I still do — and why that is remains a mystery.

However, my dad understood problems were all relative depending on who had them. One day he showed up at my house with a totem pole the Cherokee Indians in the Smoky Mountains had made for me in appreciation of my song "Trail of Tears." The totem was called Seven Hidden Eagles, he said, because there were, in fact, seven eagles hidden within the carving. The first few were easy to find; the rest got harder.

My dad drove it up to where I had my teepee and we spent a few hours digging a hole and wrestling it into the ground. I liked watching my dad work. He was six foot two and strong. He tore into the ground. And he knew how to do everything right.

Afterward, we rode horses for a while, and then returned to the teepee. We warmed up around the fire as the last bit of sun dropped behind the farthest mountain. Soon we were sitting in the dark, the big old flames dancing in front of us and casting a bit of light onto that new totem pole.

My dad chose that moment to zero in on me.

"You know, son, I'm not your manager, and I don't know much of anything about the business you're in," he said. "But it looks to me like you've got all your eggs in one basket."

"What do you mean, Dad?" I asked.

"Well, everything I hear you say revolves around whether radio stations are going to play your newest single," he said. "It's all one thing, and that limits you. I think you ought to branch out. Get one of those Kenny Rogers–Dolly Parton kind of careers. They do it all — film, television, *and* music."

"Shoot, man, I'd love that," I said. "But how? I'm not an actor."

I'd done guest spots on *The Nanny* and *Diagnosis Murder,* but neither was a real acting gig. Now I decided to up the ante. My manager put out feelers in Hollywood and some scripts came in. Most were for Westerns and romances; none knocked me out. I was content to wait for something that felt right.

At the end of 1998, I agreed to do a guest spot on a reboot of *The Love Boat,* shooting in Los Angeles. I played a singer named Lasso Larry. On my last day on the set, I picked up a trade magazine someone had left on a table and read that director David Lynch was casting for a new project called *Mulholland Dr.*

Whether *Mulholland Dr.* was going to be a TV series or a movie was still unclear at that point, but I didn't care. I was a fan of David's work. I loved both *Elephant Man* and *Blue Velvet,* so I called my agent and asked if he could get me an audition. Since we were leaving that afternoon, I knew the odds of David having time were small. Yet a short time later, I had an appointment that afternoon.

If only the rest of the day had been that easy. First off, I confirmed my meeting. Then I changed my plane ticket to a flight later that night. Tish, Miley, and Braison kept their seats on the early flight. As I helped them get into the car, we all remembered that we had two baby chickens living in the bathtub in our hotel room.

"Dad, we can't leave 'em," Miley said.

I looked at Tish. She was shaking her head, letting me know that she didn't want to carry them home along with two little kids.

Earlier in the week, we'd taken the kids to a petting zoo near the beach in Topanga Canyon. As we looked around, we discovered some baby chickens that were being raised to be fed to the large snakes. After a quick family conference, we asked the people in charge if they'd sell us the baby chickens.

When they said no, we went to plan B. We snuck around the back and stole two of the chicks, one black and one white, and took them back to our hotel, where they lived in our bathtub.

"All right," I said to Tish and the kids. "I'll take them with me and bring them back home."

So I had these guys with me when I showed up at my audition. I thought if anyone would appreciate this strange story, it would be David Lynch — and you know what? He did. But I had other concerns. My part had been sent to me less than an hour before, and I hadn't begun to memorize it or even think much about the character, Gene the Pool Man.

However, David never asked me to read the lines. Somehow he knew about Mary Magdalene Pitts and my song about child abuse, "Enough Is Enough." I told him about my dad's neighbors Calvin and Jimmy, the fire at their house, and the voice I'd heard crying, "Help me. Help me, Mommy."

When I finished, he said, "That's great. I'll have somebody get in touch with your people." Sure, I thought, that was Hollywood talk. But before I got to the airport, my agent called and told me I had the job. Now if only I could get the birds through security . . . I told them they were rare African cockatoos. "They're very nervous birds," I told 'em. "They must remain in their cage with a towel over it to shield them from the light." It worked. I got the chicks home . . . and the gig with David Lynch.

As I expected, there was a big learning curve once shooting began in February 1999. Most of it had to do with comfort and familiarity. The script was so dark, I expected David to show up dressed in black, wearing a cape, and burning candles. In reality, he wore blue jeans and a denim shirt and couldn't have been more normal.

But that's where normal ended on *Mulholland Dr.*, a psychological thriller about an actress who's involved in a bizarre search for identity across Los Angeles after befriending a woman suffering from amnesia.

For my first scene, I was in bed with another man's wife when he walks in and finds us. I lay there and said, "Forget you ever saw it. It's better that way." The husband reacts by pouring pink paint in his wife's jewelry box. Then, in the next scene, he and I fight in the kitchen. That was more complicated, and I was unsure of my performance even though David said it was good and got ready to move on to the next scene.

"Should we try it again?" I asked. "Maybe just get one more take."

"No, we're all good," he said, smiling. "Acting is about being real in the moment, and you gave me exactly what I want."

"Really?"

"I'm not your manager or your agent or anything," he said. "I'm talking to you as a director, and you're what a director wants. You come in here and play it real. I think you can be quite an actor."

Without that vote of confidence from David Lynch, I doubt I would've continued to act. After *Mulholland Dr.*, I felt like I had done something incredibly dark. My power came from wanting to share God's light and love. It fueled my drive and passion. I feared I might've tampered with a force that I didn't want in my life.

On a flight home from L.A., I prayed for guidance. If God wanted me to be an actor, he'd send me a project that he wanted me to act in. A couple of days later, I came home and found an envelope on the table from my manager. Inside was the script for *Doc*, a values-heavy family drama about a Montana doctor working in New York City.

Tish read the script first and, later that day, when I asked her what she thought, she said, "It's so *you*. It's about everything you represent."

I sat down with the script and loved it more with each turn of the page. *Doc* made me think of *Brian's Song*, a made-for-TV movie I'd loved as a kid. Although it was a very different story, *Doc* pulsed with the same kind of heart: tons of emotion, sadness, and beauty that made you feel better — or inspired to be better.

"I can see you as Clint Cassidy," Tish said that night after we'd put the kids to bed.

"Me, too," I said. "He's the underdog. He's all about overcoming adversities. And that's me."

At that point, *Doc* was slated to be a movie for Pax TV, a new cable network. If ratings were good, it would get picked up as a series. Either way, I had mixed feelings. My intuition told me that I'd get the part if I auditioned. However, I didn't know if I wanted to commit myself to the project. I had signed a new deal with Monument Records, and I was in the midst of making my *Southern Rain* album, which I loved. I also loved riding my horse, taking out my dirt bike, and playing with my kids. I loved my freedom.

My mind played this game of Ping-Pong until finally I called my manager, Al Schiltz, and said I wasn't going to do *Doc*.

"Call 'em and cancel," I said.

"Man, I think you're passing up a big opportunity here," he said.

He knew me well enough to tell me to go up to my teepee and pray about things. "Call me back tonight before I cancel your flight," he added.

I took his advice. I got down on my knees in that desperate man's prayer pose by the fire, and said, "God, I'm confused. Do you want me to go to this audition? Do you want this to happen?"

Now I know God most likely wasn't taking a time-out from the much more important matters on his schedule to deal with my career decisions — or indecisions. Then again, within a few minutes, a voice said, "Go to the audition. If they hire you, you'll know the answer is yes. If they don't, you'll know you didn't miss an opportunity intended to do my will."

That was it. I returned home and called Al.

"Keep my seat on the plane," I said. "I'm going to the meeting. It's in God's hands. What's meant to be will be."

CHAPTER 24

"Stand Still"

BEFORE *DOC* HAPPENED, I got involved in another production: the birth of my youngest daughter, Noah. She came into this world on January 8, 2000, the day the Tennessee Titans were playing the Buffalo Bills in the AFC Wild Card playoff game. Both events were memorable for the same reason — they involved a miracle.

Tish felt wonderful the whole nine months our little girl was growing inside her, and she'd scheduled the delivery so we'd be sure I'd be in town when it happened. But she woke up on the eighth feeling like the baby might be coming, so we went to the hospital early.

By the afternoon, nothing had happened. We had long ago decided to name the baby Noah Lindsey, after my papaw Cyrus, whose middle name was Lindsey. I had brought an old photograph of him preaching and hung it in the corner so he could oversee the birth of his namesake. What I liked about the picture was that it showed the woodcarving on his pulpit. It was one of his favorite sayings: EXPECT A MIRACLE.

And we were expecting a miracle.

Tish even said, "It's going to be a miracle if I can get this baby out of me."

Meanwhile, the Titans started playing the Bills. We could practically see the stadium outside the window of Baptist Hospital. Unfortunately, we couldn't watch the game or hear the cheering because the TV in our private room didn't work. Tish didn't care about the game, but I followed the doctors and nurses into a waiting room, where there was a TV that worked. Every few plays I checked on Tish. Well, sometimes a nurse went in my place because the game was so close I didn't want to leave and miss the action.

With less than two minutes, the lead changed twice. First, the Titans went ahead on a touchdown drive, and then with only sixteen seconds on the clock, the Bills took the lead on a field goal. They kicked off, the Titans received, lateraled in a crazy kind of Hail Mary, and ran the ball for a touchdown as time expired, winning the game in what became known as the Music City Miracle.

The cheers that filled the hospital's corridors turned into tense quiet as the play was challenged and brought under review. It was one of the first times instant replay was used to decide the outcome of a game. The only place the drama was thicker was in Tish's room. Suddenly it was baby time. The doctors, nurses, and I all looked at Tish, then at the broken TV, and then at one another, our expressions saying the same thing: "But the *game!*"

Then two more miracles occurred. First, the TV in Tish's room lit up. The game was on and officials ruled that the Titans had won the game. Our cheers were just in time to welcome Noah Lindsey Cyrus, whose eyes were wide open and looking around as if to say, "What's going on?"

I cut the cord, kissed Tish, and then glanced up at the game, though on the way to the TV my eye caught the photo of my papaw. He might as well have been standing there with us in person. Expect a miracle.

A miracle, indeed.

Brothers David and Gary Johnson were the cocreators and producers of *Doc*. With Andy Griffith and Michael Landon as their biggest influences, their goal was to make a family show with a strong, moral male role model. They dreamed up Clint Cassidy, a Montana doctor who takes a job in a New York medical clinic and brings his country ways to the big city.

Within the first ten minutes of our initial meeting, David, Gary, and I knew we were meant to work together. Their idea of a family show was exactly like mine. They even put Tish and the kids in a quick cameo in the pilot. If you look closely in one scene, you can see Tish as a nurse checking me out as I walk through the hall. Still, despite the good vibes, I was still plagued by doubts — but as was usually the case with me, that turned into a good thing. I just wanted to keep it real.

One day, midway through the pilot, I had to take off for a few dates that had been booked before I signed on to the TV series. My plane was delayed on the tarmac in Toronto. As we sat on the runway, with the pilot periodically apologizing for the congestion, I wondered what the heck I was doing there in the first place. It was the same confusion as before. Why am I up here acting like an actor? Why am I not playing music full time?

Feeling lost, I shut my eyes and flashed back to a time when I really was lost. I was eight or nine years old, and my dad had taken me squirrel hunting in the woods. I'd never killed a squirrel. I didn't have it in me to shoot anything. Who was I to take a life? Even a squirrel's life.

While my dad went his own way, I sat with my gun and waited. After a while, I went for a hike and headed deeper into the woods until I was hopelessly lost.

At that point, my walk turned to a jog and then my jog turned into a run. I called my dad's name. I knew you were supposed to be quiet when you hunted, but I was hollering, "Dad! Dad! Dad!" I tripped over a log and my gun snapped in two.

Finally, late that night, I staggered out onto an old country road. A sheriff spotted me.

"Don't worry, son," he said. "Your dad is right up here looking for you. I'll radio in that you're all right."

A moment later my dad pulled up in his car, got out, and ran toward me. I was thinking he was mad and might pull his belt off. Instead, he wrapped his arms around me, pulled me into his chest, and hugged me. It seemed like he might have been crying a little bit. He knelt down and looked in my eyes.

"Listen to me, son. When you're lost, stand still."

That moment was frozen in my mind as if it had happened the day before.

Now, there I was on the tarmac, a grown thirty-nine-year-old man, feeling just as lost as I'd been in the woods that day. I picked up a pen and pulled out the puke bag from the seat pocket in front of me and began to write:

> *When I was just a little boy*
> *I wandered through the woods*
> *Searchin' for my daddy through the pines*
> *I guess I took a wrong turn*
> *Somewhere along the way*
> *But the Bible said,*
> *"Seek and ye shall find."*
>
> *Daylight turned to darkness*
> *Adventure turned to fear*
> *When I finally found my way back home*
> *His words I still can hear . . .*
>
> *Stand still!*
> *When you're in the dark,*
> *Listen to your heart*
> *And pray for God's will*
> *Stand still . . .*
>
> *Stand still!*
> *Adrift in the wind . . .*
> *Your voice within*
> *Will be your best friend*
> *Stand still . . . and pray*
> *Stand still*

Now that I'm a grown man
On my own and on my way
I got my own decisions
to be made
And when I'm at the
crossroads
Unforsure and unforeseen
I bow my head
And with these words I pray . . .

After my shows, I returned to Toronto and played the song for David and Gary Johnson. I said, "Guys, I think this is a theme song for *Doc*." They agreed, and introduced me to Jack Lenz, who had been hired to score the pilot, as well as write the theme. He was a kindred spirit, someone who lived and breathed music the way I did.

During production for *Doc*, I rented a condo in a twenty-four-story building in downtown Toronto, a far cry from my Nashville farm (now five hundred acres altogether). The windows in that condo didn't even open. I hated not being able to breathe fresh air at night.

Tish and the kids flew in as their busy schedules permitted. (By this point, Brandi was showing horses and Miley had cheerleading practice after school.) I also got back home at least one weekend a month, but things were changing. The kids were growing up so fast and I longed for a simpler time. Just a few years before I had put Miley and Braison in my pickup and driven them to the farthest hill on our property, where there was a tiny clearing surrounded by forest.

There was a meteor shower that night, and I wanted my kids to see Mother Nature's best fireworks display. We got set up at our secret place, by the kids' favorite tree with a notch at the base where they hid Matchbox cars and RugRat toys. (They're still there to this day.) We had marshmallows and wieners and we built a fire. Suddenly, Miley took off like a sprinter, running full bore.

She got about four feet in the pitch-black before tripping over a tree stump. She flew an equal distance in the air and landed against the bumper of my truck. Oh man. A baseball-size bump appeared on her forehead. Blood spurted everywhere. I swung by the house to pick up Tish, and beelined it to the emergency room.

"Whose idea was it to play in the woods close to midnight?" Tish asked.

Miley looked at me. I tried not to look guilty . . . but I was.

"I thought so," Tish said. "I got five kids and one overgrown, terminal teenager."

After wrapping production on *Doc*'s first season, I was like a kid getting out of school for summer vacation. I hadn't ever worked as hard or as long in a concentrated stretch as I had making those twenty-two episodes. It was June 2001, and all I wanted to do was go out on the road and play music with my band. I took fairs, festivals, and casinos — any and every gig I could get. I just wanted to find the music, thank the fans, and be in the band.

On the night of September 10, 2001, I flew from Nashville to Toronto, reading the script for the first episode of season two. Based around my song "Some Gave All," it was the story of a Vietnam vet dealing with PTSD — post-traumatic stress disorder — who can't let go of loving his high school sweetheart even though she's married to another man and has a child.

I landed about 11:15 p.m., and by the time I got through Customs in Toronto, it was close to midnight. It turned out I needed a new work permit, but only one guy was around, and he didn't work in that department. He told me to come back in the morning when one of the officials would be there.

So I went on my way, back to my condo, and got up early the next morning. It was about five thirty; a car arrived for me at six. I remember yawning in the backseat. By eight thirty, we were rolling film on the opening scene. I was listening to the vet tell me his life story and about his inability to move on. We had begun filming season two.

We were about thirty-five or forty minutes into the scene when

somebody said, "Hey, there's been a plane crash in New York City."
At that point, we didn't know much of anything. The folks on the
morning news were waiting for details to emerge. As the crew prepared for the next take, we turned the monitor into a TV, and we
couldn't stop watching the tragic events that unfolded right before
our eyes. By nine thirty, the whole world had changed.

People would have thought I was crazy if I'd told them about the
dreams I'd had six months before this dreadful day. It took me a
while before I mentioned them to anyone, except my driver, Loren
Fredrick, who I told about the dreams the morning after they happened. I didn't even want to think about them, but I couldn't help
it. As I sat glued in front of the TV, I remembered the two startling
nightmares I'd had that America was attacked and I couldn't get
home to be with my family.

The second one was so vivid that I woke up in the middle of
the night having an anxiety attack. The only way I could catch my
breath was to get dressed, go outside, and stand by the lake with
the cold air blowing off it.

Now, with that nightmare a reality, my breaths were short
again and my chest filled with an unsettling tightness. This time I
couldn't open my eyes and make it go away, though I tried. America
had been attacked. I was in Canada. My family was in Nashville. It
was exactly what I'd dreamed.

Every fiber in my body was telling me to get to Tish and the
kids. I wanted to be with them so badly, but I couldn't. The borders
were closed. I called home and hung on the line with my wife. We
watched the news together in silence, except when one of us fought
back tears. Despite being thousands of miles apart, I had never felt
or needed to be as close, but I was so far away.

The extreme circumstances inspired us to push the episode back
two months and turn it into a two-hour tribute to firefighters, police, and the military. Our writers expanded on the original script,
and we sent a crew to New York and interviewed one particular
firehouse that had been hit extremely hard. The show became a

documentary wrapped into a dramatic episode about the coura-geous people who put their lives on the line . . . heroes. I knew it was the most important thing we were ever going to do during the show's run.

I flew to New York to help with the interviews, and while I was there, some officials invited me to participate in the seventy-fifth Macy's Thanksgiving Day parade that November. They asked me to ride on a float honoring fallen New York City firefighters. I immedi-ately said yes. The float was lined with boots and jackets belonging to fallen heroes from the firehouse where we'd done our interviews. There was a banner on the float that simply read "Some Gave All." It couldn't have been more true.

To this day, I have never had a more surreal, or even spiritual, ex-perience than I did that Thanksgiving as I rode through New York City. I could still smell the smoke smoldering with the ashes. Those heroes were not physically present, but they were very much there. You could feel 'em. Like a song you never forget; I couldn't help but feel those men and women lingering over Fifth Avenue, over the entire city, inspiring us, reminding us of the price of freedom and the cost of courage, as heroes do.

CHAPTER 25

"Amazing Grace"

ARL P. MAYFIELD WAS the biggest name on morning radio in Nashville. His show was on WKDF, and over the years, he'd become a good friend. Carl knew that many people had written me off before they even knew me.

One of those people was Waylon Jennings. Even though nearly ten years had passed since Waylon's dig at the Country Music Awards, I still remembered his putdown. I'll be totally honest: all the platinum and gold records hanging on my wall at home didn't erase the sting of a legend half-jokingly telling Nashville that maybe my tennis shoes were a little too tight.

Well, Carl knew Waylon and I had never met, and he started talking about this canker sore of controversy on the air. He brought it up every day. It became his thing on the radio. It got people in town talking. What if Carl P. gets the two of them to meet? Wouldn't that be something? Would Billy Ray get red on Waylon? If he tried, would the old outlaw shoot him?

It got pretty crazy even though I knew Carl P. had my best interests in mind. He did repeatedly say, "If Waylon would just meet my friend Billy Ray, he would totally change his mind. He just doesn't know him."

Carl P. called me in Toronto and asked when I was going to be back in Nashville. I had a break in a couple of weeks and a trip planned to see my family.

"Would you be willing to go live on the air with Waylon?" he asked. "It'll be you, me, and Waylon in the studio, live. Whatever happens, happens."

"Of course I would," I said.

When I returned to Nashville, my first appointment was at WKDF. Waylon was already in front of a mic when I walked in. The tension in the studio reminded me of the feeling before a high school football game. He watched me carefully, like a gunfighter in a bar in an old Western. He spoke first.

"Hi, Billy Ray Cyrus," he said. "I'm Waylon Jennings."

I looked at Carl P., whose face was flushed with the excitement of the moment. He got right into it, too.

"OK, Waylon, what did you mean about Billy Ray's tennis shoes being too tight?" he asked.

"I was just making an observation, you know," Waylon said.

"Well, I've got to thank you for that," I said, jumping in. "I don't know if you recall, but when you said that, I reached down and loosened 'em up, and I swear, I've felt better and more free ever since."

All of us laughed a little bit. As we continued to chitchat, Carl P. added calls from listeners, and then something unexpected happened. Carl P. took a call from a lady who said that she was with her gravely ill grandmother. Even though they were getting ready to unplug her from life support, she was coherent. She and the rest of the family had one request before they said good-bye. They wanted to hear me sing "Amazing Grace."

Talk about drama. We weren't talking about two country singers mending some manufactured bad blood for a pal with a radio show. This was real life. Waylon looked at me with an expression of, "What are you going to do now, hoss?"

For a moment, there was just silence. I had my guitar in my lap, so I began to strum. Then I just did what comes naturally to me. I started to sing.

Amazing grace . . . how sweet the sound . . .

Then Waylon began to sing.

That saved a wretch like me . . .

And then Carl P. started to sing. By the time we finished, there wasn't a dry eye in the studio or, I assume, among listeners. After we ended, Carl P. cut to a commercial, and Waylon reached over and shook my hand.

"Man, I've done a lot of things," he said. "I started my career in radio. But I've never had a moment like that."

"Me neither," I said.

"You want to come over to my place for a cup of coffee when we get done here?" he asked.

"I'd love to," I said, and with that, the show went on . . .

After playing a few more songs, I found myself following Waylon back to his house. Inside, he pointed out Buddy Holly's motorcycle and told me this and that as he showed me around. He bragged a little about his then-teenaged son, Shooter. As a matter of fact, I've never seen a daddy so proud. He cranked up one of Shooter's new tunes. It was hard rockin' and drivin', just like his old man. His wife, Jessi Colter, came into the kitchen, poured herself a cup of coffee, and joined us as he played me some new music he'd recorded.

"We've got to write a song together," Waylon said. "Do you know David Lee Murphy?"

"I sure do," I said.

David Lee Murphy was a great singer-songwriter. Still is.

"I love him," I said.

"How 'bout me and you and David Lee write a song?" he said.

The following week, I went back to Waylon's house and the three of us wrote a song. I spent the next day there, too. It was the start of a deep friendship. It turned out, Waylon was a fan of *Doc*. He knew a lot about the episodes and what Dr. Clint Cassidy was up to. When I went back to Toronto, he called me after each new episode aired and gave me his thoughts and told me he liked the letters I read at the end of every episode. I came to realize that this guy everyone thought was an outlaw and a tough, callous old man . . . Well, I don't want to ruin his image, and so I won't. But he did have a heart of gold.

One night Waylon and Jessi drove over to my house, and we were sitting around the kitchen table when Miley came in with her little guitar. She asked Waylon if he'd show her the chords to his classic "Good Hearted Woman."

I was amazed at Miley's curiosity and fearlessness. She'd once asked Ed King to show her the chord progression of "Sweet Home Alabama" and she sang "Blue Suede Shoes" with Carl Perkins. My God. Now it was Waylon and Jesse singing "Good Hearted Woman."

Waylon couldn't have been happier to show her. He took her guitar and played the song right there, as Miley watched, her face as close to the guitar as she could get. She was like a sponge.

When I went on tour in the summer after *Doc*'s first season, Waylon and Jessi came to my show at the Celebrity Theater in Phoenix. They'd moved out there; his health had declined pretty rapidly. I could see him starting to fade. But there he was, having come out to see me and my band at that theater in the round.

We'd played "Geronimo," which was as hard and as loud of a rock song as anything I'd written or performed. It was about the earth and taking care of Mother Nature. I loved it. And so did Waylon, who said, "Gosh, I loved that song, man. When is it coming out?"

I laughed and said, "It came out like ten years ago. Nobody ever heard about it. It was on my *Storm in the Heartland* album."

"I never heard of that one," he said.

"Neither did anyone else," I said, with a shrug.

"That's OK, man," he said. "The song was fantastic. I loved the whole show. I love it that you play what you feel."

I savored those words the way I did something else he'd said. It was back when we first started to hang out. One night we were sitting around the kitchen table, talking about whether being accepted really mattered if you were true to the music inside you.

Waylon listened to me complain about being ignored and slighted and locked out of Nashville's mainstream. He'd heard my rap before. Putting down his coffee, he said, "Cyrus, do you know what the definition of an outlaw is?"

"No, what is it?" I asked. I wanted to know from the man himself.

"One who has been outlawed," he said.

"Makes sense," I said.

He stuck out his hand. We shook.

"Welcome to the club, brother. Welcome to the club."

As he said that, I knew it was a moment I'd savor forever. He couldn't have given me a greater gift. Or compliment. And I took it as such.

Waylon died on February 13, 2002. A month later, country music's biggest stars gathered in Nashville for a tribute to this man whose life and music had touched all of us, and beyond. I had an idea for something that I thought might be the ultimate compliment to Waylon. Before the tribute, I sent a note to Travis Tritt, asking if he'd want to join me onstage for "Amazing Grace." I thought Waylon might like that. Once again, I don't want to ruin his reputation; still, it's kind of funny to think of Waylon Jennings as the great healer. But ain't that what music's all about?

CHAPTER 26

◆━◈━◆

"I Want My Mullet Back"

BOTH MILEY AND NOAH appeared on a number of episodes of *Doc*, which made me happy. The more they did, the more the family was together in Toronto.

Noah became a regular. Her name was Gracie; she was Dr. Derek's little girl. Miley was Kiley; ironically, this would be the original name for her character in *Hannah Montana*. If anyone was destined to be in front of the camera, it was Miley. If she saw a light or a lens, she ran toward it. A live audience was even better.

As a tiny little girl, if she was at one of my shows, I had to make sure she was locked in my dressing room with the nanny. Otherwise, if she made it out to the sound board, sooner or later she would find a way to get on the stage.

We have a classic picture of Miley when she was two years old. She's no bigger than a popcorn fart, and all done up in a pretty little dress. It was 1994, and we were in Memphis, taping an hourlong tribute to Elvis for a TV special. Miley was backstage with A.J. But somehow she broke out at the end of the show and found her way onstage as Tony Bennett, Eddie Rabbitt, the Jordanaires, the Sweet Inspirations, and I started the encore number, "Amazing Grace."

I couldn't see her from where I was, but I sensed a commotion and saw someone in the wings put his hand to his face in horror and say something about a little girl on the loose. I knew it was Miley, and I was right. One of the Sweet Inspirations caught her and they took turns passing her from one to another. Then one of the Jordanaires scooped her up. She sang into the microphone of whoever held her. But she kept breaking loose. By the end of the last chorus, Miley was in Tony Bennett's arms.

"You've got a special little girl here," he said as he handed her over to me at the end of the song.

People kept saying that about her. And we saw it, too. I knew she could sing from about the time she began making sounds. She also came downstairs with her little guitar whenever any of my friends were over and asked them to teach her how to play their songs. She was hungry to learn.

I can still picture as if it were yesterday, that time Miley asked Waylon Jennings to show her how to play "Good Hearted Woman," though I crack up because of what happened with Noah. See, we were all in the kitchen: me, Tish, Braison in the corner, Miley, and Noah, who was being cradled by Waylon's wife, Jessi. Then, as Miley practiced the chords, Waylon asked to hold the baby.

"You want to hold Cod?" I asked.

I had given Noah the nickname, after codfish.

Waylon ignored my question as he took Noah from Jessi and gazed at her with amazement and adoration.

"Don't call this baby Cod," he said with a loud chortle, which set off a chain reaction of laughter.

"I told him to quit calling her that," Tish chimed in.

"It's Cod, like a codfish," I said.

"No one gets the fish part," Waylon said.

I laughed. "Actually, Cod is Doc backwards."

As Jesse smiled, Waylon shook his head and said, "I'd stick with Noah."

During *Doc*'s first season, we went to New York, where we took Miley to the play *Mamma Mia!* During the show, she hugged me and whispered, "That's what I wanna do, Daddy." There was no holding her back. For the next three years I was in Toronto, Miley studied acting with Canada's most respected coaches, including Dean Armstrong, who was also one of the stars on the hit TV series *Queer as Folk*.

Eventually Miley left her school in Nashville to study full-time in Toronto. She appeared on several episodes. Periodically, she and Tish flew to L.A. for auditions and casting calls. Miley seemed to know her path from the start.

None of our other kids wanted to get into the business, but Noah still stood in when we needed Gracie. She loved being on *Doc*, and I loved seeing her on the show. I still smile when I picture her at three and four years old, practicing her lines. That little face and her adorable smile.

The episode "Blindsided" was kind of her coming out. In it, Dr. Herbert thinks he's going blind. Due to high blood pressure, he's self-diagnosed himself as having early signs of glaucoma. With his vision fading fast, he comes to me, crying, and says all he wants is to see his little girl's recital. If only God will let him hang on to his eyesight long enough to see Gracie dance.

It had all the emotion of *Brian's Song*, especially when it crescendoed at the recital, where he was able to see her onstage. I was next to him in the audience. As tears welled up in his eyes, I stared at him and noticed his shirt collar was too tight. It was choking him. I reached up and unbuttoned his shirt. We sat there while Gracie's show finished. I didn't say anything else.

Afterward, as we congratulated Gracie, I made a couple of hand gestures and noticed my friend saw them.

"Is your vision coming back to you, Dr. Herbert?" I asked. "How'd you know I put up two fingers?"

"I don't know, Clint," he said. "This is actually the first time that my head has not been hurting bad. I could see Gracie fine. What is happening?"

"Well, I just remember there was one little thing I learned back in my senior year of medical school," I said. "If your shirt is too tight, your vision starts to go."

It was true. And it was a light ending to a heavy episode.

As Tish will attest, I was crazy about little Noah. I knew she was going to be the last kid we'd have, and I'd vowed that every second I wasn't working I was going to be playing with that child, holding her, laughing with her, just being a good daddy.

After 9/11, I made a deal with Pax that I could use their network jet (with the *Touched by an Angel* logo on the tail) twice a month to fly back home. When I arrived, I'd take Noah to a place near our front gate where I'd put a picnic table and hung a rope swing from a giant tree branch. It was on a bluff where the property's original homestead had been a hundred years earlier. I'd push her for hours.

We shot her swinging and playing in that exact spot in the video for "Face of God" from my gospel album, *The Other Side*. I didn't write it, so I can brag about what a magnificent song it was, and still is.

I had high hopes for *The Other Side*. It came on the heels of *Time Flies*, an album I did for a small label in the middle of *Doc* that sadly got lost in the shuffle. *The Other Side* was on an even smaller label, one that specialized in Christian music. I wasn't writing many songs then. Actually, in terms of music, the show had kind of paralyzed my ability to write new songs.

Then one day I wrote "The Other Side," the only religious song I can lay claim to. I thought since God gave me an original song, He must be wanting me to cut an album. Right after, I got a call from producer Billy Joe Walker Jr. asking if I wanted to make a gospel album.

I had wanted to do a tribute to my dad for a long time. With *Doc* nearing the end of its five-season run, it was a great time in my career to say thank you to both my dad and God for allowing me this wonderful journey.

The album impressed some critics, like *Country Standard Time*'s Dan MacIntosh, who wrote, "[W]ith *The Other Side*, [Billy Ray Cyrus] deserves credit for doing a spiritual album the right way, because this 'other' side is also one of his better sides." Unfortunately, others on the gospel side of the business viewed me as an imposter and treated me as such. In a couple of instances, I'd never been treated ruder.

At times, I felt like my effort to do something different had unleashed Satan's fury. But I stuck to my message, the same one Papaw Cyrus had preached every Sunday in his church: Christianity isn't about being perfect. It's about realizing that we're all human, and that's why God sent his son to this earth — to save people like us.

It was a Sunday. I was in my condo in Toronto. *Doc* had run its course. We'd looked at the end of the series after I failed in my bid to get them to move production to Nashville. If that had worked out, I'd probably still be Dr. Clint Cassidy. I didn't want the show to end; I just couldn't handle the commute anymore. It was hard on my family, and it took me too far from the essence of my being, which was music.

For whatever reason, I hadn't written any songs in ages. But then I found myself on this rare Sunday. I say *rare* because I already knew my lines for the next day. My homework was done. And with Tish and the kids at home in Nashville, I didn't have anything to do.

I picked up my guitar like I used to do and almost immediately wrote "Wanna Be Your Joe," a song about a guy whose only goal was to be a good husband to his wife and father to his kids. I remember strumming my guitar, shutting my eyes, and feeling a yearning to get back to basics.

> *Joe works at the steel mill*
> *Works damn near every day*
> *Leaves for work when the sun comes up*
> *Drops the kids at school along the way*

When the night is falling
He gets home and hugs his wife
He says how much he missed her
And that he loves her more than life, yeah
More than life . . .

Joe will never be a rich man
No lawyer or movie star.
He may not own the finest jewelry
And he may not drive the nicest car
Joe has everything he's ever dreamed of
All the treasures that he needs
No wonder Joe is always smiling
He only aims to please, yeah

Let me be your Joe
Just want to love you and watch our babies grow
I may not be no millionaire
But I want you to know
I wanna be your Joe

You are just a woman
And I am just a man
Though I may not fill every need
I hope you understand

I wanna be your Joe
I wanna be your Joe
Let me be your Joe
Just wanna love you and watch our babies grow

I may not be no millionaire
But I want you to know
I wanna be your Joe
Let me be your Joe
Just want to love you
Just want to be your man
Just want to hold you
Love you with all that I am

I wanna be your Joe
Let me be your Joe
Wanna be your Joe

There was no mistaking the thoughts in my head. That afternoon, still feeling good about that song, I turned on the TV to celebrate. I was curious about the Boston Red Sox–New York Yankees playoff series, and the game was on. It might've been the first baseball game I'd watched in years. *Doc* — and everything else — kept me too busy.

Anyway, Red Sox outfielder Johnny Damon stepped up to the plate. I didn't know who Johnny Damon was at that point, but I saw him and all of a sudden couldn't take my eyes off him . . . or, specifically, his mullet. No one was in my room, but I started to say, "That dude's got a mullet!" It was a damn good mullet, too. It started me thinking about how much simpler my life had been when I had one myself, back in the days before "Achy Breaky Heart."

Instinctively, I grabbed my guitar, hit some chords, and started to sing:

I want my mullet back
My ol' Camaro and my eight-track
Fuzzy dice hangin' loose an' proud
ZZ Top, they're playin' loud.
A simple time, that's what I miss
Your miniskirt an' your sweet kiss
Things are changin', man, and that's a fact
I want my mullet back!

I had so much fun cranking on that riff, I went ahead and wrote more verses. In one, I threw in a line about Skynyrd, and in another I added a reference to Bob Seger. It was as much fun as I had ever had writing a song, and it was all true. I wished times could be a lot more simple. Who doesn't?

Terry Shelton and I were already at work on a new album, and "I

Want My Mullet Back" fit right in. We had a few songs, including "The Freebird Fell," my tribute to Skynyrd and Ronnie Van Zant (cowritten with the band's Ed King and Artimus Pyle), and "Country Music Has the Blues," which I credited partially to Trace just because he liked to hang out with me and the band and help us out.

The cool thing about "Country Music Has the Blues" was that Loretta Lynn and George Jones came in and recorded vocals, giving the song just the right touch of credibility. Loretta had just done an album with Jack White, and I thought, why don't I do anything cool like that? Probably because I didn't ask. So I asked Loretta, who said, "Billy Ray, I haven't seen you since our tour buses crossed paths in Branson."

And George and I had been friends for a few years. In 1999, his wife, Nancy, had interviewed Tish for her book *Nashville Wives*, and the next thing I knew, Tish hung up the phone one day and told me that George and Peanut — his best friend and driver — wanted to know if they could come over and hang out.

"Are you serious?" I said. "George Jones wants to come over?"

A few years later, I was taking George through our house and he saw the letter Johnny Cash had sent me. He was impressed.

"Where were you when you met Johnny?" he asked.

"I've never met him," I said. "And it saddens me. I always wanted to thank him personally."

"You've never met Johnny Cash and he wrote you this letter?" he said, incredulous.

"No, sir," I said. "And it saddens me. I always wanted to thank him personally."

George looked at Peanut and scratched his head.

"Peanut, isn't Johnny at the bookstore tonight signing books?" he asked. "The store down in Franklin?"

"Yeah, I think he is," Peanut said.

A moment later, George and Peanut were taking me to meet Johnny Cash. I remember asking myself, "How in the hell did my life get this crazy? I'm in the truck with the legendary George Jones, drivin' down the same highway where he infamously drove his lawn mower to the liquor store, and now he's taking me to meet another legend, Johnny Cash. I'm going to thank him for writing me a letter. It's too crazy." But hey, it was true.

"I'm proud to meet you, Cyrus," he said. "Just keep doing what you're doing and make your music because you love it."

"Yes, sir," I replied, thinking how cool it was that Johnny Cash had just called me Cyrus.

"And look at these fans," he added, casting his eyes down the long line of people waiting to meet him. "If you treat your music right and treat your fans right, they'll both always be there for you."

"Yes, sir. Well, I better let you get to 'em."

As I turned and walked away, I knew I was saying goodbye to country music royalty. But I kept thinking about the advice Johnny had given me. Treat your music right and take care of the fans. I was fixing to do just that with my next album, *Left-handed*, which Terry and I had already begun. It was going to be about me getting back to my roots with country music and some fun, bar-boogie rock like I used to play at the Ragtime. "I Want My Mullet Back" was so into that groove, and it made me excited about finishing the album. *Doc* was going to be done in a few weeks. Only a few more weeks. And then I figured I'd go back on the road. I'd play music for the fans and be in the band for the rest of my life.

I couldn't have been more wrong.

PART IV

Left-handed

CHAPTER 27

"She's Hannah Montana"

HOME WAS PERFECT. How lucky was I to be able to say that? *Home was perfect.* It was. After *Doc* wrapped, I felt welcomed back to the farm by my family and even more so, it seemed, by the land itself. My dirt bike and ATV four-wheelers were lined up waiting for me, as were my horses. Whenever I had a chance, I saddled up one of my Tennessee Walkers and reacquainted myself with the trails.

Out there I saw deer, a handful of giant bucks that believed they had as much if not more claim to this land as me, a flock of wild turkeys, and various birds, including a hawk that would sit on a hay bail and train its penetrating eyes on me. Our cow always made me laugh. He hung out with the horses . . . and probably thought he was one.

To understand me, you have to understand my relationship to this land, to the feeling I had when I first arrived on this property and said to myself, "Cyrus, you're home." I was fortunate to understand that about myself. It allowed me to mature as a man without losing the boy inside me. I identified with philosopher Henry David Thoreau, who famously said, "I went to the woods because I wished to live deliberately, to front only the essential facts of life, and see if

I could not learn what it had to teach, and not, when I came to die, discover that I had not lived."

There, at home, I could pull my family around me and take care of them. I wasn't a perfect parent. I wasn't perfect in any situation. But God had allowed me a wonderful space that reminded me of the woods I used to play in when I was a little boy. The land taught me important lessons about the basics of life, reminded me of the inevitable cycles of change and renewal, and let me feel closer to God.

I think it did the same for the rest of the family. The kids had favorite trees, they rode horses, and chased butterflies. They loved the outdoors.

So I was thrilled to enter, or re-enter, this Jeremiah Johnson phase. I didn't care what I looked like. Without cameras pointed at me every day, that stuff didn't matter anymore. For me, it was just about being at home with my family, playing with the kids, watching the grass grow, the leaves change, riding horses, being one with my Heavenly Father, my Mother Earth, writing songs, and working on *Left-handed*.

Some music writers had criticized me for chasing trends. I disagreed. Except for the one album where I gave in to the record label, I felt like the only music I'd chased was the music in me. It was an imprecise science where the goal was to first please myself, then hopefully other people.

As I wrote more songs, I felt good about *Left-handed*. It had the promise of being something special. Then something else happened, something unexpected, something special in its own right that took all of us in a different direction altogether.

Tish and Miley were in California for some casting calls when agent Mitchell Gossett gave them a script for a new Disney Channel TV series called *Hannah Montana*. It was about a girl who lives a double life as an ordinary teenager by day and a pop star by night. Miley was going to read for the second lead, Lilly. She and Tish brought the script home. They were both excited.

One day I picked it up, only intending to read a few pages. They'd gone through Lilly's part with a pink highlighter. I read all the way through to the end because something obvious jumped out at me: The main character had two names. One was Hannah Montana. The other was Kiley Stewart.

I didn't pretend to know much about TV or Hollywood. As my dad liked to say, I was just a boy from Kentucky. But before I finished the script, I knew Miley wasn't Lilly. No way. She was Kiley. More than that, she was Hannah Montana.

I found Tish.

"Did you say all this stuff underlined in pink here? I mean, was Miley reading for the part of Lilly?"

"Yeah," she said.

"Tish, Miley is Hannah Montana," I said. "She's reading for the wrong part."

"I don't think Miley's got the experience to carry it," Tish said. "And Disney feels the same way."

"Hell, man, have they heard her sing?" I asked.

"No, she hasn't sung for them," Tish said.

"Oh my God. We have got to get her on tape," I said. "Just let them hear her sing."

A song called "Goin' to the Beach This Weekend" had been floating around as a demo, and Tish and I took Miley to a studio and put her on the track. We sent it to Disney, and their reaction was exactly as I expected. *Holy crap! Let's get her back out here.* Tish and Miley returned to L.A., where she read for Kiley. They loved her. There was just one problem. They said she sings great, but she's too little. They said the girl had to be about fifteen. Miley was only twelve.

Tish and Miley returned home feeling defeated. I told them not to sweat it.

"Just you wait," I said. "If Disney doesn't change their mind, they're making a huge mistake. Miley is Hannah Montana. I know it like I know the sky is blue and the grass is green. Some things just are, and this is one of them. I can feel it. Just wait. It's meant to be."

They weren't as sure.

• • •

Time passed. Three months. Six months. Then the agent called Tish and told her that Disney hasn't been able to stop thinking about Miley. In fact, they were considering rewriting the show so Kiley Stewart / Hannah Montana could be a little bit younger. Assuming Miley had probably matured some since they'd seen her, they asked if Tish would bring her back out to L.A. for another look.

Tish told Miley the happy news, and she burst into my office like a bolt of lightning.

"Daddy, I got a callback!" she exclaimed. "They want to see me for Hannah Montana!"

I gave her a hug and said, "That is so cool, baby." I saw Tish over her shoulder. She was smiling. I gave her a hug, too.

"I'll stay here with Braison and Noah," I said. "You guys go do your thing."

Even with Disney stuck on her, Miley read with another dozen or two girls. In the next round, that number was reduced to eight or ten. Then one day I was out in the woods when my cell phone rang. It was Tish. She said that Disney Channel president Gary Marsh was really taken with Miley. She was green as grass, he said, but he saw something in her eyes that made him think she had big potential. He had used the word *star*. According to Tish, though, he also wanted to know if I'd consider playing the dad, Robbie, if Miley was Hannah Montana.

I could hear the eagerness in Tish's voice. I wish I could say I shared it.

"I don't know," I said.

I'd told myself I wasn't going to do another series. I wanted to play music.

"You don't know?" she asked.

"This thing is going to be big," I said. "I can feel it. And I don't know if I want to tie into something like that again."

I had other concerns, too. Finally, I told Tish that I'd call her back later that evening. Then I did my usual thing. I rode my horse up to the top of the hill, sat by the fire, and prayed. When I spoke to Tish again, I felt much clearer. I explained: "You have to tell them that it ain't fair to Miley or to none of those other girls to put my name in the sentence right now. As it stands, my answer is no. The first thing they have to do is decide who is Hannah Montana. I never want Miley to look back and say she did or didn't get the part on account of me. If Miley ends up being Hannah, certainly, I'll consider the other role. But for right now, at this moment, my answer is no."

After more than ten years of marriage, Tish knew short answers weren't in my repertoire. Nor were they in God's.

She told the producers how I operated, that I played everything by ear, and eventually we'd know if it was meant to be. The casting of Hannah Montana came down to two girls — Miley and another girl with more television experience. Folks at Disney were split, but finally Gary Marsh chose Miley. Later, in an interview with *The Hollywood Reporter,* the Disney executive recalled sending an e-mail that said, "Our job is not to make shows. It's to build franchises and stars. We may have a drink a few years from now and talk about whether we made the right choice, but I'm saying to you that we're going to hire Miley."

Then they focused on me. They wanted me to read for the part of Robbie, Miley's daddy. I was hesitant. I agreed to fly out, but I said, "I'll come on out, but let's play it by ear and see how it feels." I wanted to follow protocol. What if I wasn't good? What if Miley and I didn't have the right chemistry? What if there was someone better? In fact, when I showed up, some handsome dude was just walking out of an audition, and I flat out told Gary Marsh they didn't need to see me anymore. "Her father just walked out of here," I said. "Put my child with that guy and y'all got a hit TV show."

Gary and the other producers laughed. They continued to laugh as I ran a couple of scenes from the pilot with Miley. Our chemistry was unmistakable, as you might expect. We were father and daughter. There was some type of magic in our realism, I guess. A fun energy filled the room. Then Miley threw a curve ball. "Dad, you've got to sing them the song 'I Want My Mullet Back.'"

"What's 'I Want My Mullet Back'?" one of them asked.

"Oh, it's just this song I recorded," I said. "It's going to be on my new album."

"Dad, let's sing it," Miley said.

Before I could say yes or no, she began snapping her fingers and started to sing the words. I had no choice but to join in. And it's hard to describe what happened in that room, but everyone clapped when we finished. It was a special moment. It was magic.

We left and went to a studio where Miley was going to sing a song for the show. Possibly the theme song. But I really don't remember. My agent, Mitchell Gossett, had called me on the way and said, "They loved ya!" I wasn't sure, but I nonchalantly said, "Well, if it's meant to be, then it'll happen. If it ain't, it won't."

I was at the studio only about ten minutes when I saw a nice, shiny car pull up. The door opened and none other than Gary Marsh got out. He was all smiles when he found me. He stretched out his hand and said, "Let's make a hit TV show."

"Are you serious?"

He was.

"Can you stay out here?" he asked. "We're shooting the pilot in a week."

We stayed, and during that week we rehearsed the show, and two significant changes were made. One, Robbie inherited a middle name, Ray. He became Robbie Ray. And two, I kept calling Kiley Miley, until finally someone threw up their hands and said, "From now on, everything that is Kiley is going to be Miley." And the rest, as the say in Hollywood, is history.

CHAPTER 28

Spirit Mountain

IT'S NOT EASY TO lose a parent, to suffer the permanent absence of a loved one, and to simultaneously experience your own climb up the ladder of mortality. I learned that my dad had cancer at the same time I was finishing the pilot for *Hannah Montana*. He called and wanted me to come visit him. He had something he wanted to tell me in person.

Needless to say I cried the whole way there.

It was not the first time I had confronted death. In one of my craziest moves ever, I arranged for Tish's deceased father, Glenmore, to be reburied on our property. I realize this seems as nuts as George Jones taking his lawn mower to the liquor store. It was also a complete surprise to Tish.

Glenmore and his wife were the angels who adopted my wife when she was a baby. Theirs was one the greatest love stories I ever heard. They met on a Wednesday, got married on a Friday, and never spent a day without each other. They never missed one of Tish's dance recitals or a game where she was on the sidelines as a cheerleader. For some reason, though, Tish's grandmother hated Glenmore. Tish said they couldn't be in the same room together.

However, after Glenmore died of cancer (Tish was eighteen and pregnant with Brandi, who was named Brandi Glen after him), he was buried next to his mother-in-law. It wasn't enough that she tortured him when they were alive. Now she'd do it for eternity. Tish was so bothered by it she couldn't bring herself to visit his grave.

After a few years, I had an idea that I thought would help Tish. I'd exhumed Glenmore and rebury him up on Spirit Mountain. I wanted it to be a surprise for Tish. We were heading into Christmastime, and one day when Tish and I were up on Spirit Mountain I said, "Wouldn't it be great if Glenmore had been buried here?"

She nodded wistfully and said, "If he was, I could bring him flowers."

To me, she was really saying it might ease a lot of other things going on, some of the wounds she carried from the past, if he was here.

And that led me to Mammy, who was keeper of the will. I asked what she thought of moving Glenmore.

"It's a great idea," she said. "It's one of the craziest ideas I've heard, too. Can you really make that happen?"

Once I get behind an idea, I feel like I can move mountains to make it happen. Having a good lawyer also helps. My lawyer drew up papers, had Loretta sign all the proper forms, and then got my land approved as a state-registered cemetery, officially known as the Cyrus Family Cemetery.

So now Glenmore had his passport to come to Tennessee. On Christmas Eve, I rented a backhoe and a neighbor helped me dig the hole. Early the next morning, before anyone in my family was awake, Glenmore arrived at the gate in the back of a hearse. Since I knew about what time he was expected, I was up waiting on him.

It was beautiful. I was laughing to myself as I saw him through the security camera. Here comes Glenmore, I thought. I also wondered if I was crazy. It was the crack of dawn. Everybody was asleep. I bundled up and led the hearse up the hill and we got him all buried. I put a bunch of those red Christmas flowers on his freshly covered grave. I got it all beautiful and even dug up a little Christmas tree from the woods and put it nearby.

When I got back to the house, Tish was waking up. Knowing the kids were going to sleep for another hour or two, if not longer, I told her that Santa Claus had a surprise for her.

"Walk outside and let me show you something," I said.

"What are you up to?" she asked.

She knew my favorite part about Christmas was planning a surprise.

"Just come out with me," I insisted. "And dress warm."

Tish is not an especially outdoorsy person, so going outside in the cold on Christmas morning was not her ideal way of starting the day. I think she figured that I'd bought her a new car. Even then, she was reluctant to brave the cold. But I got her to bundle up and walk with me. Sure enough, as we started across the field, she asked, "Why do we have to walk out here on Christmas morning?"

"Because it's Christmas morning," I said. "It's beautiful. It's just me and you, a couple of kids from Kentucky out here in this incredible land, on this incredibly beautiful morning."

By this time she knew something was up. She thought I was taking her to the teepee. But we passed the teepee and rounded the corner. Then, after a few steps, she stopped. She saw the large rock on which I'd painted, I AM HERE NOW, a reference to a song off my *Trail of Tears* album that she loved, GLENMORE FINLEY 1922–1986.

"You didn't?" she said, as tears began to fill her eyes.

"Yes, ma'am, I did," I replied, grinning like a mischievous little boy.

"I can't believe it," she said before wrapping her arms around me. "I mean you're crazy. I love you. But you're crazy. Did you have him —"

"I did," I said.

"When?" she asked.

"He drove over this morning," I said.

"He drove?"

"Well, he didn't," I said. "But I saw him at the gate . . . and they opened up . . ."

She laughed. "This is really pretty crazy."

"I don't know," I said with a shrug. "If you ask me" — and I looked around — "this is kind of what Heaven's supposed to be like, right?"

She wrapped her arms around me and planted a big kiss on my lips. "Right."

Cletis is buried a little bit down the hill from Glenmore. He got sick in late 1997 from smoking and died from COPD — chronic obstructive pulmonary disease — or emphysema. That was not a good way to go, but at least the years he spent living in Tennessee were happy ones.

After we moved to the farm, Cletis and my mom took over my log cabin on Snead Road. I had already given them that place when we moved into the big A-frame, and Kebo got our boyhood home at 2317 Long Street. By then, Ruthie had become famous in her own right. All my fans knew Ruthie. Some days she had a hundred people from all over the world lined up in front of her house, waiting to see her.

My aunt Mary was lonely after her first husband passed away and she loved it when people came to her trailer. She remarried a wonderful man who I called Uncle Marlin, and both of them enjoyed the company of fans. She built a shrine to me and would send pictures of people standing in her trailer next to posters of me. I'd see 'em with their arm around a cardboard cutout, holding a bag of Fritos. It was hilarious.

But you know, God bless her and all those folks. People need company. I'm all for anyone feeling a little less lonely.

Cletis, in his retirement years, became very comfortable. He sat out by the pool, under a shade tree that he liked a lot. There were two ponds stocked with the hugest catfish ever. He never cast a line. He only liked to throw them corn. Every morning and every evening he went out there and fed them. He would take Miley and the kids down there and let them feed the fish. He was a great grandfather.

I admired Cletis as much as any man I ever met. He could've

turned his back on me real quick. If someone had been as mean and disrespectful as I had been, I would've said eventually enough of this shit. But he stayed with me. After I'd made it, I thanked him. I said, "You didn't have to love me. But you did anyway."

Another thing about Cletis. With all due respect to my dad, he was the hardest-working man I knew. After the railroad laid him off, he worked nonstop on other things, like driving or loading trucks. If he wasn't doing that, he was in the driveway fixing my piece-of-shit car, my minibike, his truck, or the neighbor's car. He was always busy, always fixing something.

People from all over Flatwoods would bring him their cars. I swear he was the greatest mechanic in the area. He never charged anyone. He liked to fix things. In some ways, he even fixed me and my broken family.

I was standing by his bed in Centennial Hospital when he took his last breath. He was sitting there, gasping for air. I remember reaching out and taking hold of his hand. He was in a great deal of pain. It was not a comforting sight. And then he left us. Everyone was brokenhearted but relieved after it was over. I'm sure that included Cletis. If ever there was a man who was ready to go, it was him. That disease was doing some ugly stuff to him, and it was worse because he knew what was going on. Cletis suffered.

If he had any comfort, it was that he knew where he was going to rest after he passed. He and my mom had picked their spot up on Spirit Mountain. They had begun to prepare it long before he was hospitalized. Cletis knew there was a big buck that liked to hang out in that area, and to this day, around sunset, that buck will hang around his headstone, as if he's come to watch over a kindred spirit.

My mom goes up there several times a day to pull out the weeds and keep it manicured. If there's bird poop on the marble, she cleans it off. She gets a great deal of comfort when she goes on top of that hill. Just like me. Both of us love that place.

I have it in my will that within twenty-four hours of my death I must be cremated and returned to dust. The kids won't have to hassle with anything. They won't have to worry about where to put me. They'll take me up to Spirit Mountain and sprinkle me over this pile of stuff I've found out in the field — arrowheads, tomahawks, and even a piece of a meteorite that I picked up one day while I was playing with the kids when they were little.

I've already placed a marble bust of an Indian chief in the center of that pile. I brought that bust home from Arizona years ago after I made the video for "In the Heart of a Woman." It never fit properly in the house, and then one day it hit me. "It's going to be my grave marker." Yes, indeed. And I put it on my four-wheeler, rode it up the mountain, set it down amid all the rocks and bones the kids and I had found over the years. I knew for certain that was the spot that would be my home for eternity.

I know that when I'm spread over the ground up there I'll be returned to the best days of my life: the days when I rode horses and and dirt bikes with the kids, turned rocks into treasures, roasted marshmallows and wieners by the fire, watched a mother hawk teach its babies to fly, saw a herd of deer run across the field, and stared up at the Big Dipper.

I think about death more than most people, but I don't know what it means other than life ends and another journey begins. I do believe in a heaven and hell. I believe in a soul. And I believe life is about doing good works on earth. I think we're supposed to live for the light. What's the light? The light is goodness. Try to be a good person. Try to help out. The Bible says, "As you sow, so shall you reap."

My dad really took that to heart. Helping people was the essence of his life, and nothing made him happier than when we started the Billy Ray Cyrus Foundation. We set one goal for ourselves: to help the underdog. My dad loved having the funds that I could generate with benefit concerts. When he heard the Boy's Home in Ashland had burned down, he got involved and we were able to rebuild it.

Likewise, when a little boy from Paducah was paralyzed in a car wreck, we got him a specially equipped van and a computer pad for his wheelchair so he could go to school. Such efforts made it easy to call on friends such as Dolly Parton, who performed at our second benefit. In 1999, I played a show in Arkansas the night before a tornado wiped out the little town of Mulhall, Oklahoma. One of the strongest on record, it literally erased the small town.

Instead of going home, I called my dad and asked if we could get the wheels up on the foundation. We had created it to help people in eastern Kentucky, but I wanted to head to Mulhall and clean out every Walmart on the way. My dad gave me the green light.

My bus pulled into the little town around noon the day after the tornado. I had never seen anything like the destruction the town's residents were facing. They were in shock. Every square inch of space on my bus was packed with food and water and diapers.

Kids ran over. Their parents and other adults were happy that someone cared. And if my dad's years of public service taught me anything, it's the importance of showing up and showing you care. You figure out the rest.

My dad was proud of me. I was even prouder of him. He taught me that we were all put here for a reason: to give back to our fellow man. We both shared a passion for helping others. I think as far as accomplishments go, the Billy Ray Cyrus Charities Foundation was one of the most significant.

Cut to summer 2004. I was playing Renfro Valley, Kentucky, and my dad showed up with his best friend, a man named Woody. He and Woody rode horses in Kentucky. My dad was robust and aging gracefully. But something about him looked off. He was pale and moving slowly, like he was uncomfortable, and he seemed like he'd lost some weight.

"A little under the weather," he said. "I think a copperhead might've bit me one day when I was out riding."

"Wouldn't you know if you got bit by a snake?" I asked.

"I go through them woods," he replied. "It's tough to say. Something else might've got me. Maybe a spider. I don't know."

A little more than a year later I went to his house in Cave Run. He and my stepmom had a little cabin out in the woods of the Daniel

Boone National Forest. As I said earlier, he wanted to talk to me in person, and I knew it wasn't good. I knew I was going to get the truth about my dad's health, not another snakebite story.

When I flew out from California, I found him in bed — although the man I saw there bore very little resemblance to my dad. Propped up on his pillows, he looked me in the eye and told me that he had been diagnosed with mesothelioma, a rare but virulent form of the disease that's caused by exposure to asbestos. It's like lung cancer but worse.

Back when he was in the Kentucky legislature, my dad had fought hard to get an experimental cancer-fighting drug called Laetrile legalized. It was made from apricot seeds. At the time, desperate people were going to Mexico to get it. The bill didn't pass, but it was the hardest thing I'd ever seen my dad fight for and lose, until he began his own battle against cancer.

Against my wishes, he decided on treatment with the world's leading specialist in mesothelioma at Dana-Farber Cancer Institute in Boston. Why was I against it? Chemotherapy. Although I understood that his doctor was number one, I'd never seen chemo do anything but tear people down. I didn't know how much time he had left, but I knew I wanted it to be quality time.

My dad appreciated my opinion. He investigated all the alternatives I provided. In the end, though, it was his call.

Meanwhile, Disney picked up the *Hannah Montana* pilot and ordered a series. We moved out west. I sold the land on Snead Road — the A-frames and the log cabin — for the exact amount we spent on a house with a little red door in La Cañada, a nice family neighborhood in the hills above Pasadena. I had sticker shock from that transaction. I'd traded thirty-two lush, green acres of pure heaven for a sandbox in the desert. Such was real estate in La-la-land. But Tish and the kids loved that new house, and I was content as long as I didn't owe anyone a dime, which I didn't.

As we started making episodes, I visited my dad at the hospital in Boston. One weekend in the late fall we watched a baseball game together. I played him the songs I wrote for *Left-handed*. He got a kick out of "I Want My Mullet Back." "Kids are going to love that," he said. He was right, too. It was on *Hannah Montana,* and the kids thought it was great. The last song I ever played him was called "Hey Daddy." It was off the *Joe* album. As he listened to it, especially a part in the beginning of the track when you can hear a little girl playing in the background, I saw a tear come down his cheek. "Is that Noah in the beginning?" he said in a weak voice, because by then he was on heavy chemo. I said, "Yeah," and we held each other's gaze. He enjoyed one last Christmas and New Year's. But while I never gave up hope and he never quit battling, he faded quickly.

My dad, the former steel-mill worker who went back to school and served eleven terms in the Kentucky House of Representatives, died on February 28, 2006.

We were on the *Hannah* set, filming what was the twelfth episode. Titled "On the Road Again," the story had Miley realizing that her dad Robbie Ray had once been a famous country star before quitting his career to focus on hers. She plots to get him back on the road again, and the story culminates with Miley and her brother, Jackson (Jason Earles), surprising Robbie at his gig. And guess what they help him sing? "I Want My Mullet Back." All of them wear mullet wigs, too.

Right before we began shooting the last scene — the performance of "I Want My Mullet Back" — someone from production called me over to the side and said I had an emergency call from home. I said, "It's my dad, ain't it?"

They said, "Yeah. He passed away."

I had to tell Miley. I didn't think it was fair to shoot the scene and break the news to her afterward. She'd seen them tell me, and she knew. She came to me, and I held her, not saying anything, just holding her. Finally, she said, "It's Pappy, isn't it?" I nodded, and the two of us sat on the side of the stage for a while, staring quietly into a fog of sadness.

Some of the producers came by and said they understood we probably needed to leave. We could pick up the following week, whenever we were ready. I appreciated that and thought about what we should do. Miley watched me, as kids do, knowing me better than I knew myself.

"What would Pappy say?" she asked.

"You don't want to know," I said.

"I do," she said. "Tell me."

"He'd say, 'The show must go on.'"

Miley high-fived me and stood up like a four-star general, calling out, "Come on, people! We got a show to do!" And we did the last scene.

After finishing the episode, Miley and I drove home in my old gray Range Rover. The whole family met up at the house and I got a private plane to take us back to Kentucky for the service and burial.

Unbeknownst to Tish or any of the kids, I packed the mullet wig I'd worn on the *Hannah Montana* episode. I knew there might be some sad moments with the family in the hotel and I wanted that wig in case the kids needed a lift, which they did.

On the morning of my dad's funeral, everybody was pretty distraught. As we got ready in our hotel room, some of the kids were crying and the others were on the brink. I slipped into the bathroom to get dressed for the service and came out wearing that mullet, acting like everything was normal. The family stared at me like, *Are you kidding?* But it lifted their spirits a little. It was something my dad would've done, and for that moment he was there, in that room, smiling with us.

After the service, I drove from the church to the cemetery to help lay my dad in the ground. He loved my property and the view from Spirit Mountain, but he wanted to be buried with his mom and dad at the Cyrus family cemetery in Louisa, Kentucky. However, when I got there, I saw they had dug a hole on the wrong side of the hill.

It turned out some family members didn't like the scenery from where he would've laid next to his mom and dad and brothers and sisters, so they put him elsewhere. I went ballistic. The reason he wanted his final resting spot there was to be next to his mom and dad.

"We can't do this now, Bo," one of my relatives told me. "The hole has been dug. Everyone is here. The service must go on."

I was so mad I didn't know what to say and, to be honest, I'll probably never get over it. I still get upset thinking about it. But a good friend once comforted me by reminding me my dad isn't there: "He's in Heaven with his mom and dad and sisters and brothers. It doesn't matter what side of the hill he's on. He made it to the top of the mountain. He's home."

About a week later, I had to go back to my farm to take care of a few things. I noticed the light on the phone answering machine was blinking. I hit PLAY and heard a message my dad had left after one of my visits with him the previous fall. He said that he'd enjoyed seeing me, hoped the TV series went well, and mentioned something about being able to hear all those cheers from right over that wall at Fenway Park.

"I'm doing fair to middlin'," he said. "I'm OK. Bye-bye now, buddy . . . I love ya . . ."

CHAPTER 29

———◆◆◆◆———

Dancing Fool

IN THE WAKE OF losing my dad, I realized his wisdom would always be a part of me, like my mom's sense of humor, the music I grew up hearing and loving from as far back as I can remember, the voices I heard and let guide me, as did my papaw and my dad — and, well, it always came back to music. It always would.

Even with a hit TV series, I was still about the music. No matter which direction my career headed, I'd always call myself a singer-songwriter. As *Hannah Montana* took off, I saw an opportunity to marry acting and music. I had a satchel full of songs for my *Left-handed* album, and Disney had their own country music label, Lyric Street Records. It was a perfect example of synergy. I saw it as clear as the Big Dipper above my Tennessee farm on a cloudless night.

Except Lyric didn't bite. I couldn't figure out why. The songs were there. The TV show was red-hot. Old Robbie Ray (aka me) had a whole new audience. All the pieces were in place for a hit.

Hurt and disappointed, I signed with New Door Records, a small subsidiary of Universal Music. Was it a perfect match? No. But desperate men do desperate things, and I loved my music so much I was willing to get it out at almost any cost.

The cost ended up being significant. The New Door executives insisted on changes that erased the album's rootsy flavor and emotional rawness. Remember, this album began with me wailing on my guitar in my Toronto hotel room: "I want my mullet back . . ." But if I wanted to get the album out, I had no choice but to buy into their plan.

So we removed what I thought was the coolest part of "Wanna Be Your Joe" and changed the mix. We also gave "Country Music Has the Blues" a new slick sound. Then we dropped an old Mike Murphy tune called "Appalachian Lady" and a cover of Elvis Presley's "One Night with You" and instead added several new songs.

By the time we mixed, it had turned into a much different record than the one I'd envisioned. Even the name of the album was changed. Now it was called *Wanna Be Your Joe*.

Why did I agree to such compromises? Well, I had already begun writing my next album and I couldn't move forward creatively until those songs were released. It's the way my creativity flows — or doesn't.

Wanna Be Your Joe was released in July 2006. Neither of the two singles released even charted. It was the same old story: radio didn't care. I would've been destroyed if not for the fans. Regardless of what the industry thought, they helped the album debut at No. 24 on *Billboard*'s Top Country Albums chart and proved there was an appetite for my music.

Indeed, the music lived; it had a life of its own. I went on the road, and the band was rockin' and so were the fans, and that made every date on the whole summer tour worthwhile.

From my opening concert to the last sold-out show, at the Santa Monica Pier in September, I enjoyed the hell out of being on stage and seeing moms and dads and their moms and dads and little kids having as much fun as me.

One day, after the tour was finished, I was back home on the farm, visiting my mom. She was watching the news on TV and a story popped up about a local Special Forces soldier named James Ponder who'd been killed in Afghanistan. He left behind a wife and two daughters. Something about their family touched me and

I told my brother Mick, who helps me with stuff, to reach out to them and ask if they would like me to perform "Some Gave All" at his service. As soon as they replied, I was on my way.

At the service, I found out James had been a great daddy, an avid baseball fan, and a turkey hunter. Afterward, his wife and daughters gave me his dog tags as a remembrance.

Well, the following October, I was invited to sing the national anthem at the sixth game of the World Series in St. Louis. The Cardinals were playing the Detroit Tigers. Before leaving L.A. for the game, I remembered the young war hero had been a Cardinals fan. I slipped on his dog tags and wore them when I sang. His family appreciated the tribute; even better, the Cardinals won the series.

Later, I hung his dog tags on a tree at home near my teepee where a flock of wild turkeys hung out. They're still there.

They may be the only things from that time period that stayed put. In November 2006, Miley's *Hannah Montana* soundtrack album rocketed to No. 1. A day later, six songs from the album hit the charts — a record! No other artist had ever accomplished that feat.

We were beyond proud. Disney executive Gary Marsh reacted with an I-told-you-so grin. Explaining her appeal to the media, he said she had the likability of Hilary Duff and the talent of Shania Twain. Of course, the Disney machine had also launched Britney Spears, Christina Aguilera, and Justin Timberlake, and as far as I was concerned, Miley had the same qualities that made them superstars. She was exceptionally good and 100 percent unique.

Musically, she had been what I'd call a prodigy since she was a little girl asking my friends to teach her licks, and she'd gotten only better. She'd get up in the morning, ask me to fix her a cup of coffee "Pappy style," which meant with lots of milk and sugar, and then we'd get in the car and sing all the way to work. To this day, she sings the hell out of Johnny Cash's classic "A Boy Named Sue." I wish y'all could hear her right now — or see me smiling as I think about it.

As a daddy, I enjoyed a special sense of awe and pride, watching

Miley evolve into a world-class actress. She reminded me of a little Lucille Ball. In scenes where I had to laugh or smile at something she said, I'm laughing and smiling for real. I'm not good enough to fake it. She was always funny, and still is.

In those early days of the show, the writers watched the way Miley and I joked with each other and added it to the storyline. The humor on *Hannah Montana* was our real sense of humor. Miley would crack jokes about me, and I would put myself down. People laughed. Then she might take another swing at me. That was our shtick. We were daddy and daughter, best friends, and singing partners, and it played like a dream because it was genuine. I loved that in our serious world, brothers and sisters, moms and dads, papaws and mamaws, and aunts and uncles gathered around the TV and shared laughter. We were blessed for that to be our job.

But there was a price to pay for being a part of a phenomenon. No one knew that better than me. I'd seen the pitfalls of the circus; I'd stood in the center ring, and dang if the tent wasn't pitched in my backyard again. Hell, it was inside my home.

Suddenly the Cyrus family was going in all directions, like Jiffy Pop on the stove.

Phones rang nonstop.

Agents asked for meetings.

Publicists arranged photo shoots, interviews, and appearances.

It was the same circus I'd been a part of before; same circus, different clowns.

But I got swept up in the excitement, too. I'm no different than anyone else. That kind of excitement is hard to resist. It's impossible to resist. When you're on a rocket like "Achy Breaky Heart" or *Hannah Montana* and it's taking off, you only see opportunities. Everybody loves everybody. You don't see there's an elephant in the room that might get loose and stomp somebody's brains out.

Here's what we had in our favor. After the *Hannah* pilot had been shot and picked up, we had a week or so before we had to be in California to start making the series. Concerned about the abrupt and drastic changes our lives were about to undergo, Tish gathered everyone together in the kitchen and said, "This family is going to get baptized because we're going to be under attack in Hollywood."

That next Sunday, our car pulled up in front of the People's Church of Franklin in Spring Hill. We went inside and Trace, Miley, Braison, Noah, and Tish all took a dip proclaiming Jesus Christ the Son of God. Brandi had already been baptized. When my turn came, I asked the pastor, Rick White, a remarkable man, if I should do it since I'd also been baptized back when I was in high school.

"If you feel like you need to, go ahead," he said.

I stepped forward.

"I feel like I need to," I said. "A second dip surely couldn't hurt."

Tish's premonition was right on. Soon after *Hannah* premiered, our little house with the red door became a tourist attraction. Our doorbell rang nonstop. We moved to a larger place up the hill where we had more protection from the constant traffic and intrusions. But things continued to get crazy. One day Tish took Miley to the mall to get some new clothes, and within a few minutes the store was overrun with fans. Mall security closed the doors until the crowd could be cleared.

At home, we tried to keep life as normal as possible — at least we thought we did. We gave the kids chores and made sure we went to church on Sundays, but I suspect, in reality, we were holding on for dear life.

There weren't a lot of child-star or show-business families to serve as role models. The studios and agencies didn't hand out instruction manuals for parents. We did our best, but deep down both Tish and I knew normal was over. Miley was a worldwide superstar.

It took Tish and I working together to keep Miley grounded, and I think we did a good job. I just worried it wouldn't last. One Sunday, we were in church and Miley drew a little heart on my hand. It was so sweet, but I grew sad thinking how fleeting that bond we had might be as she grew up. "You know what?" I said.

"Today is your day to do whatever you want. This is going to be your day."

Miley, who could be sweet or spiritual or wild as a buck, just like me, took my hand, pointed to the heart she'd drawn, and grinned with a mischievousness that made me worry.

"Let's get that tattooed," she said.

"All right," I said. "You got a deal."

A few hours later, we'd found a tattoo parlor in Pasadena and I had her little heart on my hand for life. When that was finished, she led me to a hair salon on Ventura Boulevard called Whackos and gave the lady there instructions on how to style my big old head of hair. I left there with the craziest rock-and-roll highlights and a lasting memory of the two of us giggling till we were gasping for breath.

Like I said, I'm far from being a perfect father. But we spent time together that day. We lived and we laughed, and that was my goal. You don't forget those times, and I haven't.

Other memories are bittersweet. For instance, Miley was invited to a dance at a friend's school. After a long day of taping, Tish and I drove her there, hoping she'd have the sort of fun we remembered from school events. Tish had bought her a dress and done her hair, and she looked adorable, like a doll, as she followed other kids into the gym.

Tish and I held hands, watching in silence. I'm sure we shared the same thought. Miley had the same kind of double life as the character she played on TV. Well, almost.

"I think this is going to be as close to normal as she'll ever know," I said.

"At least she'll have this," Tish said.

And she did. Miley called that her "homecoming dance."

As *Hannah Montana* began the second season, Disney asked if I would appear on *Dancing with the Stars,* the hit show on their TV network, ABC. It seemed like it could create some good synergy. Plus, I always loved a challenge and learning something new. At the time, following the recent loss of my dad, I needed to push myself to do something I was afraid to do. So I said yes.

I wish I would have factored in that I didn't have a lick of dancing ability. The show's producers said that didn't matter. I knew better, but I did it anyway.

For *Dancing's* fourth season, I was partnered with Karina Smirnoff, a beautiful, Ukrainian-born dancer whose trophy case included five US National Championships. Our first dance was a cha-cha, and I wanted to dance to ZZ Top's "Sharp Dressed Man." But the producers insisted I dance to "I Want My Mullet Back." As I think about it, they were setting my ass up from the word go; but I kind of knew that, and I didn't need their help. I'm perfectly capable of making an ass out of myself, as I proved when Karina and I took the stage in front of 23 million people on live television.

She wore a mullet wig, which I was supposed to pull off her on the final beat of the dance. We practiced that fifteen hundred times in rehearsal, and it worked every single time. But that night, fate had a different plan.

We got to the end of the dance pretty much as we'd rehearsed. I was a little nervous. Bruno later compared me to a bear running through a swamp. But that's beside the point. When it came time to remove Karina's mullet, I pulled and pulled. And pulled. By the third time, her eyebrows were raised and I knew that wig wasn't coming off. The mullet was dead-bolted to her skull. Or so it seemed.

You talk about experiencing a near-death moment of dread and panic; man, I saw the bright light flashing in front of me. I'd hoped *Dancing* would boost my career. In that instant, though, I realized I'd probably damaged it tenfold, or possibly ruined it forever.

On my way home, I was gripped by a crippling anxiety and had to pull over a couple times because I couldn't breathe. I puked twice between Beverly Hills and La Cañada. I was beyond embarrassed that I was sick.

At home, Tish and the kids looked at me as I walked through the door. No one said a word. They all just stared at me. So I knew it was as bad as I thought.

Somehow Karina and I made it through the elimination show. I was stunned. My fans were more forgiving than me, I suppose. We were supposed to meet early the next morning at the Y down the hill from my home. We rehearsed there to help me conserve time between the two shows. But I didn't want to get out of bed. I didn't want to face the world — or my Ukrainian taskmaster.

Then I heard my dad's voice for the first time since he'd died.

"Bo, you've been knocked down before," he said. "Take it one step at a time. Swing your right leg out from under the covers, then bring the other one behind it, and stand up. Then put one foot in front of the other, walk to your sink and brush your teeth, then get dressed, get in your car, and drive to the YMCA."

"I don't want to," I said to myself. "I can't."

"Trust me," he replied. "One foot in front of the other. You've been here before."

Karina was waiting for me at the Y. I felt sorry for her. What a stroke of bad luck for a world champion to be partnered with me. But there was no sorry in her when she saw me lumber into the room. Her eyes narrowed. If she'd had a whip, she would've cracked it, I'm sure.

"You're seven minutes late," she scolded.

"Well, I —"

"Well nothing," she said. "You're late. We've got a lot of work to do. I don't know if you noticed, but our first dance didn't go so well."

She played our next song, Johnny Cash's "Ring of Fire" and informed me that we were going to do the quick step. I couldn't even do a slow step, I thought. Now we were going to do a quick one? Oh . . . crap.

"I'm so depressed," I said.

"Why?" she asked.

"Because I suck."

Karina shook her head. "No more negativity from you," she snapped, and then began the painful process of teaching me the dance. She invited my children to watch a rehearsal, knowing I wouldn't complain as much if they were around. And she was right.

On the next show, Len Goodman praised my moves. "You calmed down," he said. Bruno Tonioli said I was "going the right way" and "the difference in a week is beyond belief." Carrie Ann Inaba added, "I vote you the most improved dancer from last week."

Over the next few weeks, Karina yelled at me, hit me, and tied my hands while I danced. She had me jump through hoops. She also switched my legs a few times with a stick. I knew her arsenal included a whip. It also included one other thing: the heart of a champion. It reminded me that winners want to win, and they get back up when they get knocked down.

Ironically, at one of my last dances, the Greatest was there, Muhammad Ali. (His daughter, Laila, was a fellow contestant.) He was sitting in the corner of the floor. Everyone has heroes, and Ali was one of mine. When I finished my dance, I went over and shook hands with him. "You're the greatest," I said. He made a fist and winked at me. I felt the heart of a champ, *the* champ. That was worth it all. And you know what? If I hadn't gotten back up after that first night I got knocked down, I never would've had that moment.

Each week, my entire family sat in front of the TV set. If they weren't at the show, they made sure to watch it — and for one reason. They loved seeing me make an ass of myself. I could only imagine their text messages: *Make sure you're home in time to watch Dad make a fool out of his fat ass in front of the entire country.*

Amazingly, I made it through the foxtrot, the paso doble, and the jive, and all the way through the quarterfinals, before getting eliminated. It was the eighth week, and I didn't have to be told that I'd stayed way longer than I should have. Nor did I have to be told why I'd lasted. It was the fans. I had the greatest fans in the world. They wanted to see me do well on the show. I loved 'em for that.

There was a payoff to my tenacity. On the night I left, Laila Ali's father, boxing icon Muhammad Ali, was in the audience. He was my hero. She graciously introduced me. I turned into a fan myself, not something that happened to me very often, and I explained that one of my earliest and fondest memories was listening to his fight against Joe Frazier on the radio with my dad and my papaw.

"Thank you," he said.

My dad would've loved hearing me tell him about Ali. Life never ceased to surprise me.

CHAPTER 30

"Ready, Set, Don't Go"

ONE ON ONE, I'M reserved and fumble for words, unsure how much to reveal and uncertain how to do it. But get one of my CDs, push PLAY, and you get a clear view straight into my heart. Take the song "Ready, Set, Don't Go." It's about a father letting go of his daughter, and it takes you straight into where I was in that precarious time during *Hannah Montana*'s second season.

The show's writers incorporated it into the thirteenth episode, in a show titled "I Want You to Want Me . . . to Go to Florida." In it, Robbie Ray injures his back and can't accompany his daughter to a show in Florida, forcing her to cancel the appearance. When she sneaks off anyway, he tracks her down and, in an emotional moment on the plane, sings her the words he's not able to say.

The story behind the song was even better. The day Tish and the kids were moving to California, I stayed behind in Tennessee to take care of all the business, secure the farm, and make sure we were ready to set up shop in L.A. I would fly out a couple of days later.

I stood in front of the house and waved good-bye as they disappeared over the hill and down the driveway. I walked slowly back into the house and, as I took my boots off, I noticed a card on the kitchen table. It was to Braison, from his little girlfriend. He'd fallen in love for the first time, and leaving her was hard, possibly his first heartbreak.

I picked up the card and noticed on the front were two stick figures, hand-drawn like a kid would do, and beneath them it read, "Ready." I opened the next page and there was a picture of the same two figures poised at the starting line of a race. It said, "Set." Then I opened up to the last page and it was just the girl figure by herself. She held her hands over her heart. That picture said, "Don't go."

I put the card down, turned around, and there was my old guitar, the one I call the songwriter. It was in the corner, waiting for me. It might as well have said, "Come on. You know that's a song." It's true. I was already hearing the words and the melody.

Within minutes, I had a written a pretty good piece of it, and then my instinct told me to call my neighbor Casey Beathard, who was a hit-song-writing son of a gun himself, one of the best in Nashville. "Hey, my family just left for California, and I got a great hook," I said. "It's called 'Ready, Set, Don't Go.'" He said, "Man, I'll be right over."

Minutes later, he showed up with his gut-stringed guitar, like the kind Willie Nelson plays, and soon the song was completed. We laid it down on my BR 1600 right then and there, and we knew it was special.

She's gotta do what she's gotta do
And I've gotta like it or not
She's got dreams too big for this town
And she needs to give 'em a shot
Wherever they are

Looks like she's all ready to leave
Nothing left to pack
Ain't no room for me in that car
Even if she asked me to tag along
God, I gotta be strong

She's at the startin' line of the rest of her life
As ready as she's ever been

Got the hunger and the stars in her eyes
The prize is hers to win

She's waitin' on my blessings
Before she hits that open road
Baby get ready, get set, don't go

She says things are fallin' in place
Feels like they're fallin' apart
I painted this big old smile on my face
To hide my broken heart
If only she knew

This is where I don't say
What I want so bad to say
This is where I want to
But I won't get in the way
Of her and her dreams
And spreadin' her wings

She's at the startin' line of the rest of her life
As ready as she's ever been
Got the hunger and the stars in her eyes
The prize is hers to win

She's waitin' on my blessings
Before she hits that open road
Baby get ready, get set, don't go

She's at the startin' line of the rest of her life
As ready as she's ever been
Got the hunger and the stars in her eyes
The prize is hers to win

She's waitin' on my blessings
Before she hits that open road
But, baby, get ready, get set, please don't go

Don't go, mmm don't go
She's gotta do what she's gotta do
She's gotta do what she's gotta do

The *Hannah Montana* episode featuring the song aired in July 2007, the same week my album *Home at Last* came out. Helped by the exposure of "Ready, Set, Don't Go" on TV, the album was my highest-charting record in years: No. 3 on the country chart and No. 20 on the pop chart. Guess who was in the top spot? Miley and her album *Hannah Montana 2: Meet Miley Cyrus*. I knew how my dad must've felt. I couldn't have been prouder. And as long as I saw the name Cyrus was next to No. 1, I couldn't complain.

In October, as "Ready, Set, Don't Go" was already climbing the charts, Miley joined in on the record with me. I tweaked a few lyrics, and suddenly there were two versions of the song — and it took off all over the world. We performed it on *Dancing with the Stars*. Two months later, we sang it again on *The Oprah Winfrey Show*. Find the video on YouTube — she sings the stuffing out of that song and you can't get a truer picture of our relationship at the time than when I sing, "Don't go," and Miley responds, "Let me go now. I'll be OK."

I went through the same thing with all of the kids. Trace had his own band, Metro Station, and like me, he was married to his music. He'd worked as a roadie for me starting when he was in eighth grade, and loved the lifestyle. All he wanted to do was change strings and ride the bus with me. He loved being part of the band and the crew, and he's like that to this day.

So is Brandi. By her late teens, she was singing and writing songs and wanting to get onstage. When I saw how committed she was, I hired her to play guitar in my band. I knew if she played with Sly Dog, she'd only get better. There wasn't any stopping her anyway. She had the music in her soul. And now she tours with her own group, Frank and Derol.

As for some of the typical teenage milestones, like teaching the kids to drive, well, I got 'em started early. Like most kids who grow up in the country, they were driving vehicles around the farm about four days after they learned to ride a bicycle. They started on four-wheelers, graduated to my Kawasaki mule, and then grew into my truck. Just in case we were out back in the woods and I had a heart attack or whatever, I wanted them to be able to get us home. At least that's how I justified it.

Unlike Brandi, who wasn't interested in boys until later on in high school, Miley liked them as far back as I can remember. During *Doc*, she fell for the little boy who played my son, Tyler Posey, who went on to star in the series *Teen Wolf*. On *Hannah Montana*, she and Nick Jonas connected instantly when the Jonas Brothers guest-starred on the show. I saw that chemistry happen right before my eyes.

Again, it was art imitating life or life imitating art. Take your pick. But everyone saw they had a big crush on each other and that things just grew to where they were inseparable. I liked him. I thought he and his brothers were very talented . . . and nice guys. By the time Miley and Nick were together, we had moved again to Toluca Lake, into a large, Mediterranean-style home behind fifteen-foot gates, and one night, hearing them come home after a night out, I hid in the pantry and jumped out when they walked into the kitchen. I scared the crap out of them. It was pretty funny, and we all laughed. That night, Nick, Miley, and I sat by the fireplace and talked for a while. The Jonas Brothers weren't really famous yet. They were just getting loaded up to take off. And so again, I knew this might be as close to a normal boyfriend relationship Miley would ever know.

They were all over the teen magazines and tabloids. Miley was in the teen magazines and tabloids every week and also pictured daily on the Internet, where celebrity websites exploded in popularity and changed the whole landscape. Paparazzi took pictures of Miley — of all of us — every time we stepped outside. They waited in front of the house, followed us to the store, and parked behind us in the drive-thru at McDonald's. We were constantly followed. It became part of normal life . . . if that was normal, though by then, for us, there was no normal. I knew from experience, the teeter had done gone to totter. People always ask if Tish and I would close our bedroom door at night and ask each other how we were going to handle things with Miley and the other kids, and I say, "Oh yeah. About a hundred thousand times."

From October 2007 through March 2008, Miley took her *Hannah Montana: Best of Both Worlds* tour around the world. I toured and recorded my own music. We stayed in touch by phone, fax, and Internet, and spent a small fortune chartering private jets to ensure family time.

But Miley's fame made even family time newsworthy. At the end of 2007, a photo of her sharing a piece of red licorice with a friend at a sleepover was leaked to a website. Suddenly, the Internet lit up with talk she was a lesbian. Miley laughed it off but felt sorry for her friend who, as she lamented to a journalist, "had to go back to school and deal with that crap."

Then, in February 2008, the *Hannah Montana: Best of Both Worlds Concert Tour* was released and someone noticed a scene where Miley and I were in the car and not wearing seatbelts. The little girls on the sleepover circuit who made the film a must-see and a box office smash didn't seem to care — or notice — but the grownups in the media turned it into a major issue.

Disney executives insisted on a response. We had numerous meetings about it. While I never claimed to be the world's smartest man and I sure as hell ain't the world's greatest parent (thank God the Internet wasn't around when the kids were little and I had them on an ATV without helmets), I understood their point. And actually felt bad about it.

"How about we say we're sorry?" I said. "That's what I usually do when I screw up."

And that's what we did. We said we were sorry and reminded people they should always wear a seatbelt . . . Seatbelts save lives.

As soon as that story went away, others popped up. Miley's cell phone seemed to get hacked regularly or her friends posted pictures that were taken at parties, sleepovers, or when Miley was out having fun. Were we happy to see a photo of her mooning a camera? I can't speak for Tish, but at fifteen years old, my idea of fun was streaking through town.

Of course it wasn't that simple for her. In April, a *Vanity Fair* magazine photo shoot with famed photographer Annie Leibovitz included a setup of Miley from the waist up wrapped only in a satin sheet. When the photo came out ... BOOM! ... another explosion. Our phone rang nonstop. E-mail poured in. Meetings were called. You would have thought Miley had posed for *Playboy*.

We were caught completely off-guard. Keep in mind, we didn't raise our children in a bubble. We were living our lives, managing careers and kids, and still trying to hit church every Sunday. Really, we were doing the best we could do under extraordinary circumstances.

Here's what I remember. Annie had shot me previously for the popular "Got Milk" ads, the milk mustache series (*psst* — wanna know a secret? that white stuff is yogurt), and I thought she and I were friends. And we still are. Annie is a great photographer. We were honored she had been assigned to shoot Miley for *Vanity Fair*. Tish and Miley's grandma Loretta and Miley's publicist were at the shoot. At Annie's request, I swung by to pose with Miley. I was on my way to play for the troops in Washington State, so I didn't have a lot of time. I took a few pictures, hung out, and then caught my plane.

After the shoot, a picture was released on the Internet. Suddenly, the world asked, "How could she? Where were her parents?" As I said, I was gone. From what I understand, the shot was the last setup of the day. Looking back, would I have stopped it if I'd been there? Honestly, I don't know. I'd a have to have been there. But who knows, Annie might have wrapped my fat ass in a sheet.

The picture was irrelevant to me. What was important to me was what Miley said. I wanted to know how she was feeling about things. And *Vanity Fair*'s profile of Miley made her sound like she had a good head on her shoulders. They described her as earnest and sincere, noted she ate a turkey-melt sandwich for lunch, liked both *Sex and the City* and *I Love Lucy,* and laughed off the paparazzi that followed her.

The writer expressed surprise that Miley seemed so "well adjusted," to which Miley said, "That's just my personality."

As for my personality, I often longed for the simpler days when I could be at home with my dogs and horses in the woods. At times, when my schedule became too much, I came right out and asked, "What am I doing?" After *Doc,* I'd vowed never to do another series. Maybe I should've listened to myself. Because then along came a script for *Hannah Montana: The Movie.* It was all about taking Miley back home to Tennessee.

Disney wanted to shoot in Louisiana for budgetary reasons. As a producer, though, I lobbied to make the movie in Tennessee. I had all the research and contacts from when I tried to get *Doc* to shoot there. I also had my daughter's best interests in mind. *Hannah Montana: The Movie* was the story of not forgetting where you came from, and I said, "Miley's performance will be out of the park if she's really coming home, if she's really staying in her room where she grew up."

My dad had a saying: Be aware of where you're at at all times. Always know where you are going. But most important, never forget where you come from. That's what this script was all about. Tennessee came to the table with the proper incentives, and Disney approved. We were going home to make the movie.

The studio put together a great cast, and Miley's performance was also incredible. But I got the most satisfaction when filming stopped and I saw her step back into the role of ordinary teenager. She and the other kids took the four-wheelers out on the trails. They found the old toy trucks and dolls they'd hidden in the hollowed-out trunks of trees where I took them to play when they were little. At night, they sped off for a late-night snack at the local Sonic. And we all spent time outside by the fire, roasting marshmallows and wieners under the stars.

A few months later, I unwittingly played matchmaker. I was hosting the show *Nashville Star,* and during the second week this young singer-songwriter named Justin Gaston was voted off. I was stunned. I said something like, "Ladies and gentlemen, keep your eyes open for this kid. They just kicked off Tom Cruise." Backstage, I told Justin not to worry and invited him to look me up if he got out to Los Angeles.

So he did. While visiting me on the *Hannah Montana* set, I introduced him to Miley, and they clicked. From that day, they were inseparable. It became a big thing in the press because he was a couple of years older than her and a devout Christian. He carried a Bible with him just about everyplace he went.

Miley was happy. She didn't have a chance to make friends at school like other kids her age. Tish and I liked him, too. He and Miley played guitar, wrote a lot of songs, and stayed at the house in Toluca Lake. In those days, we were still going to church every Sunday, and we took Justin with us, too. The church parking lot was always full of paparazzi. It was a freak show.

I was ecstatic when we celebrated Miley's sixteenth birthday in November. Both Tish and I were gratified whenever we got to give her something that resembled normal life. Not that everything about this milestone was typical. Her first party was at Disneyland. Taped for a TV special, it included guest sightings of Tyra Banks, Steve Carell, Cindy Crawford, and Demi Lovato, plus me singing "Ready, Set, Don't Go" and a four-song set from Miley herself.

We had a more private party at home where Tish and I gave Miley an SUV. She traded it in for a Prius, saying, "Thanks, guys, but I'd rather drive a car that's better for the planet." Tish and I took that as a sign our kids might be smarter and more sensible than us, and there was nothing wrong with that.

Parenting is something you do one day at a time. As we knew

from raising five kids (when they weren't raising us), some days are better than others. Miley's sweet sixteen was a good one.

Thoughout Miley's life, I tried so hard to walk the line between best friend and father, keeping in mind that that's what my dad was to me. But the line was quickly becoming blurred. She was growing up and doing her own thing, and that's a difficult phase for any parent. Back in Tennessee, when we had shot the scene on top of the hill where Miley and I dueted on "Butterfly Fly Away," I knew she was no longer the caterpillar mentioned at the beginning of the song. Out there on Carl Road, I literally saw the butterfly fly away, and I knew at that moment things would never be the same. And they weren't.

I ended the year in San Diego, starring in the movie *Flying By*. It was an indie film about a frustrated real estate developer whose twenty-fifth high school reunion turns into an opportunity to rejoin his old band and have a second chance at rock-and-roll stardom. After a cross-country concert swing, I flew there with my dog Tex, and both of us stayed on my tour bus, which came down from L.A. and parked in an alley outside the soundstage.

It seemed like a sweet setup. I was going to play a rocker, Heather Locklear had signed on to play my wife, and the producers were going to use a few of my songs in the movie. Plus, I was living right outside where I worked. But as sometimes happens when things seem perfect, it turned out to be a pretty depressing time. I missed my family, who were all out on tour with Miley, and truth be told, I missed my life, or what I wished my life could be and what it had been: trees, horses, sitting in my teepee, playing with the kids, hanging out with Tish. The reality, though, was the kids were grown up, Tish was managing the career of a superstar, and I was downright lonely.

It was a desolate time. It rained almost every day. And maybe because I had so much time by myself, or maybe because the rest of the family was so far away, or maybe because of a combination of both, it was becoming more and more obvious that our busy schedules were taking a toll on our family. I felt the strain, as if my world might be starting to unravel, like a rope beginning to fray. I knew that everything in this world comes with a price, but I asked myself: Was it worth it? I didn't know.

What I did know was that life had somehow changed and there I was, sitting on my bus not in the happiest frame of mind, with a dull thud in my heart, confusion in my head, and a sense that there might be some problems up ahead. It was a little past midnight, and I started playing my guitar. And then, as often happens, those feelings that I couldn't articulate began to flow out of me.

> *Moonlight comes callin'*
> *On my window pane*
> *Ain't seen the sunlight*
> *Lord, I've felt the rain . . .*
>
> *When will this misery end*
> *Your picture's in my head*
> *I feel my heart break once again*
>
> *You know I love you*
> *Still you chose to leave that day*
> *Lord, I've been broken*
> *There's still hope that I can mend*
> *If I could see you once again . . .*

CHAPTER 31

"Back to Tennessee"

IN 2009, I VISITED the troops in Germany, Iraq, and Afghanistan. One day, I was onstage in a giant hangar in Kabul when bombs went off nearby. I was in the middle of singing "Some Gave All." I heard the explosion and felt the ground rumble. I stopped, concerned. Then, a soldier yelled, "Keep going, Mr. Cyrus. We're used to it."

I understood. Trusting fate was much better than acknowledging fear. In my own life, that meant moving forward no matter how lost or desolate I felt inside. In fact, there was no stopping or slowing down even if I'd wanted to. That April, within a two-week period, the *Hannah Montana* movie came out, *Flying By* premiered, and my latest album, *Back to Tennessee*, was released.

Before the year was up, I made two more movies, *Christmas in Canaan* and *The Spy Next Door*, starring Jackie Chan. I was exhausted, emotionally and otherwise. But take time off — why? To do what?

Tish and I had grown apart, and that chasm kept getting larger. Communication is the key to any relationship, new or long-term like ours, but we weren't talking to each other the way we should have been.

Meanwhile, Miley made the movie *The Last Song,* her first dramatic role, and she fell in love with her leading man, Liam Hemsworth, a handsome young actor from Australia.

During the making of the movie, controversy erupted at the Teen Choice Awards. Some accused Miley of pole dancing on top of an ice cream cart. "If you don't like it," she said to those who criticized her, "change the channel. I'm not forcing you to watch me."

She wasn't Madonna, but she had the same mettle. "If you think dancing on top of an ice cream cart is bad," she said, "then go check what ninety percent of high schoolers are up to."

Soon she added a couple of tattoos, including one over her heart that said "Just Breathe" and a tiny one inside her ear that said "Love." There was no doubt that she was grown up and ready to move beyond *Hannah Montana*. "As I've grown into it," she told *Parade* magazine, "I've grown out of it. Does that make sense?"

Tish and I left it up to her as to whether she wanted to continue the series, though everyone knew it was time to pull the plug. She didn't want to do another season. She was done with the wigs and the sparkle.

We supported her. The thing people may not have realized about Miley is that she wasn't a follower. From the beginning, she had a sense of wanting to blaze her own trail. I wonder where she got that. To her, *Hannah* was just the start. She was eager to discover what was next.

Just as *Hannah* had become a chore for her, I also was ready to finish the last season. The fun was gone. Miley and I were like two roads that had run side by side for miles, then suddenly one turned left and the other right. It was hard to smile in the barrel of that camera every day knowing the truth in our real lives: things just weren't funny anymore.

The final episode was shot on May 13, 2010, Tish's birthday. Everyone was primed for a wrap party. It was well-deserved, too. Four seasons of good, funny, family entertainment was worthy of a celebration. But just before we finished the last scene, I got a phone call from Tish saying that Noah had been thrown from a horse at the L.A. Equestrian Center and was lying semiconscious in a hospital emergency room.

So I went there and sat till we got word our little baby was going to be fine. She'd suffered a minor concussion. I skipped the party and sat with Noah that night. That's what daddies do.

I moved on from the *Hannah Montana* phase quickly. The proof was on my left arm. In early June, I spent an absolutely crazed forty-eight hours getting a sleeve of tattoos, including Chief Joseph, the Mayan calendar, and lots of words that meant something to me, including BELIEVE, HOPE AND MUSIC CHANGES EVERYTHING, LIE TO ME, and the one that said it all: a broken heart with the word LATELY written across it and an arrow running through it.

Afterward, the guy inking me noticed the word *Faith* was blurry. He wanted to fix it. I'd been with him for two days straight; another hour wasn't going to make a difference. But I looked at it and said, "You know what? It's a pretty perfect articulation of how my faith feels right now. I think you actually might've nailed it. My faith *is* blurry."

It fit with my new music. For the past few months, I had been writing a new batch of hard-edged rock songs, and I formed a new band to play them. Brother Clyde consisted of Jamie Miller, Samantha Maloney, Dan Knight, and Dave Henning. I gave us a simple mantra: No rules. No limits. No preconceived notions. In other words, there was no asking what is Billy Ray Cyrus going to sound like? What is Billy Ray Cyrus going to look like? It didn't matter. As always, I wanted the music to speak for itself.

And that's exactly what Brother Clyde was about — the music. It was hard and dark, epitomized by our single, "Lately," a dark, Sabbath-like rock anthem that came to me from Morris Joseph Tancredi and Jonathan Rivera and included a rap from King Phaze. The album also featured a country rocker called "The Right Time," which Morris and I wrote for Dolly Parton, plus a cover of Johnny Cash's "I Walk the Line," recorded with a bunch of friends (Ed King,

Mike Estes, Johnny Neil, among them) one night in a basement in 1998. My son Trace also added vocals on the song "Alive."

We debuted in June at a Harley-Davidson store opening in Kansas City. The two-day event was dubbed Worthstock. The mostly biker crowd embraced Brother Clyde's take-no-prisoners repertoire, which ranged from "Crawl," a grungy rocker I'd written while watching news coverage of the 2008 terrorist attacks in Mumbai to a cover of Mountain's classic "Mississippi Queen."

At the end of July, we rattled the walls at the Roxy nightclub on the Sunset Strip. It was a full-on attack that I closed with a chestnut from the old days, my cover of Billy Idol's "Rebel Yell." I will always love singing that song. A few weeks later, we headlined the annual motorcycle rally in Sturgis, South Dakota. During a break, a guy in the crowd yelled that he'd been at my show in Afghanistan when the bombs went off.

"You were there?" I asked. "In that little hangar?"

"Yes, sir," he said.

We shook hands, grateful to be back on safe and sturdy ground in the United States. But it was when I left Sturgis and met up with Tish and Miley in Detroit that I realized the ground was still littered with land mines, the emotional kind. I arrived there on my tour bus. Miley was making the movie *LOL,* and they'd set up camp in a little house. I had my dogs, Tex and Fluke, with me, and as best as I can remember, I got there, took a look around, and realized everything I had ever thought about my marriage and what was going on in our lives — just the whole thing — was no longer the reality.

Long before Tish and I met, I had vowed that my own kids, if I had any, would never see me argue the way my mom and dad did when I was little. I didn't want to deal with that scenario, but I knew that's where we were headed. There was too much bullshit in the air. I tried to ignore the lies and the façade that had been woven around me because the truth just hurt too damn much.

So I called this place I knew in L.A. and had them send a Learjet to Detroit to help me make a jump. A short time later, my dogs and I were headed back to Tennessee.

It was good to be home. I retreated into the woods just as I did as a kid when something bothered me. During the day, I roamed the trails. At night, I stayed in my teepee. I built a fire and stared up at the billions of stars in the Milky Way. I searched for answers. How had this happened? Why had it happened?

Why, why, why? That word filled my head. *Why?*

Fittingly, a storm blew in. The temperature dropped. A tornado touched down on the property and nearly blew away my teepee. One day it snowed. The bleak weather matched my mood. Then the most astonishing thing happened. Both Miley and Braison came to me, separately I should say, and said, "Dad, we know what's going on. We know you've tried everything except one thing. Now you've got to do it."

I could tell they came to me out of pure love, not anger or a wish to hurt their mom. They were trying to figure out answers, too.

I had a million thoughts about what was going on . . . more than I could make sense of . . . more than I could handle . . . I kept going back to the word *why*. It wasn't just a word . . . it was a question . . . Why? This time, though, I came up with an answer that gave me the strength my kids must have had when they approached me. It was what my dad had told me back when he and my mom were getting a divorce. Life ain't fair.

Life. Ain't. Fair. Well said, Dad.

It was time to stand up for myself, something that didn't come easy to me. I called my attorney.

"Have you ever been around a powder keg after the fuse has been lit?" I asked him.

"No," he said. "What are you talking about?"

"Get ready for an explosion," I said.

It took him a few days to draw up the divorce papers. On October 27, he came out to the house so we could go over the documents and make sure everything was accurate before he pulled the trigger.

That evening, just before sundown, I walked with my dogs down to the gate to let him in. I was nervous as hell. I could feel another storm blowing in. Moments before he showed up, I heard tires squeal. I looked up just in time to see a beautiful deer jump out of the cornfield in front of the car. Then BAM! The deer was killed instantly. Blood was everywhere. I took it as a sign.

CHAPTER 32

"Change My Mind"

ASK ME THE DEFINITION of insanity now and I will tell you it's me being hunkered down in a teepee on top of Spirit Mountain, with a fire going, while helicopters full of paparazzi circled in the sky above and more photographers and reporters hid their cars and vans in the cornfield in front of my gate. It was early November, less than a week after I'd filed the divorce papers, and it appeared I was under attack.

I remember leaning back and looking at my dogs, Tex and Fluke. They stared back at me with looks on their faces that seemed to say, "You really stepped in it this time."

They were right. I had done what no one, including me, expected. The powder keg had exploded. My dad always said, "The more you stomp in shit . . . the more it stinks." Right again. A dark cloud descended over the Cyrus family. We went into shock and were overwhelmed by an onslaught of pain, confusion, second thoughts, regret, anger, and sadness.

Despite all the advantages, adventures, and blessings in my life, I rediscovered a fact I knew all too well: people are just people, and heartbreak is an equal-opportunity pain. It don't care if you're famous, live on a big farm, or parent one of the world's most famous kids. And that's the way it was through November.

It was my darkest hour. I felt sick 24/7. I didn't eat. The pain-killers couldn't ease the pain, and the sleeping pills couldn't put me to sleep. I didn't want to talk to anyone. I stalked the woods, built fires, and stared into space, thinking about what I could have done differently as a parent and a husband.

On November 23, Miley celebrated her eighteenth birthday at a bar in Los Angeles. Days later, a video of her with a bong appeared on the Internet, and within seconds it appeared at the top of every celebrity website and blog in the world.

Miley proclaimed her innocence. She said she had been smoking salvia, a legal herb in California. Publicly and privately, it upset everyone involved, from Miley to us, her parents. The folks at Disney were incensed. It didn't matter whether the video was stolen from a friend's phone or whether it was the stupidity of teenagers pressing SEND before they thought of the ramifications. We had to do something. But I felt helpless.

I chose to step out front, and go on offense. I took to Twitter, my first mistake. "Sorry, guys. I had no idea," I tweeted. "Just saw this stuff for the first time myself. I'm so sad." Then, just because I wanted to get my side out, I added, "There is much beyond my control right now."

I felt bad for Miley, but I felt even worse for all those kids who looked up to her and loved her so much. I knew their hearts were broken, as was mine. Everyone got hurt. Once again, it was a blood-bath of emotion. But quite frankly, I do realize also that I'd done some things when I was her age. If I'd been famous and the Internet had existed, I probably would have gone to prison, and possibly still be there.

In the midst of that despair, I let a reporter from *GQ* magazine come to the house. Mistake number two. It was a bad idea perfectly executed. Let me explain: A new album was supposed to come out; it didn't. But by then, I ended up giving a very bleak and damaging interview. In short, I blamed Disney and *Hannah Montana* for ruining my family. I didn't mean it. Nor did I realize what I was saying at the time. But by the time that article appeared, it was too late.

And I still had to get through the holidays. My brother and my mom visited me at the house. Otherwise I spent them with my attorney, my accountant, and my dogs. At one point, I buried my head in my hands and muttered, "This is not how the story goes."

In short, I wanted the family to heal. I wanted the hurt to stop.

Here's the reality: I could have walked away from the marriage and everyone would have been fine — fine in terms of having enough money to live, eat, and continue life comfortably. But I was from a broken home, and that was not what I wanted for my children or my family. That's not what daddies do.

Daddies stay by your side. They shelter you from the storm. They ease your pain. They don't give up on their family.

If I had learned anything from my years of studying the habits and philosophies of successful people, it was this: every goal, every dream, begins with desire. After that, it's about taking the steps to make that desire a reality. I knew that every monumental task begins with a first step. For us, it was a phone call, then a talk, then Tish told me a story she'd read about redemption. As I broke that word down, something about its root, *redeem*, stuck in my head and rang true in my heart. I wanted to put the family back together, and I wanted us to heal.

In January 2011, Tish and I went to a movie near our home in Toluca Lake. Brandi and Braison joined us. We didn't care if we were spotted out together, which we were. We ignored the circus. We were patching things up and in that place couples go where walls can crumble all around and you don't notice. In early March, Tish went on Facebook and posted a bunch of family photos, including one of us in a passionate embrace. I loved it. The shot could have been taken ten years earlier. In fact, it had been taken only a few days before. Our feelings for each other were deep and strong. I was so gratified we hadn't given up.

The truth is always in front of us provided we open our eyes, and so it was with me. "All this time I was chasing after dreams," I had sung on the song "Back to Tennessee." "It was right in front of me. I was lost without her."

The next day I began what my manager Stuart Dill referred to as the Apology Tour. The *GQ* story had come out and I needed to make amends for the statements I'd made about Disney in print. We met at Stuart's office. I situated myself behind his desk. One by one, he dialed studio executives and I explained that I had spoken without thinking during a difficult time for me. I made it clear I was proud of *Hannah Montana* and grateful for all the opportunities it had provided my family. I was there for quite a while.

My mood was good and confident a few days later when I appeared on *The View*. I was in New York City, promoting my latest album, *I'm American*. It was finally available five months after its original release date. I performed my single "Runway Lights," as arranged, but I had a surprise for Whoopi Goldberg, Joy Behar, and the others during the question-and-answer segment on the couch.

Knowing they were going to address my recent troubles, I decided to play offense instead of defense. When they brought up my marriage, I revealed that I'd withdrawn my divorce papers. It was the first anyone outside of my immediate family heard that news, and I could see the surprise on their faces. I think Joy said, "Really?" and I confirmed it with a nod of my head.

"I'm not divorced," I said. "I dropped the divorce. I wanted to put my family back together."

What viewers couldn't see was the executive producer's jaw drop. As the ladies kept up conversation, he sprinted backstage to where my manager was watching and asked if I'd really withdrawn the papers. Stuart said he was hearing the news for the first time, too. The producer raced back to the stage and instructed his hosts to keep asking me questions. It was great TV for them. For me, once again, my life was playing out on the world stage.

I covered my relationship with Tish and the family ("the best it's ever been"), Miley ("we're the daddy and daughter we were before *Hannah Montana*"), and fatherhood ("I wish there was a manual on how to be the perfect dad. I think what's obvious is if there is, I didn't read it"). Tish offered her support on Facebook. "Hope everyone got to see Billy Ray on *The View* today," she wrote.

"Big thanks to all of our family, friends, and fans who have kept us in their thoughts and prayers," she added. "Our family weathered a huge storm and I feel we are stronger than we have ever been!"

I felt the same way. I learned that the most meaningful things in life are the ones you have to work the hardest for. I had always known that. I knew life was about sacrifice. And that night, in my room at the Trump Soho, in New York City, I wrote the song that says it all for me, "That's What Daddies Do."

> *I was just a young boy*
> *The day I learned to ride my bike*
> *I asked daddy are you sure if you let go*
> *I'm gonna be alright*
> *He said trust yourself my boy*
> *Keep your faith and know that dreams can still come true*
> *And know I'm her to catch your fall*
> *'Cause that's what daddy's do*
>
> *That's what daddy's do*
> *They shield you from the rain*
> *Shelter in the storm*
> *There to ease your pain*
> *Wherever you may roam*
> *What you're going through*
> *Know I'm by your side*
> *'Cause that's what daddy's do*
>
> *Now that I'm a grown man*
> *With my own family*
> *Pictures of my daddy on the wall*
> *Of that fade memories*

I can still see him standing there
The day he read the doctor's news
Though he tried to hide his pain
He smiled and said, Son that's what daddy's do

That's what daddy's do
They shield you from the rain
Shelter in the storm
There to ease your pain
Wherever you may rome
What you're going through
Know I'm by your side
'Cause that's what daddy's do

Yeah, know I'm by your side
'Cause that's what daddy's do

CHAPTER 33

Hillbilly Heart

L IKE EVERYONE ELSE, MY life is a work in progress. All of us have problems. None of us know all the answers. We try to fit the pieces together, if we can even find those pieces. Good or bad, it's always something. With me, I try not to be my own biggest obstacle. I'm at my best when I think less about how I'm doing and focus instead on my original mission, using my music to share God's light and love.

The music is still the best definition of who I am, where I've been, and where I'm going. Consider the honesty in "Hillbilly Heart." I think it's as true to my musical roots, influences, and my personal attitude as if I was looking in a mirror and seeing my reflection. The lines on my face, the scars on my body, the sincerity in my eyes . . . It's all still there, a window into my soul. "Hillbilly Heart" is a picture of who I am, past, present, and future.

> I was born in the holler
> Down among the hills
> Never had a lot of luck
> But Lord, I had some thrills
> Keepin' it country
> Keepin' it country all the time

Country is as country does
Country is what country loves

Walkin' by the river
Down along the tracks
Always tried to look ahead
But Lord I love lookin' back
Keepin' it country
Keepin' it country all the time

Well, I've been this way from the start
I've got a hillbilly heart
Lord I love the guitar
Love to hear it loud
If you don't like what you hear
You should leave this crowd
Keepin' it country
Keepin' it country all the time

This southern twang here is my art
I got a hillbilly heart
I love my truck
Love to drive it fast
If you don't like the way I drive
You can kiss my ass
I'm keepin' it country
Keepin' it country all the time

You can change every part
Except my hillbilly heart
'Cuz I've been this way from the start
I've got a hillbilly heart

In June 2012, I was arranging to release my song "That's What Daddys Do" online as a free download on Father's Day. I had supposedly retired from making albums, but who was I kidding? I'm a singer-songwriter from Flatwoods, Kentucky; this is what I was born to do. I wanted to give something to the fans, many of whom had not only supported me the past twenty years, but had grown up with me and were now raising families. Giving them a song was one little way I could say thank you.

Then Miley burst through the kitchen door, her legs and arms and hair flying in every direction just like it did when she was a little kid. "Daddy!" she screamed. "Dad!"

A moment later, she wrapped her arms around me and stuck her finger in front of my face. I was staring at a diamond ring — a pretty sizable chunk of diamond, too.

"I'm engaged!" she said. "Liam asked me to get married."

Liam followed her into the room, and Tish was not far behind. All of us hugged and smiled. I was even happier because they had recently come down from Miley's house in the hills and moved into our old house, which Tish and I had recently vacated for a smaller, cozier place around the corner that had previously belonged to Miley. Basically, we traded.

Although we weren't sure when young Mr. Hemsworth was going to pop the question, Tish and I both knew it was on the horizon. He had come to us and said, "I'm getting ready to ask Miley to marry me. What do you think?" At nineteen, Miley was young. But she had an old soul. She'd seen a lot and grown up fast. And she sure did seem happy around Liam.

I'd had a good feeling about Liam from the first time I laid eyes on him — and that was before Miley saw him on the set of *The Last Song*. Tish was working with a casting company to find the male lead for the movie, and they were down to three or four contenders when I looked through a stack of pictures and pulled out Liam's photo.

"I could see that guy being her boyfriend," I said.

Tish looked up at me.

"Wow, me too," she said. "But he's not one of the finalists, and I don't want to cause a stir with these people."

"Hey, you're a producer on this movie, right?" I said. "If you feel like that, voice your opinion."

She did. Then they brought in Liam, and everybody fell in love with him, including Miley. He was from a part of Australia that reminded me of eastern Kentucky . . . in a way. He and his brother, Chris, are talented actors, and his family are good people. Most important, Miley and Liam have a lot of fun together, and they're good friends.

So when Liam asked if he could marry my daughter, I gave the only response that made sense. I said, "Can you get me in one of your brother's movies?"

Hey, it was only a joke. Of course, in a more serious tone, I said the truth: "Sure, it's cool with me . . . if it's cool with her. Miley's the boss. You know that. Hey, but make me one promise. You guys be good to each other . . . and don't ever stop being best friends."

A few days later, Brandi came to me with boyfriend trouble. Then Braison had to be rushed to the emergency room after his tonsils burst while he was asleep. I heard him choking — on his blood, it turned out — and woke him up. The doctor said it was a freakish occurrence that could have killed him. It was always something. Tish and I knew neither of us could have managed our brood alone. I promised her a nice porch and a rocker for our old age if we survived our kids.

History had proven our durability. More than twenty years after "Achy Breaky Heart" became a monster hit and catapulted me into the limelight, I was still going strong. In late 2012, I released my thirteenth album, *Change My Mind,* and made my Broadway debut as Billy Flynn in the award-winning play *Chicago.* I know what you're thinking right now. Broadway? How does a hillbilly like you end up on Broadway?

Well, I wanted to become a better actor and learn something new. I had never challenged myself to discover all I could about acting, not just being a personality on the screen, but being an artist. Going to Broadway was definitely a way to climb the ladder and acquire new skills.

But what I really learned was: never underestimate life. Instead, expect the unexpected. I went to New York thinking it was about me. I'm going to be a Broadway star. I'm going to learn this.

I'm going to do that. Then Hurricane Sandy hit and everything changed.

What I learned was what I already knew. It wasn't about me. God had put me right where I was supposed to be — in the eye of the storm. I was there in the darkness to represent his light and his love, striving for purpose to find a moral to the story.

Where do I go from here? What's my next chapter? I wish I had an answer. Or maybe not. Maybe it's better not knowing all the answers, not understanding everything, and enjoying the mystery of tomorrow. The only thing I do know is, I don't know nothing. I play life the same way I play music. I play it by ear.

What you are is God's gift to you.
What you do with yourself is your gift to God.

— LEO BUSCAGLIA

AFTERWORD

"Forgot to Forget"

L ATE ONE AFTERNOON, SHORTLY before my dad got sick, the two of us sat in a couple of chairs I have on Spirit Mountain, about twenty yards from my teepee. The spot looks down on pastures and straight across the land that rises again into more tree-covered hills. Sitting there creates a mood and perspective perfect for sitting and thinking or talking and reflecting about life, and my dad and I were doing just that.

Topics ranged from his horses to my travels and family. As we talked, the sun went down and the sky turned black, revealing billions of stars above us. Talking with my dad was one of my life's greatest treasures. He was a great dad and a wise man who shared his knowledge generously. He didn't look down on people, and he knew how to forgive mistakes.

He was equally good when the conversation paused and there was just silence. He was the one who taught me that ninety percent of a conversation is listening. I remember the wind blowing through the trees and both of us leaning back and enjoying the sound.

"Dad," I said. "Let me ask you a question that I don't think I've ever asked you."

"Sure, Bo," he said.

"Well, it's like this. Do you really believe in heaven?"

He turned to me with a troubled look in his eyes.

"I mean if we do the right things with our life," I continued, "and believe in Jesus, do we get there?"

Instead of saying anything directly to me, he put his hand on my back, shut his eyes, and bowed his head.

"Bo, we're going to pray," he said. "Heavenly Father, my son asked a question and needs an answer. If I heard him right, I want you to know that the fact he doesn't know the answer, that he has any doubt, causes me a great pain."

I wanted to interrupt him and apologize, which I suppose my dad knew, because suddenly the arm he had placed on my back pulled me closer. My dad was holding me like he did when I was a boy and got lost in the woods that day. He wanted me to pay attention.

"Mom and Dad," he said, "if you are up there in heaven right now, will you please show my son a sign so he believes . . . Amen."

We opened our eyes, and as soon as we did, a bright light shot across the sky right in front of us. I swear it was like Halley's comet . . . only bigger. It only lasted an instant. But both of us saw it. Neither of us said a word. I was about to say something, but then my dad started walking off into the darkness. I remembered what he had taught me long ago: sometimes silence speaks louder than words.

DISCOGRAPHY

SOME GAVE ALL (1992)

- Could've Been Me
- Achy Breaky Heart
- She's Not Cryin' Anymore
- Wher'm I Gonna Live?
- These Boots Are Made for Walkin'
- Someday, Somewhere, Somehow
- Never Thought I'd Fall in Love with You
- Ain't No Good Goodbye
- I'm So Miserable
- Some Gave All

IT WON'T BE THE LAST (1993)

- In the Heart of a Woman
- Talk Some
- Somebody New
- Only Time Will Tell

- Ain't Your Dog No More
- Words by Heart
- It Won't Be the Last
- Throwin' Stones
- Right Face Wrong Time
- Dreamin' in Color, Livin' in Black and White
- When I'm Gone

STORM IN THE HEARTLAND (1994)

- Storm in the Heartland
- Deja Blue
- Redneck Heaven
- Casualty of Love
- One Last Thrill
- I Ain't Even Left
- How Much
- Patsy Come Home
- A Heart with Your Name on It
- Only God Could Stop Me Loving You
- Roll Me Over
- Enough Is Enough
- The Past
- Geronimo

TRAIL OF TEARS (1996)

- Trail of Tears
- Truth Is I Lied
- Tenntucky

- Call Me Daddy
- Sing Me Back Home
- Three Little Words
- Harper Valley P.T.A.
- I Am Here Now
- Need a Little Help
- Should I Stay
- Crazy Mama

SHOT FULL OF LOVE (1998)

- How's My World Treating You
- Under the Hood
- Give My Heart to You
- Busy Man
- Shot Full of Love
- Rock This Planet
- Missing You
- Touchy Subject
- His Shoes
- Time for Letting Go
- The American Dream

SOUTHERN RAIN (2000)

- You Won't Be Lonely Now
- Southern Rain
- All I'm Thinking About Is You
- We the People
- I Will

- Love You Back
- Burn Down the Trailer Park
- Everywhere I Wanna Be
- Crazy 'Bout You Baby
- Without You
- Hey Elvis

TIME FLIES (2003)

- What Else Is There
- Bread Alone
- The Way It Is
- She Don't Love Me (She Don't Hate Me)
- Time Flies
- I Luv Ya
- I Still Believe
- Without You
- Hard to Leave
- Nobody
- Tell Me
- Close to Gone
- Stone Still
- Back to Memphis
- Some Gave All

THE OTHER SIDE (2003)

- Face of God
- Wouldn't You Do This for Me
- Always Sixteen

- I Need You Now
- Love Has No Walls
- Tip of My Heart
- Did I Forget to Pray
- Holding On to a Dream
- I Love You This Much
- The Other Side
- Amazing Grace

WANNA BE YOUR JOE (2006)

- Wanna Be Your Joe
- I Want My Mullet Back
- The Man
- I Wouldn't Be Me
- What About Us
- Country Music Has the Blues
  (with George Jones and Loretta Lynn)
- The Freebird Fell
- I Wonder
- Lonely Wins
- How've Ya Been
- Ole What's Her Name
- Hey Daddy
- Stand (with Miley Cyrus)
- A Pain in the Gas

HOME AT LAST (2007)

- Ready, Set, Don't Go

- The Beginning
- The Buffalo
- Flying By
- Brown Eyed Girl
- Don't Give Up on Me
- You've Got a Friend (featuring Emily Osment)
- You Can't Lose Me
- Can't Live Without Your Love
- My Everything
- Put a Little Love in Your Heart
- Over the Rainbow
- Stand
- Ready, Set, Don't Go (featuring Miley Cyrus)

BACK TO TENNESSEE (2009)

- Back to Tennessee
- Thrillbilly
- He's Mine
- Somebody Said a Prayer
- A Good Day
- I Could Be the One
- Like Nothing Else
- Country as Country Can Be
- Love Is the Lesson
- Give It to Somebody
- Real Gone
- Butterfly Fly Away (with Miley Cryus)

I'M AMERICAN (2011)

- Runway Lights
- We Fought Hard
- Keep the Light On
- Stripes and Stars (featuring Amy Grant)
- I'm American
- Old Army Hat
- Nineteen
- Some Gave All (featuring Darryl Worley, Craig Morgan, and Jamey Johnson)

CHANGE MY MIND (2012)

- Change My Mind
- Once Again
- Hillbilly Heart
- Tomorrow Became Yesterday
- Good as Gone
- Forgot to Forget
- That's What Daddys Do
- Hope Is Just Ahead
- I'm So Miserable
- Stomp

Credits